HEART

CENTERED

MARRIAGE

HEART CENTERED MARRIAGE

Fulfilling Our Natural Desire

for Sacred Partnership

SUE PATTON THOELE

BARNES
&NOBLE
BOOKS
NEW YORK

To Gene Thoele,

my friend and my beloved,
who anchors my life in love and security
while sprinkling it with laughter and fairy dust!

Deep, heartfelt thanks to:

The unseen Muse who guides me on this mysterious journey called writing.

*Mary Jane Ryan, my publisher and editor, whose gentle advice
allows me to bring my passion to fruition.*

*The wonderful team of people at Conari Press, with
special thanks to Ame, Brenda, and Emily who not only
believe in me but are unbelievably patient with me.*

*Mike, Brett, Paige, Lynnie, and Shawn who share the fire of our
sacred family circle.*

Mother and Dad for the love and security they provided.

My sister, Gayle, and her husband, Larry, for the connection we've established.

*Jo, Roy, Sarg, and Ray who welcomed me into
the Thoele clan with open arms.*

Annabelle Woodard who is an unquenchable light.

Judith, Susan, Bonnie, and Patti, my soul sisters.

*Each wonderful woman in our Woman's Group for providing a safe haven for
laughter, tears, magical learning, and unconditional love.*

CONTENTS

A Deep and Holy Hunger

There is within each of us, I believe, a deep and holy hunger for sacred union. Our souls yearn to unite, to live in concert and connection with other souls. Collectively and individually we are crying for the solace of reconnection with God. On earth this deepest and sweetest desire for sacred union is most often expressed in a committed, compassionate, and soul-filled partnership with another; we long to interlace hands and hearts with a beloved as we make the pilgrimage toward our own spiritual evolution.

In this sense, marriage can be a crucial part of life's spiritual journey because it, like nothing else, can take us to the sacred places in ourselves. The mystery of mystical union with another gives us a glimmer of *re*union with God—a union experienced in faint and fleeting glances and touched in dream and meditative states. Sacred partnership provides a gateway to God, an opportunity to practice love daily, a chance to enhance our heart connection through commitment and consistent gentle kindness to someone else. Although we may not always feel like being loving, we intuitively know that we must honor our promises to love and cherish all life if we are to open our hearts—the door through which God can enter.

Our holy hunger for sacred union can also be expressed by our yearning to love wholeheartedly. The words *whole* and *holy* originate from the same root, meaning to be undamaged or inviolate, and thus our desire to love freely, cleanly, and with great clarity reflects our heart's deep striving toward wholeness. I have found in my twenty years as a psychotherapist that, although outwardly more often expressed by women, the craving for the sacred in marriage is not gender-specific. Both men and women yearn for the satisfaction of a marriage that feeds the hunger churning inside us. We each long to feel whole, complete, and undivided, that is, holy.

None of us gets married hoping for a bad or humdrum marriage, and yet many of us end up with one. I did, my first time out. In fact, it was the heartbreaking failure of my first marriage that catapulted me into a search for what love really is and how it can be expressed and received within the circle of marriage. Why, since we yearn so for love, does it still elude us so regularly?

This haunting question led me to graduate school, a degree in counseling psychology, and, eventually, a private psychotherapy practice. But the most important *and* most challenging continuing education is my second marriage, now in its twenty-second year. In my marriage to Gene, there is daily opportunity to uncover my own "stuff"—old and newly acquired stuff that gets in the way of my being able to be open to or give love. Over the years, it was sometimes pretty rough going and I wasn't sure I was really up to opening my heart and having the sacred partnership that I yearned for. But, here we are, twenty-two years and four children down the road, and I can thankfully say that Gene and I have a complementary partnership that supports both our collective and individual dreams and facilitates our emotional growth and spiritual evolution. Much of the time our marriage feels sacred; more times it feels safe, secure, and supportive; and a good majority of the time it is a lot of fun. Believe me we have worked—and still do—on our capacity to keep our hearts open to each other, which, I think, is the secret of maintaining a sacred partnership.

It is from this passionate commitment to the journey of sacred partnership that this book was born. Written from a woman's perspective, *Heart Centered Marriage* is geared toward heterosexual couples who are in search of ways to enact their commitment to its fullest depth and breadth. I know, of course, that sacred partnership takes many forms. Committed relationships of all kinds, our friendships, and the incredibly close bonds we have with our children and other family members are sacred blessings to be held in awe and appreciation. But the majority of this book concentrates on our deep and holy hunger for sacred partnership in marriage. I deeply honor the sacred union that marriage can be, and passionately feel that, in its highest form, marriage is truly sublime and, conversely, that from the hell of its depths we can mine the gold of personal growth and understanding.

Heart Centered Marriage is an offering from my heart to yours. Throughout the book I share many stories from my own marriage journey as well as examples from the lives of my clients and friends. It is my fervent hope that from our triumphs and failures, our quiet joys and noisy struggles, you may get a clearer picture of what can help you and your mate to expand and deepen your own sacred bond.

As well as offering examples and stories, I have tried to illuminate the deep yearning for heart centered marriage with the light of practicality, suggesting how-to's to facilitate and gentle the process. First we will explore the poetic aspects of love, such as why we yearn so to fathom the mystery of sacred partnership, and how the alchemy of relationship helps us discover the gold of our spiritual essence. Then we will delve into the practical but potent ways to create heart centered marriage. How do we become artisans in the craft of love? Finally, what gifts does sacred partnership bestow upon us and upon the greater whole?

FIRES OF CHANGE

As most of us realize, the institution of marriage is going through the fires of change. We know what doesn't work, as shown by our divorce rates. It seems that what we've tried to do to make marriage work has not succeeded, maybe because we have come from a solution-oriented place of trying to "fix it" rather than heartfully moving into an understanding of what marriage needs to *become*. Can we, in this ecologically aware time, recycle our marriages? Restructure, reframe, reenergize, and transform them into safe harbors for love, self-realization, and service? I think we can. *Heart Centered Marriage* is grounded in my optimism about the trend toward sacred partnership that I see emerging throughout society.

Gene and I are a good example of a marriage that was founded on very traditional, even old-fashioned, ideas and is evolving into new ways of being that better fit our more mature selves. Our personal changes parallel the shift from authoritarian to egalitarian beliefs that society as a whole is experiencing. We personally can vouch for the fact that making changes is not easy nor done quickly, but is possible. So, as you begin your journey in this book, I want to encourage you to take heart; the metamorphosis to sacred partnership is not always smooth. For no matter how divine we are at our core, we are each very human in the here and now, and that can cause the road to be quite bumpy.

In challenging times, I find it very helpful to remember that those of us consciously working on our relationships have an important mission to redefine marriage and family, to move into the very essence of relationship, altering it in ways that are necessary for the protection and reemergence of love, compassion, and soul. For the well-being of our children, our selves, and our planet, we must stoke the fires of change in our own lives and learn to come increasingly from our hearts rather than our heads.

Poets and prophets have long known that love conquers all, but the exciting thing is that there is currently a huge groundswell of grassroots advocacy for the idea of love as healer. Businesses, schools, and even government are beginning to think in terms of love and acceptance, of working together for a common cause and to a common purpose. Cultivating and harvesting the fruits of this transformation in ourselves and our marriages can lay the cornerstone for a society—even a civilization—that lives and acts from its heart. It's a big dream, but by clearing the weeds in our own patch, we can help heart centered living come to fruition. It is my prayer that *Heart Centered Marriage* brings a spark of inspiration to you that will help fan the flame of this vitally needed transformation.

AT HOME IN GOD

As Gene and I have walked the path of sacred partnership, I have come more and more to see that having the intimate marriage we deeply want is predicated on our desire for and commitment to having an intimate and enduring relationship not only with ourselves, but with God.

Although many of us were told that we were created in God's image, we have not yet integrated that concept into a deeply felt belief in *our* individual souls' sacredness. Both the desire to reunite with our source and to believe in our own goodness are worked out in primary relationships—most notably and nobly, with our mates. Our mate is our chosen one, the person upon whom, ideally, we pour our very best. But of course, this is almost impossible until we can let that same love stream onto ourselves. For loving and valuing ourselves makes it possible to truly love and value another. Thus, to create deeply satisfying relationships, we must continually nourish our own hunger for self-love and acceptance. Loving ourselves is not selfish or unnatural, as we may have been taught. It is, instead, one of our highest and hardest life tasks.

As a little kid, I was naturally cozy with God, whom I viewed in the traditional way: white-robed and long-bearded. I would sit in my bedroom window basking in the moonlight and write poetry to my friend, God. Even though I always went to church, when I got older, my relationship with God became more distant, much more heady, and I regularly forgot about him altogether. That changed with the advent of my divorce. Embroiled in the trauma and reeling from my wounds, I didn't just turn back to God, I scuttled under his wings and began a real love affair of the heart.

That love, although it ebbs and flows, is the cornerstone of my life. Constant but ever-changing. Sometimes full of certainty, more often questioning and exploring, but always grounded in a faith that the God I know and love is good and cares about all of her creation. From the immeasurable security of being at home in God, I have been able to heal giant fissures in my self-esteem and develop a strong and loving relationship with myself. Of course, being human, I slip up on that one often.

The blessing of this gift of trusting God did not just land on my doorstep one morning with the newspaper. It is the product of much struggle and searching until I was finally able to surrender to the Mystery, realizing that the answers that would satisfy both my analytical mind and my hungry heart were not to be found *out* there, but only *in*side myself. One thing that I am sure of is that because I believe that God and I are in eternal, sacred partnership, I have the courage to pursue creating sacred partnership with Gene. On occasion, this very human partnership may not *feel* sacred, but the belief that it is holds steady even in really difficult times.

GOD NOTE

Because I believe that the sacred partnership we hunger for in marriage is conceived and birthed in the holy relationship we have with ourselves and with the Divine, I have referred to God by many names throughout the book. I want you, the reader, to know that I am not using the terms as indicative of a purely masculine deity; in fact, I mix up the pronouns *he* and *she,* in relation to God, as the spirit moves me. Those who know me will chuckle as they read this because they are well aware of how passionately I feel about reclaiming the Sacred Feminine voice in women *and* men for the good of our planet and all people everywhere.

I call myself a Celtic Christian because, for me, that phrase encompasses the mysticism, awe, and reverence for Feminine Energy in nature and spirit, a deep affinity for Christ—both the person and the Power—and an indefinable chalice into which I can pour my evolving understanding of the Mystery. No matter what name I give this Mystery, please know that I embrace the Loving All, and encourage you to feel free to replace any name that I use with whatever term resonates with your heart.

As you read, please let my words flow over and through you like music to be heard, absorbed, and interpreted by your heart's most cherished desire, allowing your soul to open to your own deep and holy hunger for sacred union.

Part One

THE MYSTERY
OF
MARRIAGE

*Why do we yearn to fathom the mystery of
love and sacred partnership?*

*W*hat, besides the miracle of birth, is more mysterious than love and its fraternal twin, marriage? It is no wonder that most songs and poems have love as their theme. And it is no surprise that love is discussed endlessly among those who have just fallen in love as well as those who feel the lack of it. We dissect, bisect, and trisect love and the feelings it inspires, but for the most part it remains a mystery—unfathomable, inscrutable, yet deeply yearned for. The only thing we know for sure about love is that without it, we wither.

When it comes to the workings of love, the Western "just the facts, Ma'am" approach very rarely helps us. That's because love is not rational; through the experience of love, we are being invited to surrender to its enigmatic pull on us, relaxing into the wonder and awe with which it fills us. When we do this, we become poets and artists of love rather than engineers and technicians. By melting into love, we can find in our hearts an intuitive knowledge about how we can best love, rather than laboring over this or that technique. By swimming with the current of love's mystery rather than trying to harness and solve it, we can be happier and more serene.

That's not always easy to do. When I first started writing this book, I put our relationship under such a high-powered microscope that my husband, Gene, was squirming like a butterfly impaled by a pin. According to the impossible magnification I was suddenly viewing us through, he could do very little right, and didn't particularly care to do right. I did not fare well either. I kept muttering to myself, "What the hell *is* sacred partnership?" I became convinced that if I *could* figure it out, we surely didn't have one! How could I presume to write this book? We were a mess, and it was not much of a mystery why.

So often people do to their relationships just what I was doing to mine—scrutinize them to death instead of looking at them with gratitude and delightful discovery! It was weeks before I regained my perspective and could once more become enthralled by the mystery of the marriage Gene and I have, and how it unfolds each day as we explore our hunger for unity with each other, ourselves, and God. What a relief!

As you read *Heart Centered Marriage*, I invite you to do so with a spirit of love and generosity, not blame, toward your mate. Allow the ideas and concepts to permeate your heart, sowing in it the seeds of great honoring for the mystery of love and marriage. From the seeds planted within you, sacred partnership can become a fruitful reality.

Chapter One

THE CALL
OF
SACRED
PARTNERSHIP

*Emanating from the intuitive wisdom of Feminine Energy comes the
increasingly urgent call toward heart centered marriage,
the equality and intimacy of sacred partnership.*

$\mathcal{S}$omething is stirring in our society, within the smaller circles of our family and friends, and within ourselves. Something good. Something desperately needed. At a basic level, perhaps born out of the shocking examples of inhumanity and cruelty witnessed daily on the news and in the papers, we are inviting soul—and particularly the heart energy embodied in the Feminine— back into our lives. We are reawakening to the necessity of embracing the Golden Rule, "Do to others as you would have them do to you," as a minute-by-minute intention, not a vague Sunday School memory.

From the macrocosm of our entire planet to the microcosm of our inner selves, we are in the midst of a renaissance of the soul. This is a time of deep awareness of the need for a new way of nourishing one another and Mother Earth. The very meaning of *renaissance,* which is to acquire new life, strength, and vigor, ensures that this period of change will be filled with chaos and confusion. Moving from the old to the new leaves a void of reliable and remembered experiences, reactions, and outcomes. We are in unfamiliar, uncharted territory. Living on the cusp of a newly emerging paradigm, as we are now, usually creates a vortex of fear. From fear comes violence, judgmental behavior, and desperate clutching at the known.

Even though change is often chaotic, at the basis of the current renaissance of the soul is a heartfelt cry for more depth and meaning in everyday life. We are becoming aware of a certain anorexia of the soul suffered both personally and globally. Even though many of us realize that self-realization, love, reverence, and purpose are necessary soul foods, it is so easy to neglect giving our souls the time and attention they need. Luckily, souls are not gluttons. With a small but consistent amount of nourishment, they can be encouraged to flourish and thrive, bringing us a sense of completeness and wholeness as we return to our essence, which is love.

Although in the past several thousand years we have emphasized our minds over our hearts, and accomplished a great deal in the process—building empires and harnessing nature—now is the time to integrate the mind and the heart in ourselves, our relationships, and our world. Somewhere inside of us we know that the next step we need to take is to live in love. Love of self, love for others, and for our beautiful home, Earth.

FROM PATRIARCHY TO SACRED PARTNERSHIP

One of the biggest reasons why modern day marriages are failing at an alarming rate, or simply not feeling rewarding to the partners, is that we have been marrying for the last several thousand years into a world that is overbalanced in masculine mentality. Although masculine energy is absolutely essential for the smooth—or attempted smooth—running of our planet, it is not animated by the heart and soul, the way feminine energy is.

When I speak of masculine and feminine energy, I'm not talking about men and women per se, but masculine and feminine energetic principles. All of us, *both* men and women, have aspects of masculine and feminine energy as a part of our make up. Generally speaking, men carry more masculine traits and tendencies than do women, and women carry more feminine traits and tendencies than men. Each gender is likely to express more of their particular energy, although we all, of course, know exceptions. When either sex concentrates solely on masculine or feminine energy, it is thrown out of balance and harmony with the natural order of things, and can experience rigidity, judgment, and loss of heart as a result.

Ideally, the world—and the individuals in it—needs a balance of masculine and feminine, for, when they are out of balance, the dark sides of each begin to emerge. Negative masculine energy tends to act out its need for control from a deeply entrenched sense of entitlement, demanding domination and control of others through power and superior physical strength. On the other hand, negative feminine energy, hungry for control, will more likely manifest in a manipulative or guilt-evoking way. Neither fosters heart connections.

This is what we've been experiencing in the past two thousand years through the rule of patriarchy—the manifestation of negative masculine and feminine energy that has disconnected us from our hearts. In sacred partnership, the head bows to the heart and soul. Not so with patriarchy, the rule of the masculine principle. Patriarchy bows to no one and no thing! Patriarchy can be described as the separatist "head" approach of conquering and competing and is equated with the philosophy of control. The desire for control is deeply embedded in all of us, men and women alike. Before we'll be able to come from a heart centered space of compassion and connection, we need to be ruthlessly gentle in searching out our own attachment to power and control, our desire to dominate and *use* resources and people to our own advantage without thought about the eventual consequences for others.

I'm not bashing men when I passionately lobby for partnership instead of patriarchy, but I do strongly believe that we *must* balance ourselves energetically. For the quality and meaning of our private and public lives to be enhanced, patriarchy must be replaced by a civilization based on partnership, one that respects and honors *both* feminine and masculine energies and attributes. Men are as beleaguered as women by the patriarchal paradigm, and our planet is in desperate need of a balance of energy. Without a huge infusion of the feminine-heart energy of compassion, connection, and cooperation, we may very well do ourselves in.

Fortunately, a new paradigm is emerging, one that incorporates the best of ancient nature-based matriarchies with the best of the technology-based patriarchies. From this new paradigm, a revitalized form of relationship is evolving: sacred partnership. I have great hope that, from this uniting of soul and intellect, heart and head, the mystical sacredness of marriage will be one of the most rewarding and essential treasures discovered.

Maybe an example from my own life will help illuminate the ways we, in the inner circle of our lives, can courageously hold tightly to the new ideals. As I said earlier, Gene and I had a pretty traditional arrangement when we married. Although our agreement was mostly unspoken, we both knew the rules: I was to be the homemaker and Gene the provider. Being immensely tired from four years of single parenting and going to graduate school, I felt being taken care of was a really good deal for me. Much to my chagrin, however, it became very apparent that Gene's role as provider also seemed to entitle him to be the one in control. We had lapsed into the micro-patriarchy of love, honor, and *obey*. I was informed of decisions, but often not included in them. Gene was king of the castle and top dog in the pack, and I was struggling for a foothold in my own family. It took quite a bit of self-examination to see that out of my desire to be taken care of, I had set us up for a patriarchal hierarchy. It was then that I realized that I wanted, and was ready for, true partnership.

Well, as those of you who have gone through readjusting roles will know, it ain't that easy! As I began to assert myself, Gene and I went through a very rough period of redefining our relationship. I can remember one crucial conversation that turned the tide of our power struggle toward the oasis of partnership. We were having a discussion (argument) about my not wanting to be in control in the relationship, but definitely not wanting to be bottom dog either. I wanted to be equal dog! The phone interrupted our talk, and when I got back to him, Gene had time to really think about how he felt. His response was, "I'm used to being top dog. I don't like the idea of being equal dog." Ahh, that could be a caption for the whole patriarchy cartoon! Instead of being appalled, I applauded his honesty. *Now,* we could move from that place of recognition to what eventually became the equality of love, honor, and *cherish*.

In bringing about the change in our relationship, Gene and I both had to face fears we had hidden from ourselves and each other. Indeed, most of us on our way out of the patriarchal paradigm into the partnerships for which we hunger will need to gently venture into the dark inner territories where fear keeps us chained to the old ways of doing and looking at things. Bringing the light of understanding and healing to our fears will unshroud our souls and allow them to shine forth in love. Only by facing our fears and moving *through* them can we have the courage to change the status quo and become dedicated to creating healthy, wholesome, and heart centered partnerships. It isn't easy, but we can do it and we must.

Partnership is a process of patience, persistence, and practice containing large degrees of commitment, communication, and caring. Establishing our marriage in the richness of equality and heart centered partnership allows us to inherit a treasure chest of security, creativity, and joy.

JOINT HEIRS

The word *partner* originally meant "joint heir," and still does in legal jargon. I think that archaic definition is applicable for us now. As we evolve from the current patriarchal paradigm into one of partnership, we can begin to think of women and men as joint heirs to the joys and responsibilities of living in our society.

Joint heirs walk and work hand in hand, knowing that each is a valuable and worthy recipient of whatever inheritance there is to be experienced. Thinking of ourselves as joint heirs to all—the good and the difficult, the beautiful and the heartbreaking—helps us remember that partnership from the heart does not dominate or subjugate, but invites us into becoming more fully who we are at our sacred core.

RECLAIMING THE SACRED FEMININE VOICE

Marriage has been parched by the mind-oriented patriarchy in which all that is fertile, emotional, and intuitive—all that is *feminine*—has been labelled as suspect at best, and abnormal or demonic at worst. Unable to be destroyed, the moist, rich, fruitful *feelingness* of the Feminine has been stored in the womb of our semi-conscious yearnings, waiting to return. The time is now ripe.

Returning to the honoring of feminine energy is definitely a *reclamation* of a previous widespread attitude toward the feminine as sacred. In much of what is referred to as prehistory, the Feminine reigned supreme. Historians have shown us, through archeological discoveries, that God was seen as female long before she was cast in a male role. Dating back as far as 25,000 B.C., statuettes and figurines have been found that honored the Feminine as the Goddess of fertility and source of all life. In the Old Testament, Wisdom, or Sophia, expresses the archetypal feminine, but Jewish Philosopher Philo of Alexandria as well as New Testament writers replaced Wisdom/Sophia with Word/Logos. Even before the word was made flesh in the form of the male Jesus, the feminine aspect of the divine, revered for at least 25,000 years, had all but disappeared from religious tradition.

But She is making a comeback. Having plumbed the depths of masculine domination for the last several centuries and found it devoid of the qualities that make relationships sing, we are again ready to welcome an equilibrium of masculine *and* feminine energy into our lives. My notion of the Feminine's struggle to survive in male-dominated cultures can be likened to the moon being required by the cosmos to remain in a constant state of waning. We are acutely aware that now is the time to acknowledge the waxing and the waning of all our energies, thereby inviting ourselves to return to a state of balance and wholeness.

SILENCING THE FEMININE VOICE

In the summer of 1993, I was privileged to go on a pilgrimage entitled "Women's Mysteries Abroad." Fourteen of us, led by two extremely knowledgeable and wonderfully spiritual women, explored ancient sacred sites in Ireland, England, and Wales. Frankly, I didn't know much about the places we were going but was, nonetheless, compelled to join the group. It turned out to be a magical and life-changing experience seemingly orchestrated from above. No one understands how I received the brochure since I wasn't even on the mailing list!

Before the trip, I regularly felt extremely angry with myself and other women over the extent of our fear of men and our overwhelming concern about how they felt about us. Why in the world we were such wimps? Then I began to learn of the reality of the gender holocausts that have taken place over the centuries. I've come to believe that the fear engendered by those holocausts has embedded itself into the collective female psyche, passed down through the ages, from mother to daughter, woven in the very fabric of our ancestral line by the memory of atrocities almost too hideous to recount. Far from being wimps, we women have been incredibly wise and courageous, protecting the Sacred Feminine voice until a time when it could safely be heard and honored again.

Examples of extreme disregard for and devaluing of the feminine include the fact that in some societies unwanted girl babies are routinely killed soon after birth. Although it seems unbelievable, female infanticide is still happening today, particularly in China. Perhaps this kind of contempt for the feminine is what prompted Saint Teresa of Avila to say, "Just being a woman is enough to make one's wings fall off."

The most notorious annihilation of women happened between the 14th and 17th centuries during the Christianization of Europe, although America joined in with her own Salem, Massachusetts witch trials in 1692. These years included the Inquisition, in which millions of people were murdered as heretics for disagreeing with the Catholic Church.

But, as reported by a recent PBS program, "The Burning Times," one of the most shocking revelations is the fact that, during these years, 85% of those killed for the crime of witchcraft were women. What was termed witchcraft? Not black magic as you might imagine; midwifery, herbology, and not obeying one's husband were favorite accusations. Alleged intercourse with the devil was a popular crime, and many women did confess to this and many other sins. But these "confessions" were just as fraudulent as the accusations, since they where extracted during intense torture.

As hard as it is to fathom, sometimes *all* of the females in a village—grandmothers to tiny baby granddaughters—were tortured and killed because they carried the sinful stigma of being born female. Six generations of children watched as their mothers were burned at the stake for honoring and speaking out from their own feminine wisdom. Just writing these words makes me physically sick; is it any wonder that we women have been secretly frightened to share our intuitive feminine voices?

We do have several instances in our collective past of the masculine and feminine working together spiritually in complementary cooperation. One that I was pleased to learn about on my trip was that the Celts, Druids, and early Christian mystics very happily shared their wisdom with each other and, in some cases, willingly adopted certain beliefs from one another. In secluded areas, this natural compatibility continued uninterrupted for centuries. Unfortunately, most of these enclaves have now been "modernized," and the feminine voice has been effectively muffled in them also. But thankfully, we are now moving into a time when many of us—men and women alike—can and are renouncing the sacrificial voice of subservient fear and are regaining the Sacred Feminine without being subjected to rejection, abuse, persecution, or projection. And when we are faced with these negative responses, we're finding the courage within ourselves to speak out anyway.

SWEET MUSIC OF THE FEMININE

What does this past extermination of the Feminine mean in terms of our hunger for sacred union with our partners? Much, for the Feminine is the teacher of relationship! Our marriages can only hum with the song of love if they are filled with the Sacred Feminine voice, for she *is* the song of love. She is the harp upon which the strings of compassion and connection quiver. From the Feminine comes the sweet music composed by living complementary lives with those we love. Although she has never stopped singing in the privacy of intimacy and love, and has remained a constant, quiet celebrant at both births and deaths, the Sacred Feminine voice is now openly vocal in many, many of us. And in others, both men and women, she is awakening slowly but undeniably.

Relationships, if they are to thrive and be the safe and supportive harbors that we need them to be, must have a *balance* of both masculine and feminine energy. However, at this point in history, the scale needs to be weighted toward the feminine aspects of our being, for the Feminine is what carries the energy of compassion and connection capable of satisfying our deep need for sacred union. As Marion Woodman, Jungian analyst and internationally known teacher says, "The task of the feminine is to contain, as the mother contains the baby. The eternal Feminine is that loving, cherishing, nurturing principle which looks at the life that is becoming and honors it, celebrates it, allows it to grow into its full maturity."

Without love we cannot mature in a healthy way. But when our marriages are contained in the nurturing Feminine and are sheltered by love and acceptance, we will birth sacred partnership by encouraging each of us to develop into the beautiful beings that we are meant to become. Of course, none of us can sustain this all-encompassing feminine stance of loving at every moment, but we can, by choosing the qualities we want in our relationships and becoming educated about them, create an atmosphere in which love can grow into its fruitful maturity.

Familiarizing ourselves with the feminine qualities necessary to make relationships work is equally important for men as for women. It is vital that each of us is able to express all of who we are, and now that women are exercising more of their masculine energy, it's very important for men to claim and act out of their feminine strengths.

QUALITIES OF THE FEMININE AND MASCULINE

The key qualities of feminine energy are inclusion and the ability to accept and honor the process of whatever is happening. Perhaps this is often easier for women because we are physically and emotionally programmed to honor the cycle of conception, pregnancy, and birth and to welcome and include whoever may be born from that long, mysterious process.

Contrary to the idea that women are over-emotional, the Feminine is well-grounded emotionally, and has the capacity to bring all of her energy to exactly where she is in the moment. Feminine energy accepts the paradoxes of life and realizes at some basic level that there is unification possible within even the most disparate incongruities. Feminine energy also resonates with and deeply connects with the earth and all of her children, feeling for and with them.

The following list of feminine qualities, the songs of the Sacred Feminine voice in relationship, is by no means complete. You will be able to add many of your own.

FEMININE ENERGY IS . . .

- ♥ *Inclusive: recognizing the value and worth of all people and things;*
- ♥ *Honoring of Process: able to allow circumstances, ideas, and experience to unfold;*
- ♥ *Intuitive: holistic, accessing immediate perception rather than rational thinking;*
- ♥ *Compassionate: empathetic, warm, open hearted;*
- ♥ *Complementary: lives in concert with others, augmenting the whole with her presence;*
- ♥ *Connective: desiring to link hands and hearts;*
- ♥ *Cooperative: able to work with others without needing to be in control;*
- ♥ *Diffuse: perceives and understands a wide range of stimuli;*
- ♥ *Relational: interested in preserving and deepening relationships;*
- ♥ *Receptive: open to receive the new, different, and wondrous;*
- ♥ *Empowering: awakens others to their potential;*
- ♥ *A Be'er: introspective, drawn to the spiritual and the philosophical;*
- ♥ *Healing: carries the ability to heal body, mind, and spirit through talent for listening deeply to her internal, inherent wisdom.*

Pondering these attributes, it is easy to see why relationships flourish when they are present. In contrast, consider the following list of masculine qualities.

While each is vitally important for the art of accomplishment, many don't do a lot for fostering sacred partnership.

MASCULINE ENERGY IS . . .

- ♥ *Judgmental: something must be understood rationally to be accepted;*
- ♥ *Goal oriented: the shortest distance between two points is most desirable;*
- ♥ *Logical: believes that anything can be thought through;*
- ♥ *A Protector: sees it as a holy calling to protect those who are vulnerable;*
- ♥ *Conquering: it is his job to do it and do it well;*
- ♥ *Competitive: it is his job to do it and do it best;*
- ♥ *Controlling: his way is best;*
- ♥ *Focused: able to use a laser beam of concentration;*
- ♥ *Self-contained: sharing inner awareness is often difficult;*
- ♥ *Closed minded: the new is frightening or merely incorrect;*
- ♥ *Power seeking: needs to be top dog;*
- ♥ *A Doer: brings ideas and intuitions into fruition;*
- ♥ *Hard working: brings that which is conceived by feminine energy into the world as concrete reality.*

While the emotional side of relationship is firmly rooted in feminine attributes, the practical aspects run best when oiled with the masculine's willingness to create reality from ideas and to protect and provide for those in his care.

Again, each of us possesses these qualities in greater or lesser degree. In reviewing these lists, it became quite apparent to me that Gene, at this juncture of our journey, embodies more feminine qualities than he did when we met, and has lost none of the wonderful, responsible get-it-done energy that first drew me to him. I, who now thrive on getting-it-done-well, had very little masculine energy twenty years ago and definitely needed more balance in my life. We're a good example of a couple who has needed to recognize and enhance other aspects of our being in order to keep our relationship from tilting out of existence.

REPLACING CONTROL WITH CLARITY OF FEELING

No matter what balance we need to bring into our selves and our relationships, the masculine trait of control is one that we *all* must guard against and replace with clarity of feeling if we want to have loving partnerships. Control suffocates marriage. Controlling behavior binds and gags the Sacred Feminine voice and renders relationships sterile and unsatisfying. Knowing that the need to control usually comes from deep-seated fear and insecurity gives us a glimpse of insight into the areas we need to explore within ourselves. If control is an issue in our lives, fear, insecurity, and their brother righteousness are likely hiding around the corner.

Only we can look into the alcoves of our psyches and draw out those aspects that need healing and transforming. This personal introspection is the laboratory in which we become candidates for sacred partnership with our beloved. By becoming familiar with the feelings that prompt us to attempt to control other people and circumstances, we can work toward releasing their grasp on our actions. Without clarity about the driving forces behind our need to control, they will remain firmly planted in the driver's seat, and we will be virtually at their mercy. Healing fears and insecurities is often painful and difficult work, but it is a soul task that we cannot shirk if we long for intimacy and sacred partnership.

WOMEN AS TEACHERS OF LOVE AND RELATIONSHIP

At this juncture of history, it is the job of Feminine Energy to teach Masculine Energy how to have heartfelt alliances. It's no surprise to anyone that men, conditioned by the limitations of our society, have been more cut off from their feminine nature than have women. Because of the disassociation from their feeling nature, men often have a more difficult time reclaiming their Sacred

Feminine voice within. They need gentle but persistent encouragement from women as they go about this task. We women must be the teachers, for although we may have kept silent about the Sacred Feminine, we have, for the most part, kept its wisdom secure in the deepest reaches of our hearts.

Women seem to have an intuitive knowledge that heart connection is the essential ingredient our souls long for in sacred partnership. Probably because we have been born female and therefore carry a great deal of feminine energy, many women also have an innate gift for fostering the emergence and evolution of this much-longed-for heart connection in marriage.

Therefore, it is our great mission and sacred task to create a climate in which the feminine energy—love, compassion, inclusion, intuition, and acceptance—can blossom, and the masculine energy—both within ourselves and within our men—are balanced and harmonized with the Divine Feminine.

I know that sometimes this responsibility feels like a giant burden to us women and that we often resist being the relationship teachers. That's okay, as long as we eventually come back to an acceptance that right or wrong, fair or unfair, it's just the way it is. A few months ago I was walking with a young woman named Jodie who was discouraged with her role in her relationship with James and resisting it to the point of considering breaking up. "Do I *have* to be his teacher? Who can I find that I don't have to *teach*?!" she asked me, and wasn't altogether thrilled with my answer of "Probably no one. The reality is that the feminine is usually the tutor as far as love and relating goes, but he has much to teach you, too."

I shared with her some of the ways that Gene and I have been one another's teachers and mentors over the course of our relationship and told her that I, too, felt rebellious and discouraged at times. But, in actuality, things just worked better and more naturally when I accepted that, in the intimate relationship arena, I am the one who knows more innately how to do it. Something must have clicked for her, because I will be performing Jodie's and James' wedding ceremony soon.

Resistance to teaching our men only silences the feminine voice within that knows how to love. Accepting the role of Teacher of Love will help us sing our song and fulfill our mission of creating emotional and spiritual sanctuaries in our marriages. For sacred partnership to exist, the feminine voice must ring loudly and clearly, yet *gently*. We must always remember that a man (or woman for that matter) who feels defensive and attacked probably won't manifest much receptivity, intuitiveness, or compassion. Rather he will retreat as fast as possible to the security of the masculine principles of control, judgment, and closed-mindedness.

But if we proceed gently and lovingly to heed the call of sacred partnership, we can all make progress. Together, hand in hand, we can couple the nobility of masculine-mind with the compassion of feminine-heart and not only share our vision of sacred partnership with others, but live it courageously. It is an all-important charge from the very core of our souls. The core of Love.

Chapter Two

RETURN
TO THE
HEART

Our hearts are the rivers through which God's love flows.

$\mathscr{F}$rom the very essence of our being, we have a deep desire to live compassionate, caring lives; to gently provide heartfelt solace, nurturance, and fun for ourselves and each other. Nowhere are we hungrier for a return to the heart than we are in our primary relationships. In the sacred circle of our family, the need for kindness and consideration is intensely felt. Tired and worn out from the battle of the sexes and sickened by abuse of all kinds, we long for a safe harbor in which to rest and revitalize. We yearn to move into the creative, compassionate waters of living gently with ourselves and others, able to relax and trust our relationships without being constantly on our guard or on the offensive.

The good news is that we can learn to do that. It all begins with becoming openhearted.

BEING OPENHEARTED

An open heart is marked by an ability to express compassion and understanding and to live from a deep desire to serve. Behavior that comes from the heart is welcoming and tolerant, while behavior that pulls us from our hearts is usually rooted in fear and expresses itself in defensive, suspicious, and attacking ways. Although fear and self-contempt often keep us from expressing our true nature, beyond the armor and defensiveness of our doubts, wounds, and prejudices, we are all naturally loving and openhearted. It's a matter of remembering that on a daily basis.

We all see wonderful examples of people opening their hearts to others when we watch the way humans respond to disasters. Perfect strangers risk their lives to save the lives of others or to help ease their pain in both tangible and intangible ways.

You may be thinking that it's easy to be compassionate toward a traumatized stranger during a flood but not so easy to allow our hearts to expand in the face of criticism and painful circumstances. I agree. But because society as a whole is becoming more familiar with psychology and personal empowerment, we are realizing more than ever before that we have choices about how we view the things that happen to us. We are moving away from a poor-me victim stance of how *they* or *God* or *it* is out to get us and realizing that the lessons in our lives can be seen as fodder for our soul's growth and evolution. There may be nothing we can do *about* circumstances, but there is definitely a lot we can do *with* them and gain *from* them through our responses. Moving from the fear-based position of helpless victim to the strength of being a willing student of life's assignments is a firm step toward heart centered living.

Elisabeth Kübler-Ross, noted expert in the field of death and dying, often talks about people who have had Near Death Experiences (NDEs) as people who can teach a lot about heart centered living. The vast majority of persons experiencing NDEs return from their encounter with death blessed with illuminated attitudes. NDEs *know*, in the depths of their hearts, that God is Love and that we are sparks of her divinity. If God is the galaxy, we are the stars. While the experience is still fresh and uncontaminated with earthly energy, NDEs' heart centers emit a pure and loving energy. It is a blessing to be in their presence.

While still in his thirties, Joe, a friend of mine, had a NDE following a severe heart attack. He had talked only to his wife about his experience because it was very precious to him and he felt any cynicism toward it would be extremely painful. Knowing that I worked with death and dying, he courageously shared his experience with me.

Joe had many of the phenomena described by others—a dark tunnel and then bright light, friends and relatives greeting him, and a river between himself and the personification of the Light. As a Christian, his image was Jesus. The wordless wonder of being in the presence of Jesus opened his heart. Joe, like almost all NDEs, said that the love emanating from Christ was indescribable. They chatted and Jesus told him that it wasn't time for him to stay. My friend, although he had a wife and three little babies whom he adored, desperately wanted to remain in the light of this incredible love. He didn't, but he did bring a reflection of it back with him. To this day, he is one of the happiest and sweetest people that I know. He loves life and is solidly centered in his heart, emanating love and acceptance to everyone he encounters.

Most of us will not have the opportunity for such a dramatic heart opening. But we don't have to. We can set our intention toward becoming openhearted and then activate our will to help bring it about. We are miraculous "stars" of God, and we can move into our hearts by simply asking for the love of God to flow through us. It will happen. Our job is to clear the debris from our emotional and physical bodies in order for our spiritual bodies to be purer channels through which unconditional love can flow. It's what we're here for.

WHAT IS UNCONDITIONAL LOVE?

The highest form of openheartedness is unconditional love. Unconditional love is the expression of God's love flowing through us, with no strings or expectations attached. Using our hearts as a channel for the Divine to love in this unconditional way brings us into the transpersonal realm. Transpersonal means above and beyond the physical, emotional, and mental parts of our ego selves and into our soul, the spark of God-love within us that is not connected to personality, ideas, or feelings.

Edith R. Stauffer, author of *Unconditional Love and Forgiveness*, has graciously agreed to let me share her definition of unconditional love. Edith is an inspiration to me. In her eighties, she is the director of Psychosynthesis International, a practicing psychotherapist, healer, and seminar leader, *and* witty lady! "Unconditional love does not mean keeping the object of our love happy and comfortable on a personality level. It means using foresight and wisdom to keep alive those qualities which will stimulate the growth and well-being of our loved ones. Love guards, stimulates, and protects, yet it does not hinder freedom. Unconditional love engenders a sense of personal responsibility.

"Unconditional love is expressed and experienced on all four levels of our being. On a physical level, unconditional love is a lightness, a sense of relief, a warmth which is often felt in the chest and throat—we feel relaxed and free of tensions.

"On an emotional level, we feel unconditional love as a sense of freedom, non-defensiveness, and joy. We feel open and responsive. We have a sense of well-being. We have a feeling of liking ourselves—our self-esteem is at optimum and we highly regard others.

"On a mental level, we are accepting and able to understand all points of view without blame and judgment. We feel free to express our beliefs and our opinions because we are not attached to our ideas. We give others the freedom to express their ideas and opinions and we seek to understand them without prejudgment.

"On a spiritual level, we experience unconditional love as a sense of positive creative energy. We feel compassion and a desire to give and relate to others and unite with them. We feel trust and a deep inner security of knowing that, for self and others, all is well. We are able to relate to all people with a warm acceptance and with outgoing goodwill."

All aspects of our beings grow and flourish in the light of love; therefore, nowhere is it more important—and often most difficult—to love unconditionally than in heart centered marriage. Our hearts are called to become the rivers through which God's love flows to our beloved. Partnership *becomes* sacred as it marinates in the safe freedom and spiritual mystery of unconditional love.

LOVE OF SELF AND OTHERS

So often, instead of being unconditionally loving and openhearted toward ourselves and our partners, we toss our most lethal salvos, ripping and shredding ourselves and each other mercilessly. He doesn't do this or that well, she should have done thus or so, I shouldn't have said yea or nay and on and on. Such condemnation undermines our inner security and wounds our spirits so completely that we can only act and react from our bleeding guts, losing touch with the soft, gentle yet incredibly strong nature of our hearts.

Monitoring and gentling how we treat and speak to ourselves and one another is a lifelong process. For example, I particularly need to watch myself very carefully when I am immersed in a writing project. It's very easy for me to upbraid myself about such things as the slow pace of my progress or triteness of the content. When I am in the throes of chastising myself or Gene, my heart squinches up and I am, for the moment, lost to myself and to those with whom I'm trying to relate.

Only when we become deeply committed to exploring and healing our own fears, in order to open our souls to radiant and deserved self-love, will we be secure enough to truly open our hearts to life and loved ones. Then we can be the bright, serviceful people we are meant to be. Once we have the courage and ability to transform our fears, and the intuition to discover what we are genuinely feeling, we will find our inherent talent for living from our hearts where, if it *feels* right, it probably *is* right!

DOES IT COME FROM THE HEART?

When we are wondering if we are acting from our hearts or *re*acting from a wounded place or old habit pattern, a few good questions to ask are, Does this come from my heart? Would I be happy for those whom I admire to know how I am acting or feeling right now (especially the person in the mirror, the all-important friend who lives inside my skin)?

Also helpful is to become more acutely aware of our hearts. Two simple ways to do this are to lower our heads while in meditation or prayer so that our closed eyes are directed toward our heart. This brings meditative focus to our heart center, which energizes and opens it. Simply putting our hands over our heart and gently thanking it for the work it does and asking for its guidance can also bring profound changes in our actions and feelings.

Sufi Master Atum O'Kane says that the language of the heart is sighs, laughter, and tears. In order to return to our hearts and assuage our hunger for giving and receiving love, we need to accept our sighs, while comforting the inner sigher; unleash our stifled laughter, thereby freeing the one in us who longs to laugh; and hardest of all, dip into our vulnerable well of tears, while tenderly holding our interior weeper in the shelter of loving arms. As we can surrender into the mystery of God as love and ourselves as reflections of that same love, we will return home to our hearts.

HEART OF THE MATTER

Some of the key ingredients for heart centered relationship are summed up in the following little acronym:

H umor

E nthusiasm

A ppreciation

R espect

T rust

Humor is an important leavening agent in marriage. Without it, things can fall very flat, but with a dose of humor, dark situations can be brightened and lightened. In the past, my obsession with writing has created discomfort for Gene, and been a great source of guilt for me. When I started the countdown on this book, I decided to face the issue head on and asked Gene to tell me if he felt abandoned or neglected. Alerting me to his feelings would help me considerably since I didn't want to have to keep one eye on him, gauging his mood, while attempting to engage with my creativity and computer. He agreed that he would let me know, and then with a twinkle said he would wear a name tag, saying "Hello . . . my name is . . . ." His humorous approach allowed us to laugh at something that had, in the past, tainted my writing joy. I could then plunge ahead guilt-free.

Enthusiasm for life in general and our partner in particular is also essential to an open heart. Too often we can get caught in "adultism" and repress our spontaneous Inner Child and Magical Mystic in the all important and ever-so-responsible things we must do as adults. In general, when our enthusiasm begins to wane, a thin gray pallor of dullness covers everything we see and touch. On the other hand, life becomes much more brilliant when colored with enthusiasm—it's the difference between being a mud hen and a macaw.

Appreciation stirs the coals in our sacred fire of partnership. We all need to be seen and acknowledged for what we do and who we are. Action without appreciation can turn to resentment or rebellion, whereas admiration and recognition can spark us into movement and creativity. We've all had the experience of talking with someone who is an especially appreciative audience. In the warmth of their attention, we're likely to catch fire and become more articulate, funnier, and wiser than we ever knew we were.

Respect comes as we learn to understand where a person has come from and what motivates, terrifies, or enthralls them. Talking about your personal histories with each other is a great way to gain respect for your mate. What is the genesis of your values and desires? As the trite but true statement says, it is so much easier to respect someone when you have walked a mile in their moccasins. Being in our partner's shoes, if only through empathetic conversation, helps us understand why they act and react as they do. With understanding comes acceptance and respect.

Trust is the infrastructure of marriage. Trust, if lost, can and must be regained for sacred partnership to exist. For, while falling in love is strongly influenced by involuntary soul chemistry, staying in love depends largely on the continuity of commitment and trust.

THE MYSTERY OF FALLING IN LOVE

Meeting and falling in love is a little like plunging into magical madness. For an enchanted moment in time, our individual boundaries dissolve into an intense feeling of being "at home" with our newly discovered love. The deep desire to be connected to and known by another at a soul level is satiated. We are in a state of gluttony, not able to get enough of the other person. Untiringly and with great interest and fascination, we explore each other physically, emotionally, and spiritually. Obsessed with thoughts of our beloved, all else tends to dim in the light of our love for this one chosen person. We are blinded by love.

Meeting Gene was one of the most magical experiences of my life. On a whim, a friend and I decided to go to Hawaii. Since we had very little money, we camped out at the tiny apartment of a woman I had worked with in the past. It didn't turn out to be a very good situation for any of us, so my traveling companion Patti—who wasn't known for assertiveness in those days (were any of us, then?)—became very aggressive about getting us out of Honolulu and to a neighbor island. Reserving airline seats was an almost impossible feat since there was an army of Shriners in the islands for a huge convention. Finally Patti found us two tickets to the island of Maui.

Maui was beautiful, a true paradise for lovers, which only underscored how lonely we both felt, she because her boyfriend was in New York and I because there was no boyfriend, period. Sitting on the lanai before dinner, I said, "You know, Patti, I'm *finally* over my husband and really ready to meet someone." That night we screwed up our courage and ventured, *unescorted,* into the hotel bar. I know this sounds incredibly old fashioned, but twenty-some-odd years ago we were pretty sheltered women. Not being familiar with bar etiquette, we arrived too early. Gene was the only person there. I was immediately attracted to him. The fact that he was tall, tanned, and handsome helped, but there was some other mysterious allure. I felt as if my soul recognized his. Although I'd never believed in love at first sight, that night I experienced it. Later, while walking the beach, we saw five falling stars in the space of twenty minutes. The very heavens seemed to be rejoicing at our meeting.

Although most meetings are not quite so dramatic as ours, they nonetheless contain one similar ingredient—an overwhelming desire to be together no matter what the odds may be. Why?

Although we can offer many psychological explanations for attraction, we really don't know why are we drawn to this *one* person out of all the other people we've met. When we can answer these questions, "Does this person call forth the best in me?" and "Is this relationship one in which I am empowered and, in turn, empower and inspire my partner?" with a resounding "Yes" then it's safe to surrender to the mystery of attraction, acting on the premise that our soul can be trusted to have our best interest at heart, and that our higher self is behind our choice.

Once it feels right for us to commit to marriage, one of our most important tasks is to trust that we, at our soul's insistence, have made a wise choice. Only then can we relax and invite the unknown, paradoxical, and yet-to-be-discovered to be an integral part of the ongoing process that is sacred partnership. Believing in the wisdom of our soul, and in the rightness of our union with our beloved, we can more freely trust what occurs.

The magic of meeting can naturally extend into the mystery of marriage when we nurture the idea that there are sacred facets to our coming together, many of which will be revealed only when we are much further down the path. What does our soul see as the purpose of this partnership? What wisdom did the two of us listen to when we made a commitment to live with and for each other? How does being in this relationship bring us closer to God and to our own spiritual core?

STAYING IN OUR HEARTS

Most of us find it easy to come from our hearts during the magical time when we first fall in love and are basking in the luminous light of shared excitement about finding each other. But it is subversively easy, after the first blush, to begin to function mostly out of our heads in order to handle the myriad details of making everyday life work. How easy, but how deadly! If the majority of our energy is transferred from the magical realm of our hearts to the mechanical region of our minds, the relationship begins to dry out, becoming brittle and breakable. If we notice this happening, it's a great time to bring out the photo album and have a memory-extravaganza where we re-explore the fairy dust that so brightly sparkled at the birth of our love. Recapturing the eyes of love through which we first viewed our beloved can melt many difficult situations and moisten the arid stretches of our journey together.

The first passionate feelings created by new love are etched and imprinted onto the very cells of our bodies and stored in the memory banks of our psyches. They are a savings account that can be "cashed in" during times of stress, hopelessness, or distance. Remembering the high emotional impact of the magic you felt during the early phase of your relationship can lubricate many a rough and sticky spot farther down the road.

INTERTWINING SOUL STRANDS

As all of us who have been in a relationship know very well, each partner has much to learn from the relationship. Our mates, because they know us so well, are very often our most resourceful teachers. While this truth may be self-evident, it is frequently difficult at any given moment for us to be good students.

One way to become an eager, or at least a willing, pupil is to realize that we intertwine our soul strands with those of our marriage partner when we agree to build a life together. From the weaving together of our individual spirits emerges a much larger picture, that of our soul's work, both individually and conjointly.

Keeping that larger soul perspective is vital. To get an image of this joining, sit quietly with your eyes closed and meditate on the two of you. Allow positive energy to flow from your heart to your mate's. See or imagine your soul strands rising from the top of your heads. Watch as those beautiful and unique soul strands mingle together, dancing to the music that only your partnership can compose. Delight in the joy of your souls' harmony. Visualizing like this helps us rise above some of the human issues that often cloud our higher sight, and allows us to travel into the realms of insight about our souls' commitment of the heart.

COMMITMENT OF THE HEART

We have been seduced away from the "heart of the matter" in many areas of our lives, and marriage is no exception. There are techniques for loving, positions to increase sexual pleasure, and handbooks on creating workable partnership. Any of these may be beneficial and enhancing to a relationship *if* they come from a heart centered commitment to the soul of the person and the situation.

Commitment is integral to the success of marriage, but commitment without heart involvement is merely a business arrangement. A beautiful piece of music, well-formed technically and even flawlessly performed, can still seem flat if it's not done with heart. So it is with marriage. Therefore, in order to feed our deep hunger for the sacred partnership we long for, it is necessary to make a commitment of the heart with our mates.

Commitment of the heart means myriad things, but one of the most crucial is that we allow ourselves to surrender to the mystery of love by giving up our need to direct its manifestation. Unless we let go of the certainty required by the mind, the heart cannot blossom; there's simply no room for it. Somehow a marriage of the mind doesn't sound as nourishing as a marriage housed in the heart of mystery. More secure, maybe, but not a stimulus for the soul.

Of course, surrendering to the process is hard to do, especially for perfectionists, who firmly believe that their life-scripts are already masterpieces, or for those of us who find it almost unbearable to do without the security of being in charge. A commitment to surrender brings all of our trust issues up for reevaluation. But by putting our individual scripts on the shelf, we make room for the wisdom of our higher selves to orchestrate an even greater work of art than we might have imagined. As we let intellect, brain power, and logic relinquish their tyrannical hold on the center ring of our lives and seek the wisdom and compassion to be found in the folds of the heart, we will know the joy of being committed to the soul of another person from the depths of our own.

THE FLOW OF LOVE

There are times when our commitment to our mate is more a decision than a feeling. When that is the case, we can allow *agape,* or the impersonal love of God to flow *through* us to them. Yielding to God's love flowing through us, instead of relying on our own abilities to send unconditional regard, is especially necessary for the times that we do not, on a human level, give one roaring toot whether this totally icky other person is loved or not.

I learned a great way to do this from my spiritual mother and mentor, Annabelle Woodard, when I was sloughing through the quagmire of my divorce and my feelings were anything but sweet and loving toward my former husband. She taught me to sit quietly with my eyes closed and begin a positive flow of energy from my heart by imagining the recipient of my energy stream as someone or something that I felt absolutely loving toward. Often I used one of my children, a puppy, or a flower. When the heart flow was solidly established, very, very slowly I let the picture fade and allowed the image of my former husband to take its place. If the flow stopped, which it often did, I would put the easier recipient back in place and begin the exercise again. To tell the truth, I was really doing this more for me than for him because I was deeply committed to being free of the hate and rage I was experiencing, knowing that they were blocking my ability to open fully to love.

When we block our love to and from another person, we cut off our own energy supply. Energy from our soul, or higher self, stops flowing into us when we shut off our heart center. We are short-circuited. As soon as we can restore harmony in ourselves and reactivate our willingness to send unconditional love (it's perfectly all right if it is *impersonal*), healing energy begins to flow to us from our higher self, and then out to the other person. A closed heart can neither give nor receive, while an open heart is a direct conduit for The Beloved to love her children and her creation through us.

Loving is essential! We *need* to love in order to access the wisdom of our higher selves and live out our souls' dream. Matthew Fox, founder of the Institute of Creation Spirituality and champion of heart centered living, says, "When we are joyous and full of heart, we are emanating wisdom. Wisdom is not in the head but in the heart and gut where compassion is felt."

SONGS OF ANGELS

I've heard it said that relationships are the songs of angels made manifest. This being true, is it any wonder that relationships are the perfect vehicles for learning to sing in concert with God? I don't know about you, but I have a lot more rehearsal time than I do performances! Every now and then I feel that God and I have sung a little ditty in perfect harmony, but I'm often wondering if I'm really on key in my relationships, or in my life in general. I imagine that's how it is with many of us, and I also fantasize that God understands. We are, after all, God's *children* and, as with all children, we're learning. Where better to learn than in the sacred circle of marriage and family?

All growth and spiritual maturing begins within ourselves and is then brought into the haven of our relationships. When we believe ourselves to be a worthy channel for the voice of the Divine, we can more readily see others as divine instruments also. No matter how discordant or out of tune we may think we are, we need to accept and love ourselves as an instrument of God. From the expansion of our hearts toward ourselves will flow an ever growing acceptance of others. Nowhere is this self-awareness more required of us than in the holy halls of marriage, where love and acceptance are the cornerstones.

Knowing that relationships are sacred avenues for divine expression helps us orchestrate a marriage filled with spirit and a family overflowing with love. Our intention to sing the mysterious song of the angels in our relationships is extremely important. What we *intend* to do, we are more likely to *attend* to and accomplish. To be sure, it isn't always easy! In fact, it's rarely easy. But with the soul-fed perception that life is a sacred gift to be treasured, we will more readily turn our hearts toward an ever-increasing ability to hear the melody of the Divine as it longs to be played through us.

SIMPLY QUIET

"Great Solitude—Hath one thousand voices and a flood of light. Be not afraid, enter the Sanctuary, Thou wilt be taken by the hand and led to Life's own fountain...!"
—Elizabeth, Queen of Rumania

Acting on the whispers of our souls is often not nearly as difficult as hearing them in the first place. Without a commitment to listen intently, the softer, less insistent melody of God can be easily drowned out by the incessant cacophony of a busy life. Indeed, one of the reasons that we feel estranged from God and our loved ones is that we are very rarely simply quiet. Without having times when our mind is simply quiet, we become strangers to ourselves and then distant from others. Being *dis*engaged from our Self makes it almost impossible to fully *en*gage with others. Spiritual teacher White Eagle says, "The secret of strength lies in the quiet mind." Without the soothing balm of quiet, we are in danger of drying up and becoming brittle.

Unfortunately, there is much in our daily life that silences all but the loudest voices. The confusion and profusion of children, pets, and problems offer us scant time for a private shower, let alone solitude and meditation. It's hard to find the time or energy to stop and listen *inside* to the still small voice that teaches us our heart's unique tune.

So much of our life seems to insist that we whirl around in a maelstrom of productivity. Carting children to activities, struggling to make deadlines at work, keeping a house in order, taking some time for friends and leisure activities, keeping informed of current events, volunteering for worthwhile causes, and even collapsing in a heap and sleeping—all of this seems to loudly scream at us. When I was a single parent with two very active little boys, working part time and going to graduate school, there were many times when I lost track of my wise inner voice and thought that if I *could* hear it, all it would probably say was, "Get some rest!"

If the thought of carving out one more little niche of time, even to tune in to your inner self, is absolutely overwhelming, it's best to take tiny little steps. For instance, when circumstances create chaos and multiple interruptions in the day, maybe the best we can do is to breathe a simple little prayer before getting out of bed, asking not to become totally deaf to the music of our spirit. The prayer that I find comfort in saying regularly is only three words long, "You through me. . . ." With this simple request, I have set my intention to be a voice for the Divine. I have alerted my inner being that, contrary to how it may appear during harried hours, my desire is to sing the song I am meant to sing. Combining this short prayer with deep breathing, saying "You" on the in-breath and "through me" on the exhalation makes it more effective and invigorating. It can be done anywhere, even the checkout line of the market.

Another simple way to start acquiring the habit of a quiet mind is to take just a minute or two several times during the day to close your eyes, put your hands over your heart, and listen until you can feel, and maybe even hear, the beat of your own heart. Simply tune in to the rhythm. In much the same way that the beating of its mother's heart soothes a newborn, we can be soothed by touching and listening to the heart of our sacred inner Feminine.

It might also be a good idea for you and your beloved to make an agreement about finding a sacred space and time to be simply quiet each day—even if it is only ten minutes. Each of you could then help the other achieve that goal. Maybe you could agree to take turns babysitting, cooking a meal, or leaving the house for a while so that your partner can enjoy solitude and quiet. The compensation for such a commitment will be increased peace of mind, inner awareness, and ability to love.

Designate a nook or cranny in your house as a sacred space. Only in the sanctuary of simple quiet and meditation can we discover the spiritual being we really are. In his book *The Power of Myth*, Joseph Campbell states, "You must have a room or a certain hour of the day, where you do not know who your friends are, you don't know what you owe anybody or what they owe you— but a place where you can simply experience and bring forth what you are and what you might be . . . at first, you may find nothing's happening . . . but if you have a sacred place and use it, take advantage of it, something will happen."

Simple quiet restores our souls to equilibrium and allows us to remember to live from our hearts. Life becomes simpler and more intimate when we make the effort to gift ourselves daily with being simply quiet and listening for the soul-talk of our hearts. When we are attuned to our inner voice, the still small murmurings of our soul will seep into the fabric of our days, feeding our hunger for union with the Divine and with each other. Silence is necessary to keep the chalice of our being full and overflowing.

LOVE AS CHALICE

As Riane Eisler explains in her book *The Chalice & the Blade,* throughout history the chalice has symbolized the power to give and nurture, and, in some prehistoric civilizations, this feminine strength was held to be the supreme ideal. On the other hand, during most of recorded history, the warlike blade, symbolizing the masculine, has been idealized. In order to return to our hearts and create the sacred partnerships for which we hunger, we need to once more elevate the chalice to a place of honor. As a sacred container for feminine energy, the chalice can become symbolic of the love we long to bring to our relationships.

Perhaps the definition of chalice that first springs to mind is of the cup used by Christ at the Last Supper, its modern counterpart being the wine goblet present now at Holy Communion. Another connection made with the chalice is the legend of the Holy Grail that reportedly disappeared during the last years of King Arthur's Camelot. Writers in the Middle Ages popularized the idea that the two were the same vessel.

Joseph Campbell, noted mythologist, says that the Grail is what is realized when a person lives her life from her uniqueness. I would expand on that idea to say that the Holy Grail can also be realized when two people come together and create a relationship that expresses its sacred uniqueness. We can each choose to quest for the Holy Grail within ourselves, our partners, and the marriage that we are creating. When we do, our work will be to create, inside ourselves, a chalice of love that can contain our intention for sacred partnership with ourselves and another.

No matter what our belief system, the chalice remains a symbol of a consecrated, honored, and revered article of great value, a bestower of grace, and union with God. When we bring this kind of awe and reverence to our marriage and our love for our partner, will we be as likely to take either for granted? I don't think so. Filled with reverence and gratitude, we will, instead, hold this God-given vessel of marriage in awestruck hands, marveling at its beauty and at our good fortune in being able to intimately enjoy it daily.

PARTAKING OF COMMUNION

Picturing our partnership as a chalice from which the sacred wine of our personal communion is served thrusts us into the immeasurable mystery of marriage and helps us retain a commitment of the heart toward our mates. Communion is not only partaking of bread and wine at church, but is also defined as an intimate relationship rooted in deep understanding, the act of sharing our thoughts and emotions with someone else. In the sanctity of marriage, we have ample opportunity to give and take this kind of communion regularly.

By holding a sacred attitude toward communion with ourselves and our mates, we create a vessel of love, a pure chalice of our purpose for being together. To create such a chalice we will need to be mindful of our attitude, keeping it as heart centered as we can. It's easy, and very human, to forget that our partnership is our personal holy grail. When we get tied up in outer circumstances and inner irritations, we often lose sight of the sacred altogether. That's okay, because recreating the chalice of love is only a thought away, as near as our next breath. We can return to our hearts by simply *remembering* that it is our intention to view our marriage as sacred. The corresponding feelings will eventually follow.

By embracing the attitude that marriage is a holy estate, we can consecrate ourselves to the highest good for both of us. Doing so will feed our souls, that are hungry for spiritual union. Rainer Maria Rilke, the wonderful Modernist poet, writes that, "Love consists of this, that two solitudes protect and touch and greet each other." In Rilke's vision, love is truly a chalice, a holy container for the growth and solace of lovers.

CULTIVATE BELOVEDNESS

Since our hearts are the rivers through which God's love flows, love is not so much what we *do*, but what we allow to flow *through* us from our essence. The Sufis say that, "God is the Great Beloved who kisses the individual on the *inside* of the heart." Wouldn't it be wonderful if we could wake each morning with the thought that God was tenderly kissing the inside of our hearts? With the warmth of that waking thought, we might feel so full and cared for that love from our own hearts would effortlessly overflow onto those whom we met during the day.

If love is our nature, what dams up the flow of love through us? We do. We forget to listen to the melody of the Divine during the day, we get swept up in what we *have* to do or *should* do and get sidetracked from our heart centers. We become blinded to who we essentially are. Sometimes we're like smudged and dirty windows, unable to let light shine in or out. If the window of our beloved-ness is clouded over, we need to discover how best to clean it in order for our essence to radiate through. No one knows better than we do what dirties our windows and keeps love and light from flowing through, although our part-ners can often see our dirt more clearly than we can.

Let me give you an example. For me, being too busy renders my love-win-dows almost opaque. I can't give or take love, and my belovedness quotient wouldn't even register on the most sensitive Richter scale. For times when do-ing too much is doing me in, I have a little refrigerator sign, similar to the circle and slash in the "no smoking" signs. Instead of a cigarette, I inserted the word RUSHING to remind myself that, if I'm to embody the love that I want to, there can be only minimal rushing allowed in my life. Now, as soon as I can, when I find myself rushing around tight-jawed and closed-hearted, I try to remember my little sign and prioritize accordingly. Often Gene will see the indications long before I do and say, with a little grin, "No rushing allowed, remember?"

When Gene reminds me of my commitment not to rush, he gently helps me return to my intention to live from my heart. In sacred partnership, we act as mirrors for each other. Mirrors that are held up with love and acceptance allow us to see our foibles in a softer light. Maybe even with a little humor.

Belovedness is not just sighs and bedroom eyes, although that's a lot of fun; it is also helping each other to be the best we can be. In the chalice of love, we assist each other to be our most authentic selves by being gentle and loving observers of our mates' process, knowing that they, too, are sacred souls whose heart is kissed on the inside by God.

It might be a little easier for us if we could look at life, and the relationships in it, as a school whose main curriculum is guiding us toward graduating into the knowledge of our own spirituality and oneness with God. The wonderful statement, "We are not human beings having spiritual experiences; we are spiritual beings having a human experience!" is a great one to remember when we feel we've strayed from the realm of love and need to reconnect with our essence.

Belovedness is the melody of the Divine. In order to sing the song, we must treat each other with kindness and thoughtful consideration, gently caring for our own and our beloved's soul.

BE LOVE AND BE LOVED

Being love means that we are in the process of uncovering and expressing who we really are, bringing to our beloved, family, and friends our authentic self, as best we know it. But we need to be tolerant with our process and keep in mind that becoming more clearly acquainted with our authentic spirit is a lifelong endeavor.

Sometimes we worry about our lovability, and wonder if *we* are lovable. But, as we return to our hearts and listen to the call of our souls, we move into a commitment toward love-ability—*our* ability to love. Perfecting love-ability is something that we will probably not accomplish in this life, but we can sure give it a go. A good question to keep in the forefront of our hearts as we strengthen our ability to love is, "How much mercy, compassion, and kindness can I bring to myself and my beloved, or this situation, today?" Another good query for love-ability is, "Does this action or statement come from my heart? Will it bring me closer to understanding and a feeling of oneness with those around me?" Thoughtfully considering these questions before acting will help us live in the kingdom of belovedness.

If we have a sincere intention to embody love, we will not need to worry about being loved. For like attracts like; when we are loving, we will attract love to us.

CALL OF THE BELOVED

As we increase our ability to personify love and quietly live from our hearts, we are much more likely to hear the call of the Beloved. The call of the Beloved is a summons from our essential nature, which is basically spiritual lovingness. We can't repress or ignore our essential nature forever if we are to follow the divine design for our lives. Eventually, as the yearning within us intensifies, we will listen to our inner oracle and give our assent to following its urgings. For peace of mind and expansion of spirit, we need to answer the call of the Beloved and allow a new rite of passage to begin.

Our quest will be none other than mystical marriage with the Beloved of our soul, a profound partnering with the sacred inner core of our being that has never been and will never be separated from God. Our dreams reflect this yearning to remember and reunite, as does a general feeling of being out of the flow in our daily lives. Or the call may take the form of finding ourselves drawn toward a new path like a moth to a flame. Mythologists and sacred psychologists would say that during times like these we are being called to the hero or heroine's journey, which means that we are being asked to die to our conditioned self in order to be reborn into our natural, essential self.

Each one of us experiences these calls, and the quality of our life and learning rests in our willingness to answer them no matter how difficult the journey. We all *have* answered the call of the Beloved in our lives, even though we may not express it in those terms. We have wanted something badly enough to work diligently for it, no matter what opposition we faced. For instance, you may have gone to night school while working full time in order to earn the degree you needed. Or you may have married in opposition to your family's desires because it felt like that was what your soul was urging you to do.

My friend Patti recently graduated from seminary at the age of fifty-five, having been unable to ignore the call of the Beloved to become a minister. She tried to resist. There were real obstacles to overcome. Money, time, commitment, and fear, to name a few. Finally, the command was so insistent that she simply had to say, "Yes." The journey began: commuting to school, learning to study again, dying to outgrown beliefs and self-doubts, examining her soul deeply and then having "authorities" question her on what she discovered. Maintaining and sustaining her marriage and relationships with children, grand-children, and friends all were a part of the challenge. It was a hard road to travel, but as a result of Pastor Patti's answer to the call of her essential nature, her relationship with herself is stronger than it's ever been, and her marriage is deeper, richer, and fuller also.

This is not surprising when you consider that internal mystical union with the Beloved will naturally be outpictured in our primary relationships and all others whom we touch. When we are profoundly partnered with that which is sacred within us, our other partnerships will become sacralized as a result. The ripples imprinted on the soul of the world by mystical union with our essential nature—the sacred path of partnership both within and without—cannot be measured or even fathomed by us, so great are their significance.

ALLIES, ACCOMPLICES, AND ANGELS

When we answer the call of the Beloved by following the divine design for our lives, the universe will support us in wonderful and loving ways. Teachers will appear, synchronicities will abound, opportunities will present themselves. I experienced this phenomenon after my divorce. Each day I faithfully affirmed that I was becoming clearer and clearer about the direction my life was to take.

Although confusion reigned at first, I kept repeating the statement, tried to maintain belief in it, and concentrated on keeping my heart open to the call of the Beloved.

One day I was driving by a local university and, on an impulse, turned in. The idea of becoming a therapist had been vaguely swimming in my mind, but I had basically held its head under water through self-doubt and worry. Almost without realizing it, I found myself in the registrar's office inquiring about graduate psychology programs. I was told that they were already closed for the upcoming semester. I must admit that relief flooded through me. Ah, what a great excuse. I'd tried. Now I could go home and remain *safe*. Just as I'd breathed my second sigh of relief, the registrar suggested that I audit the preliminary classes and register the next semester.

Reluctantly, but with mounting excitement, I agreed. All barriers began to fall. The head of the department took me under his wing and registered me in spite of the closure. My mother, without being aware that I had enrolled in school, sent me some money she inherited from her aunt. And, as you might have guessed already, it was the *exact* amount needed to pay for my entire master's degree. I felt absolutely loved and looked after. Plus, it seemed to me that the Beloved of my soul was saying, "Yes, this is the right decision, Sue, and I will support you in it." I could almost hear the flutter of angel wings.

Even though we have guidance and help on the journey toward our authentic selves, it can still be a rocky path filled with pitfalls and challenges. That's why it's important that we surround ourselves with allies and accomplices as we travel. We need companions, like-hearted people with whom we gather to explore the outer reaches of our current thinking and dreaming—people who resonate with our souls and who support and challenge us to stretch into the outward boundaries of our soul's calling. Ideally, our partner will be among them.

When one of these special persons is our marriage partner, the mystical aspect of sacred partnership takes on new and wonderful proportions. But if our partners are not eager to join us in our unique pilgrimage, we can still enjoy sacred partnership to whatever extent we do resonate with each other's souls.

We are different. Feeding our need for sacred union does not mean that we must share the *same* path, only that we accept and honor our partner's path and support him or her along it as best we can.

PEACE OF PARTNERSHIP

Hearing the call and moving into an intimate partnership with the Beloved of our soul brings with it a peace so profound that it exemplifies the peace that passeth all understanding about which Christ spoke. When our souls are deeply connected to the Beloved, we know at our very core that we are intensely and intimately loved by what Jean Houston refers to as "a divine personality that the universe uniquely assumes for each person." It doesn't matter whether that personage is Jesus, Mary, Kuan-Yin, The Buddha, Yahweh, or whoever resonates with your soul. What does matter is that the deeply embedded *knowledge* that we are loved brings a quiet, peaceful unexplainable elation and unshakable conviction that, no matter how it appears, some mysterious and benevolent purpose is at work in the universe.

Hand in hand with the Beloved, we are increasingly able to live from our hearts. Protected by the river of love, we are able not only to endure, but grow through, any initiation fire provided by our soul's wisdom for the working out of personal kinks. Steeped in the awareness of God's love, we can sing in harmony with the melody of the Divine and bring increased love, affection, and awe into our partnerships with each other and with our essential Selves.

Chapter Three

INTIMACY
AS
INITIATION

*The mirrors of love
reflect our deepest wounds
and our highest visions.*

$\mathcal{I}$n the indigenous cultures of our foremothers and forefathers there were formalized rituals to initiate young people into the life of the village or tribe. Not only did the rites signify that a child had become an adult, they created a vehicle for these young adults to discover themselves and test their strength and resourcefulness. Rites of passage also provided an avenue for union with the Divine by creating a space in which the initiate could discover his or her soul's purpose. These ceremonies allowed a young person to succeed while becoming an acknowledged part of the group.

The advent of the Industrial Revolution stripped us of most sacred ceremonies; our society's "heady," intellectual approach to most things has created a culture lacking in experiential, feeling-oriented rites of passage.

It is, therefore, important to find new ways to gain for ourselves the valuable insights of self-discovery that these early rites provided. Toward that end, many of us have accepted marriage as the ritual for ushering us over the threshold of adulthood. But marriage is neither a cure-all for life's problems nor a guarantee of "happily ever after." Quite the contrary, it is an initiation into the mysteries of intimacy, in which we take turns being initiator and initiate. Within the familiarity of sacred partnership, there is an ever-flowing weaving between the roles of student and teacher, lover and friend, ally and initiator. By taking vows of love and commitment to another person, we agree to share our life's journey with them, to welcome them as the most important "other" in our lives. Sharing our outer journeys, while also learning to know and share our inner explorations, is an extremely important initiation that can lead to intimacy of body and soul.

MIRRORS OF LOVE

Allowing intimacy to act as an initiation invites us to look at our relationships as vehicles for revealing, recognizing, and reclaiming our authentic selves. With intimacy as our initiator, we will see mirrored, in the eyes of our beloved, who we are, who we have discarded, and who we want to become. As Goethe said, "Marriage is intensive learning in which I go back home to spirit." We, too, are catapulted back to spirit by coming face to face with ourselves, daily, in the eyes of someone who sees us at our best and worst, our most loving and most selfish, our most courageous and most fearful.

The mirrors of love reflect our deepest wounds and our highest visions. In the intense intimacy of sacred partnership, there is no place to hide, nor at the soul level do we want to, for uncovering our true spirit is to be connected to our core and, hence, to God. Our partner is the perfect person to show us the dark side of our moon, but, conversely, he or she can also illuminate wonderful parts of ourselves that we may not have the self-concept to perceive. A partner who believes in us, even when we are having difficulty believing in ourselves, keeps a spotlight focused on our spirit's potentiality.

More often than not, when I'm having a bad day and am convinced that I'm a lousy mother or am berating myself in some way, Gene is able to hold the vision for me. His clarity helps me plow through the emotional underbrush of my funk until I can find my way into the light of self-understanding and acceptance. Given the fact that we're all very human, there are times when each of us is blinded to our own and others' good qualities, and gropes around in the dark for a while. Actually, those times are often periods of deep initiation, for a large part of the initiatory process is being able to act in spite of fear and loneliness.

In the bright light of our love for each other, as well as in the dank and confusing tunnels of our disillusionments, disappointments and fears, intimacy invites us into the conundrum of vulnerability. In it we are asked to surrender ourselves to the profound mystery of caring for another as much as we care for ourselves. Not to surrender in the neurotic sense of losing who we are, but rather in the vulnerability of surrendering our little selves to the service of our higher selves and sharing this inner journey with our mates. Sharing at such depth will naturally make us feel exposed at times. But isn't this what God asks of us also—that we expose our authentic selves to him and, in our deep and holy hunger for sacred union, surrender into the heart of the Divine? Such sacred surrender in human form is the initiation that we are participating in with our beloved.

THE FIREPIT OF FEAR

One of the main reasons why intimacy is such an initiation is that it can send us directly to the edge of the firepit of our fears and demand that we walk bare-hearted across the coals. In order to satisfy the deep need within us for sacred union, we must navigate through the limitations that fear places on us.

For fear divorces us from our heart. Fear, not hate, is the opposite of love. Actually, fear is basically the opposite of all good things and the queller of our higher nature's ability to show the love that it naturally embodies. Fear is a curtain through which no light can shine; since fear energy and positive energy cannot co-exist, each moment filled with fear is a moment lost to love.

Because fear is such a powerful emotion, it is supremely important that we heal and transform any fears that are blocking our ability to live and love to our full capacity. In order to be able to engage ourselves, our beloved, and the Beloved in the dance of sacred partnership, we need to explore our own firepit of fear. Luckily, I've found, both in my own life and in the lives of my clients, that once we gather up the courage to stop running away and face our fears *as they arise,* they are not only manageable, but also invaluable to our spiritual growth.

During the dance of courtship, the law of attraction, coupled with our deep desire for union, often drowns out the voices of our fears. But after the intensity of first love subsides and the hubbub of putting together a wedding is over, our fears begin to stick their feet out around the corners of our lives and trip us up. When this happens, the challenges and conflicts of initiation begin that will forge our spirits, making us stronger, more complete human beings.

Accepting fear as an essential element in our own evolution helps us not to blow it out of proportion. Discovering how intimacy ignites our fears, realizing whether we face or flee them, and asking our fears what they have to tell us is a huge part of accepting our soul's challenge to forge who we are meant to be.

THE BEAR TRAPS OF ABANDONMENT AND ENTRAPMENT

Although the intimacy of relationship stirs up most of our fears, two of the biggest bear traps that threaten us are abandonment and entrapment. In fact, it would be surprising if at least one were not present in any relationship.

One of the greatest stresses that a relationship can sustain is the insecurity that results from one, or both, partner's fear of abandonment. Insecurity—a kissing cousin of fear—and love have a difficult time living side by side. If we are unconscious of our fear of abandonment or don't work it through, we will likely either smother our partner or abandon him or her, because we believe it is inevitable that he or she will eventually leave us.

On the flip side of abandonment lies the fear of entrapment, which totally stymies intimacy. A person who fears entrapment is super sensitive to closeness and views even the merest hint of it as claustrophobic. Consequently, suffering from fear of entrapment makes anyone a poor candidate for the commitment required in sacred partnership, if he or she is not willing to face that fear and overcome it.

REFLECTING AND DEFLECTING FEARS

As partners, we can play a significant role in each other's growth by reflecting *our* feelings to our partner in response to their attitudes and behaviors, by explaining how it feels to be in relationship with someone who is acting in the way he or she is. This is usually a better approach than interpreting our mate's actions and labeling their fears. We are our partner's advocate, not therapist.

For instance, Ruby had a deeply embedded, but unconscious, fear of abandonment, which caused her to create continual crises, from which her husband,

Chuck, could bail her out. Subconsciously, she believed that as long as she couldn't get along without him, he wouldn't leave her. So her Queen of Crisis act kept her fears at bay and made her feel safe. Not so for Chuck. His white horse was getting dingier by the day, and he feared he would be trapped forever as her Knight in Shining Armor.

Finally at the end of his rescuer's rope, he told Ruby that he realized he had not been doing their relationship a favor by galloping in to save her. He explained that he was exhausted, losing interest in her as a person, beginning to see her only as a fix-it project, and could no longer be counted on to step into the middle of her crises. She was furious and defensive, but probably not nearly as closed as she would have been if he had told her he thought she had a huge fear of abandonment, which was causing him to think of fulfilling that fear. Fortunately, Ruby was smart and suggested they go to therapy.

Courageously, hand in hand, Ruby and Chuck began to unearth the fears that kept them and their relationship from flowering. One hot little coal at a time they became aware of their fear-based actions and responses and worked on overcoming them.

In the process of therapy, Chuck learned to deflect Ruby's fears away from him, dodging those that seemed to have little to do with him. Without Chuck as an absorbing target, Ruby's fear boomeranged back where it belonged. To her. Faced with her own stuff, she began strengthening herself by exploring, neutralizing, and transforming her own fears.

Each of us is a little like Ruby and Chuck, and marriage provides a great initiation ground for the acknowledgment and elimination of fear. But fear is not something that is purged all at once; rather, it is soul work that we continue to dance with throughout our lives. It helps immensely when partners are courageous enough to join together in the waltz away from the firepit of fear.

INTERIOR INTIMACY

Ancient alchemists and modern metaphysicians believe that we can only create in our own image. Because our thoughts often create our reality, what we think of ourselves will be manifested in the world. If our self-image is puny and limited, or filled with doubt and self-recrimination, then what we create will probably be insignificant and infertile. Only when we know and accept what is authentic and vibrant within us can we create our lives in that image. So many of us are caught in the leaden web of trying to create what we think others want from us rather than finding out what *we* want from us. When we are really who *we* are meant to be, we will be expressing the gold of our souls. That gold reflects precious light onto ourselves and our loved one.

One of the ways to express the magnificence of our being is to accept and explore all of our experiences *as they are* rather than trying to program them into what they *should* be. Attempting to fit our experiences into a permissible preordained script diminishes them, and robs us of the priceless soul lessons they provide. David Whyte states this concept beautifully in his book, *The Heart Aroused,* "To create the golden moment, we must know where the gold lies in ourselves, but we must not have narrow, tidy images of what makes up our 'gold.' Without the fiery embrace of everything from which we demand immunity, including depression and failure, the personality continues to seek power *over* life rather than power *through* the experience of life." Through mining the precious treasures of our unique experiences, we can become intimate with the very core of ourselves. From that authenticity, we can then express the essence of who we are to our mate. Having a heart centered, sacred partnership with another is built on our desire and commitment to having one with ourselves. Thus, the first step on the path to sacred partnership with God and our beloved is to put our personal soul work first by creating interior intimacy with ourselves, regularly connecting with the essence of our spirit.

EMBRACING OURSELVES

The greatest challenge of interior intimacy is learning to love and accept ourselves as flawed but infinitely interesting and charming creatures, inherently worthy of love through our lineage from God. In keeping with that task, I would create a complementary saying to the well-known quotation, "Know thyself and the truth will set you free" by stating, "Love thyself and that love will set you free." Why is it so hard to embrace ourselves with compassion and delight? I think it's because we've been wrenched away from the Sacred Feminine voice of our hearts. The feminine, remember, compassionately loves and nurtures us while *honoring the process* of our maturation into more soul-full beings. Do we shower on ourselves love laced with the feminine qualities of our hearts? Probably not. Most of us come closest to loving our children in this manner, but don't very often cradle ourselves in unconditional compassion.

Maybe it wasn't true for you, but I grew up believing that loving myself was sinful and selfish. Changing that belief has been a primary theme of my adult life. I've come to interpret the biblical commandment of loving my neighbor as myself to mean that it's essential for me to love myself before I can really care deeply for my neighbor. It's hard to give water from an empty well, but genuinely effortless to give from an overflowing one. By filling up our inner vessel with the holy water of self-love, we can freely pour it onto those who need us without becoming drained in the process.

One great way to begin getting into the habit of gently loving ourselves is to refocus our inner eyes, meaning that when we are finding it hard to be kind to ourselves, it is very helpful to see our self as a little two or three year old who is having a hard time. Even the most selfish and poutiest inner two year old can warm our hearts and help us lighten up on ourselves. During the last few months of her life, Ginny, a wonderful hospice patient of mine, was struggling with what she saw as her major shortcoming—being judgmental. No matter what I said, she continued to berate herself. Longing to help her gain peace of mind around this issue of self-criticism, I led her in a guided meditation where she first listed all the ways in which she was judging her tendency to judge. After she had recounted her inventory of misdeeds, I asked her how she felt about herself. It wasn't great. Then I had her see herself becoming younger and younger. We named years and she described how she looked at the different ages. When we got to about two years old, I asked her how she felt about this little girl, knowing that she would have a tendency to be judgmental as an adult. It took several repeat versions of this meditation before she was able to accept and love her little child.

Moving back through the years gave Ginny a chance to review the process that had created the woman she had become. Examining the hardships and the hurdles that she had overcome, as well as the achievements and honors accomplished, helped her feel forgiving toward herself. Also, she realized that she had made herself the brunt of most of her judgments, and had really judged others no more harshly than most of us do. It was a freeing experience for Ginny to be able to combine her quick mind energy with her guilty gut energy and love the inner little girl—and consequently, her adult self—with the compassionate feminine energy of her heart.

Applauding Inner Angels

As with Ginny, most of us find it easier to dwell on our inner demons than to accept and applaud our internal angels. A large part of creating constructive interior intimacy is learning to see our own excellence, rather than always turning over the rocks looking for grubs and worms. Sometimes we become intoxicated with our own wounds and deficiencies—they make us special—but hanging on to suffering or low self-esteem can be an excuse not to acknowledge our own beauty and uniqueness. Sharing our beauty with those we love is one of our soul's callings.

Angeles Arrien, anthropologist and gifted teacher, says that many native peoples ask this profound question of themselves, "Is the good, true and beautiful as strong within me as the beast I am wrestling with?" If the answer is "yes," they can continue as they are, but if it is "no," they realize that there is inner work to be done.

A simple but powerful exercise for accepting that there *is* the good, true, and beautiful within us is acknowledging that we are related to God. When we can believe, at the very core of our beings, that we are sparks of the Divine, it will be natural for us to applaud the truth of our own goodness, reconnect with our souls, and act from our hearts. For the beast that we wrestle with is disbelief in our own spiritual wholeness. This doubt separates us from our source and causes the well of our hearts to go dry. So, contrary to what we may have been taught, self-love does not make us selfish but, rather, taps into the energy of God and creates a flow of love that anoints all souls whom we touch.

CONNECTING WITH ESSENCE

Interior intimacy requires time alone to peruse and ponder our own internal process. We are filled with hidden treasures longing to be found, but, unfortunately, finding them is not as easy to do as it is to talk about. We're so geared in this society to action rather than contemplation that we could more accurately be described as "human doings" rather than "human beings." Hard as meditative alone time is to take, it is absolutely essential if we are to know and understand who we are and, from that awareness, be able to connect with the essence of our soul.

Noted psychologist Carl Jung built a stone tower in his yard with his own hands. For Dr. Jung, working with his hands was soul work. Existing simply and alone in the completed tower, if only for short stretches of time, helped connect Jung with his essence. The zoning board would probably frown on your building a stone tower in your yard, but what self-tower can you construct for the purpose of solitude, introspection, and listening to the still, small voice within?

When I notice that my soul is suffering from a bout of anorexia, I need to pause and make some tough decisions. I usually find that I need to prioritize and simplify, simplify, simplify. Often not easily done, but experience has taught me that making the effort is worth it. Consciously working on simplifying my life and concentrating on reconnecting with my soul's essence brings me back in touch with the Sacred Feminine voice of God. Peace of mind is my reward.

NEW BELIEFS, ANCIENT FEELINGS

We all have new beliefs about life, love, and relationships, but often automatically act out of ancient feelings still fermenting in our subconscious mind. Not sacrificing ourselves on the altar of old emotions and outworn assumptions is one of the challenges faced in the intimacy of sacred partnership. Intimacy forces us to look at feelings that may be in the way of our evolution into heart centered living. What growth did our soul desire when prompting us to choose this partner? What does being in relationship with my mate offer in terms of self-knowledge and acceptance? How am I called to stretch and grow by being intimately involved in my beloved's life?

Since many of our old beliefs and corresponding feelings were branded into us on the prairies of the patriarchy, they will often include ideas revolving around the need for women to submit to the control of men. A perfect example of this is seen in a story told to me by a friend. Cathy was in her female doctor's office in the midst of an appointment when her doctor's husband and medical partner came in. He noticed some blood on the floor and jokingly told his wife to clean it up. Without thinking, my friend's doctor murmured an apology and dropped to her knees to do as she was directed. This woman, who had just as much education and just as fine a medical practice as did her ex-Marine husband, automatically acted on an ancient, inner belief that she must "hear and obey."

While we might not fall to our knees to clean up blood, we probably do sometimes act out of ancient, unconscious feelings. Nowhere are these feelings more exposed than in the intimate relationship with our partner. Becoming aware of the feelings that prompt our automatic responses allows us to decide to update them. Only by healing and transforming the ancient feelings that restrict us can we re-choose our responses to complement the new beliefs about sacred partnership that we hold dear to our hearts.

KIN AS KILN

Going through the process of changing ancient feelings and honoring new beliefs in relationships is akin to creating a piece of pottery. In the intense heat of a kiln, pottery is fired to its optimum strength. Impurities are burned away, making it more resistant to breakage. In a like manner, intimacy creates a kiln in which we, too, are strengthened and tempered, and our impurities consumed to reveal the sacred nature of our souls. No part of ourselves remains unchanged, particularly our egos.

In the kiln of relationship, our egos are fired, reformed, and seasoned. While some schools of thought suggest that egos need to be incinerated altogether, I don't happen to feel that way. I believe that our egos are vitally important to our emotional well-being, and was, therefore tickled to hear a talk recently at a psychological conference entitled, *Come back, Ego, all is forgiven*! Rather than dastardly vermin to be exterminated as soon as possible, the speaker saw egos as I do, implements of awareness, the cameras through which we view our self and the world. Unless these cameras are focused *exclusively* on our own wants and needs, they are necessary and valuable assets.

To be sure, having an inflated ego or being neurotically egocentric is not the optimal way to live, nor is it conducive to sacred partnership. An inflated ego is actually a weak ego and results from low self-esteem and insecurity. Because of their inordinate need to ensure security, people with underdeveloped and unhealthy egos can even become despots by controlling their environment and the people with whom they relate.

Rob is an excellent example of an immature ego attempting to reinforce itself through control over his wife, sons, and employees. No employee works for him more than a few months, as he is a master at recognizing their vulnerabilities and then criticizing them in those areas. He demands more work than is possible, and demeans employees who protest. There are several complaints registered against him from former employees, one from his sister-in-law. Because his wife's parents wrote letters to their other daughter's (his former employee's) attorney saying they had never known her to exaggerate or lie, he has forbidden his wife and three sons to see or have any contact whatsoever with her parents. Since his wife and sons are terrified of him, relationships that had been warm, nurturing, and supportive are now severed. Because of his wound-edness and fear, masked behind self-righteous and rigid behavior, Rob and his family occupy an ever-contracting world. I only hope a miracle occurs that allows him to heal and his family to regain their freedom.

Recognizing that a faulty ego is a fearful ego and needs our love and protection just as much as any other anxious part of ourselves does is the first crucial step in creating a healthy and mature ego. And a healthy ego is something we all need.

Several years ago, in my private psychotherapy practice, I saw a few people from a spiritual community that believed in getting rid of the ego as a path to sacred union with God. Many of the clients I had were people who had joined the community in their late teens or early twenties. They were extremely sincere and struggled desperately to follow their teachers' advice to conquer their egos. For most of them it didn't work very well. Without being allowed to ripen into maturity and mellow in their own time, their egos would often erupt—as anybody having raised teenagers can imagine—and display inappropriate behavior. Then my clients would feel ashamed and berate themselves for having betrayed their own higher selves and the tenets of their community. Often, after they became aware of the ramifications of trying to reject their egos, a little loving kindness and acceptance was all their egos needed to become constructive allies.

Our egos want and deserve to be forgiven and welcomed home! And the kiln of relationship provides a great vehicle for doing just that! As we return to our hearts and reclaim our Sacred Feminine voices, our egos can be transformed into higher expression and incorporated into our lives in loving ways. They may even be so thankful to be invited back from exile that they will delightedly serve our souls, our own and our partner's growth, and the good of the planet in general.

DANCE OF COMPLETION

Our souls embrace out of a mysterious, ancient, and elemental wisdom. At some level we have agreed to join with each other in the dance toward completion. We are drawn to each other because our souls have issues to complete, wounds to heal, or missions to accomplish. Often reuniting with the soul of our partner is the fulfillment of a promise to meet again. Perhaps our souls know of a transformative purpose for which we need to work together as a team. Maybe our reunion is a reward for growth and service already accomplished.

Souls' purposes for relationships are as varied as the people involved. For me, the purpose of my marriage to Gene is to teach me how to really love, both myself and others, and really *be* the person I am meant to be. The meaning of our relationship is more diverse, but also centers in the love that we share with each other and those who come into our orbit. Actually, that's not an unusual vision for the meaning and purpose of relationship.

One woman—a survivor of abuse—told me that the purpose of her marriage was to teach her to stand up for herself and be assertive with an important male figure. Being able to protect herself, as well as put herself forward, is very meaningful to her on several counts. It means that she is worthy of respect and good treatment and that men can very often be trusted to provide that. For other partners, the purpose of marriage may be to learn unselfish attitudes and behaviors or to provide the vehicle through which their children can be born. When asked, Gene shared that his purpose in marriage was, "To maximize my potential." Queried further he said that he feels that the support and encouragement he finds in our marriage allows him to become more and better than he would be without it. I feel the same way.

It may be both fun and illuminating for you and your beloved to explore this question. What *is* your soul's purpose in experiencing the intimacy of partnership with this chosen person? What is his or hers? Asking one another this question and listening deeply to the answer can help you understand what evolution your hearts have agreed to. Such understanding of our souls' deep purpose steadies our steps when the dancing falters.

PATTERN MASTERY

In the kiln of intimacy, our egos face the white-hot heat of transparency. We can't often fool our families because they are the people most likely to see all our faces—comedic, angelic, and demonic—as well as those to which we are blind. Honest relationships keep us authentic and accountable by reflecting both our divine and shadow sides. All too often it is the divine side of us that we keep shrouded in the shadows of old perceptions.

Intimacy unmasks patterns that we have developed over the years to protect ourselves. Exposure can be frightening to the parts of us that need protection. When threatened, we will want to reinforce familiar patterns that aren't compatible with intimacy. If we can remember that patterns of behavior are often our soul's desire to master certain themes, it will be easier for us to look at them more closely and objectively.

Patterns that Gene and I have wrestled with over the years include my emotional dependence and excessive responsibility for the "health and happiness" of our relationship and his need to be in control and to withdraw from anything seen as confrontational. In our early days, Gene's fear of confrontation was equal to my fear of rejection, so we didn't talk through a lot of things—or if we tried, it was pretty unsatisfactory for us both. But our souls were persistent, presenting us with opportunity after opportunity to face our fears and, consequently, work through the themes presented by our patterns of avoidance and dependence.

Many of the nitty gritty ways we worked through these patterns will be discussed throughout the book, but underscoring all of the techniques and self-examination has always been—and continues to be—the conviction that our souls were drawn to each other for our own, and our children's, evolving happiness and *growth*. Both of us have bridled against that inner conviction on more than one occasion. But here we are twenty-some years down the road, having weathered many storms and mastered some pretty detrimental patterns. Also, because of our successes at working through many things, we're more open to learning from the patterns winking at us on the horizon. Both of us know that things usually work out when we can keep an open heart and a gentle attitude and, consequently, we're much more comfortable with the *process* of mastering the patterns.

HEALING HATCHERY

In their desire for evolution and healing, our souls will usually magnetize to us a partnership that reactivates childhood wounds. They're ornery that way! Or wise. For instance, if we had a distancing father or mother, we may choose a partner who is emotionally aloof. His actions, or lack of action and attention, will then trigger in us the same feeling of abandonment or unworthiness that we experienced as a child. Or maybe we were over-protected while growing up and need to come to terms with the fear of entrapment that was instilled in us. If that is the case, we may be attracted to another smotherer, or to a person who exhibits just the opposite characteristic of not enough concern. Either extreme is out of balance and will bring us up against our own need to heal and harmonize.

Relationship provides a hothouse for healing, and part of the sacred trust of intimacy is to help each other heal. No one can do our healing for us, and we can't do anyone else's for them, but we can provide a climate of warmth and acceptance in which our partner—and, of course, ourselves—can develop the courage to explore and transform woundedness. We all know that a chick cracks its egg from the *inside out* and that we can't *make* it peck out on our demand. What we can create is a warm, safe, and accepting place where the baby chick will be sheltered once the protection of the shell is broken.

Intimacy, at its best, offers such warmth and gentle support. True intimacy teaches us how to be a soothing and accepting presence to our lover in his or her woundedness. We need to be able to stand beside our partner while he or she struggles, but never allow ourselves to be abused or used as a scapegoat by accepting blame or the projection of his or her feelings onto us. If we can remain true to ourselves and our soul's survival by protecting ourselves from emotional fallout, we will be able to remain present to our beloved's pain, neither abandoning nor inundating with advice or admonishment.

In order to stand by ourselves and our mates as we deal with distress of any kind, we must become comfortable with the idea that pain is part of life's process. When we make a commitment to view intimacy as initiation and return to living from our hearts, we agree to become consciously aware of any blocks between ourselves and others, God included. Emotional and spiritual blocks are cemented in place by congealed pain. To free ourselves from them we will need to melt and transform that pain. Moving through the flames of pain, we are strengthened and purified into the vessels that we are meant to be.

Our Sacred Feminine, because she honors process of all kinds, can be with people she loves, accepting their pain while holding a sacred place in which it can be transformed. Supported by her loving presence, the wounded can more easily emerge from their shells of limitation.

SWISS CHEESE CONNECTION

Another reason that intimacy is such a wonderful laboratory in which to uncover our true selves is that we are attracted to people who have what we lack. I call this the Swiss Cheese Connection. Each of us has gaps in our adequacy, like a piece of Swiss cheese has holes. In order to fill in our gaps we are drawn to people who have different gaps. Overlaid with them, we form a more complete piece of cheese. Or so it would seem.

The trouble is that we can't get what we lack from someone else, for wholeness needs to come from inside. What often sabotages us in the Swiss Cheese Connection is that it appears to work at the beginning. When first in relationship with someone who has qualities that we need, we feel more complete. We're whole, at last! But as we move more deeply into intimacy, it becomes obvious that the changes we desired are not happening.

In my own case, I was tremendously attracted to Gene's sense of personal empowerment. He was confident, creative, and very independent, all qualities I needed. Strangely enough, after we'd been married for a while, I didn't feel empowered by his strength; I felt dominated. Fortunately, although the Swiss Cheese Connection does not give us the attributes we hoped to gain, it does shine a bright light on what *we* need to develop in ourselves. Being in the presence of Gene's strength and power, I became acutely aware that I'd better work on acquiring my own or I'd constantly feel like second banana and treat myself accordingly. I gave up thinking he could do it for me but did look to him as a model for myself as I aspired to my own inner empowerment.

By contrast, Gene has learned to be more open-hearted, flexible, and funny by being in relationship with me. When we can see our partners not as the fillers of our adequacy gaps, but as mirrors accurately reflecting what we need to generate in our own lives, we become more patient with our individual soul growth gleaned from the Swiss Cheese Connection.

PATIENCE WITH UNSOLVED MYSTERIES

Learning to be patient with the unsolved mysteries of our hearts and psyches— to live and love our questions—is an important spiritual practice, especially for those of us from Western cultures to whom waiting is an anathema and solutions need to be immediate. In reality, the fruit of our soul needs to be allowed to ripen naturally on the vine of our being.

By becoming adept at the art of patience with those soul questions not immediately answered, we will naturally extend that patience into our relationships. Love flows from acceptance—of ourselves and our beloved, and of the unsolved mysteries of one another's being and the relationship itself.

When I was younger, patience was definitely one of the gaps in my Swiss cheese slice, and I writhed in emotional agony when life presented me with unsolvable problems or an unfathomable future. (Maybe that's where I picked up my habit of reading the last pages of a mystery novel before finishing the book. At least *there* I was in control of knowing the outcome!) It will come as no surprise that I was also impatient with myself, my children, and anything else that thwarted me. The growing ability to be patient with myself has splashed over into my life as a much greater tolerance for the cloud of unknowing, as

Saint Teresa stated, and also with people in general. One of the joys of aging and maturing is relaxing into the questions and not insisting that all answers arrive full-blown *now*.

But the change didn't come easily. Only by hurling me to the mat, via divorce, did my soul grab my attention and cajole me into quieting my mind, relaxing into the questions—of which there were a multitude at that time in my life—and inviting my inner voice to guide me.

INVITING THE INNER ORACLE

Intimacy itself is a mystery permeated by both grace and peril. Having the courage to become intimate with our beloved is to also have the courage to be initiated into the spirit realms within and above us.

We spend a lifetime engaging in the process of self-realization, and yet only scratch the surface of our real being. It isn't that we don't commit ourselves to self-knowledge, or that we do a bad job of learning about ourselves. It's just that we're structured very much like icebergs with the majority of our awareness submerged beneath the surface of our conscious mind. We do, however, have within us an Inner Oracle, an all-knowing ambassador from our higher Self who delights in helping us explore the lower reaches of our iceberg-consciousness. This exploration into the depths, paradoxically, puts us in touch with the higher realms of our souls, the internal and eternal Beloved.

Although our Inner Oracle is always with us, it's often hard to hear and understand, or we don't like what it says, so we ignore it. I sometimes feel that God writes directions to me in the sand right before high tide. By the time I get around to noticing that there is a message, it's been blurred by the rushing waters of life. Fortunately, the important messages recur over and over again, and we have a witness, our mate, to help us fathom what is being said.

To be privileged to traverse this initiatory path of discovery with our mates is one of the awesome bonuses of sacred partnership. Sharing our inner journeys, listening to the wisdom songs of another person's oracle, is to return to our hearts and sing the melody of the Divine with them.

Since the voice of the Inner Oracle is a sacred gift, a treasure to be mined gently and with reverence, we must hold any sharing that our mate does with us as a sacred trust. Newly discovered inner wisdom is a delicate and vulnerable bud. In order for it to fully bloom, the voice of the Inner Oracle must always be met with sensitive acceptance. Any scoffing, disbelief, or judgment will stifle that inner voice until the proper climate is created in which it can be heard with respect.

Thoughtlessly, we can abort the very intimacy that we crave by not holding our partner's inner process reverently in a chalice of love. However, with tender and gentle encouragement, inner oracles can become a trusted source of wisdom and guidance. When they speak, we must listen with as much awe, respect, and openness as we would if a winged angel were to appear in our midst.

SHARING PERSONAL PARABLES

The voice of our daytime Inner Oracle may be overpowered by all of the stimuli around us, but her voice rings crystal clear every night of our lives in our dreams. Researchers have discovered that whether we know it or not, all of us dream each night and one of the main functions of dreams is to syphon off excess energy gathered up during the day. Working off the extra energy through our dreams keeps the circuits of our brain from overloading. Deprived of dreams, people and animals very shortly begin to exhibit the characteristics of insanity.

Besides being essential for our physical well-being, dreams are gateways to divinity. Dreams are God's way of saying, "Hello, Dear One. Your wisdom teachers and I will be presenting you with a personal parable tonight. See what you make of it. How does it relate to your unanswered questions? How does it congratulate you on your life? What can you learn from the plot and characters?"

As with the messages written in the sand, dreams *are* elusive. Without commitment and concentration on our part, they will slide like quicksilver out of our awareness as soon as we awaken. The best way that I've found to retain a firm hold on a dream is to lie perfectly still after I wake and go back over the dream in my mind. Moving even a little bit seems to shake the dream right out of my head like sand running through an hourglass. After I've rerun the dream, then it's safe, and very important, for me to title it and write it down on paper kept beside my bed.

Without being titled and jotted down, dreams have a tendency to drift off. The insights and rewards derived from dream work are rich and fertile. Therefore, when a dream feels as if it has a meaningful theme or message from the Inner Oracle, it's important that we take the time to remember it and work with it.

Sharing dreams with our beloved is a wonderful way to start the day. Simply talking about the content of our dreams gives us a glimpse into each other's rich inner domain and helps enhance intimacy. Making a connection through dreams, and the sprinkle of divinity they symbolize, allows us to savor another aspect of the sacred partnership for which we hunger. Dreams can also provide a few good heart-lifting laughs.

Gene and I started consistently sharing dreams in the morning when I first began this book. This personal ritual has become a sweet connection between us. It started out because I needed to process a series of grisly dreams that agitated me greatly. Unless I released the energy of them by speaking them aloud, I carried a residual malaise with me throughout the day. As I shared each morning, Gene and I both became increasingly aware that this sequence of dreams was symbolic of my fear of being inadequate to the task of writing *Heart Centered Marriage*.

Because he had patiently listened to the nightmares, it was even more rewarding when I could begin sharing with Gene the series of dreams that followed, in which I birthed very verbal and heavy babies and was always able to feed and care for them. In another dream, heralding the hope that I had moved through the worst of the terror, I was handed an eagle feather and told to reach for higher goals and know that I could achieve them.

Without the loving attention Gene gave my fearful, then inspiring, dreams I don't think I would have been able to overcome my fear of inadequacy as quickly. Although the book-terror dreams were pretty easy to interpret, other dreams can be much more mysterious, their meaning cloaked under layers of symbolism. Verbalizing them to our beloved gives our mind and spirit a chance to see them from a different angle. From their familiarity with us, our mates will often have an intuitive insight that illuminates an aspect of the message that we might have missed altogether.

The most important truth about dreams that we need to remember is that we are our own experts. No matter how many well-defined archetypal symbols may appear in our dreams, it is up to us to give our personal parables their ultimate meaning.

JEWELS OF INTIMACY

As we share our deepest selves with one another, intimacy becomes both an opportunity and an incredible challenge. Intimacy smooths our edges. In the tumbler of initiation that true intimacy provides, we are allowed to heal our wounds and expose our souls. Although not always comfortable, intimacy has the capacity to polish our souls to a jewel-like glow.

Part Two

The Alchemy
of
Marriage

*How does the alchemy of relationship
help us discover the gold of our spiritual essence?*

$\mathcal{L}$ove is magical. It changes those whom it touches. Since alchemy is the art and science of transformation, defined as "a method or power of transmutation; especially the seemingly miraculous change of one thing into something better," alchemy and love are closely akin. The word *alchemy* originated from a combination of Arabic and Greek words and means the "art of transmuting base metals into gold." Being in love often does give us the feeling that the dross of our being has been miraculously burned away, leaving us shiny clean and pure, like blazing golden fire.

Love in its highest form *does* transform and ennoble the human spirit. Even faulty, flawed, human love can't help but be a transformative experience. Carl Jung was well aware of the alchemical possibilities of love when he said, "The meeting of two personalities is like the contact of two chemical substances: if there is any reaction, both are transformed." One of the intrinsic longings we have about marriage is that there will be an alchemical reaction between the two of us that promotes our transformation from material-bound people, struggling to keep our noses above the water of disillusionment, into spirit-inspired humanitarians who have an ongoing connection with one another and God. We have a deep longing to wed ego and soul and, by so doing, know that we are loved and are, in turn, the embodiment of love.

This inborn yearning for spiritual awareness is actually homesickness. We *are* spiritual beings who, like amnesiac little kids sent off to summer camp, long for the safety and solace of something we can't quite remember. Alchemists answer the call of the homesick soul by aspiring to combine and transform base elements into pure essence. As a system of mysticism, alchemy is permeated by sexual emblems symbolizing the synergistic alliance between masculine and feminine energy, the sacred marriage of body and soul. In heart centered marriage we hope to do the same: unite two human beings and, through their connection, create mystical union.

From Separation to Synergy

Alchemy presumes a passion for the possible. The alchemist believes in the possibility of transforming something ordinary into an extraordinary essence. Now, more than at any time in recent history, we are called to be alchemists ourselves by believing strongly in a new paradigm for marriage and relationship in general. We need to tap into our passion for the possible by having faith that we can reclaim the Sacred Feminine voice; this, in turn, will mean the reclamation of unity.

The new paradigm for marriage and relationship is not only a reconciliation between the masculine and feminine, but also a mending of the body/mind/spirit split that has fragmented us and our world for many centuries. The new paradigm, as I see it, is an open-armed welcoming of difference and diversity into the wholeness and synthesis of partnership. Philosophers see synthesis as the unified whole in which opposites are reconciled.

This is what we need to do—rescue our relationships from the separation fostered by the patriarchy's gender entitlement and elevation of the intellect, and reunite women and men, spirit and mind, as essential elements of the Whole. Then, rather than enduring the separation of either/or, we will meet in the embrace of both/and. As we repair the rift between opposites, we will reclaim and refurbish our inner and outer lives, allowing for the synergy of cooperation to flourish. In the art of synergy, cooperative forces work together to form a greater total effect without losing any of their individuality.

At this very important time in our evolution, we are called to melt into the mystery of alchemical marriage by creating a complementary circle of love and wholeness with our partner. With the intention to live in the alchemy of equality, we can transform the separation caused by fear, competition, and alienation into a union dedicated to cooperation for the highest and best good of all.

In the new paradigm of alchemical equality, people choose to be together because it makes both partners more joyful and enhances their ability to uncover gems of spiritual reality within themselves. By interlacing our hearts we support each other's underlying energy for moving toward the spiritual essence that we are here to recover and embody. Our partnership can become a sacred space in which the intrinsic desires of our heart and soul can take root and flower.

Chapter Four

Two Shall Become More:
Creating Complementary Interdependence

*Two solitudes interlacing hands and hearts become
temple pillars providing sanctuary, solace, and soul growth.*

Two people marry and become one. No! Why would we want to go into a relationship that by its very definition diminishes both participants? Clearly this is a reductionistic concept, and what we hunger for in love and marriage is expansion, growth, and deepening. As a friend of mine so aptly put it, "For centuries the idea was that you married and became one . . . and it was *him*!" Unraveling that long-held, thoroughly unrealistic and erroneous concept is one of the tasks of sacred partnership.

In a truly synergistic union, one plus one actually equals three. He and She create We, without losing He or She. Two individuals form a union that, as a separate entity, is expansive and evolutionary, a container where both individuality and partnership can flourish. At the soul level, we do not want to lose ourselves *or* consume another in marriage; instead, we have a basic yearning to live in concert with another person to enhance each individual self as well as create a whole that is bigger and greater than its parts.

Muscles and organs of the body are good examples of individual parts working together synergistically. But when I think of a more alchemical symbol for the synergistic combination of opposites, the yin-yang sign comes to mind. In it, light and shadow fit together in a graceful curve—each containing a circle of the other within itself. Intertwined, they form a perfect circle, which is a universal symbol of wholeness and infinity.

The yin-yang symbol.

INTERLACING HEARTS, INTERTWINING LIVES

I've heard it said that marriage is a mystery between two universes. That makes sense to me for, as inextricably as planets are bound together in the cosmic dance of synchronistic orbiting, the lives of marriage partners are intertwined. A more earthy symbol of the interconnectedness of marriage is the huge marine ropes that tie ships to their moorings. These ropes are made up of thousands of tiny individual strands, woven and coiled together to form an enormous and effective whole. In marriage, our lives also become coiled and woven together; if this joint weaving remains only on a pragmatic and functional level, it becomes more a business merger than a sacred partnership. But, when our hearts are interlaced with our partner's in an awareness of the great mystery of marriage and the renaissance of the soul in which we are both participating, our need for sacred connection is satisfied, our hearts open, and our souls expand.

To be united by intertwining hearts, living together, emotionally, as graciously and beautifully as the lovers in Moscho's sculpture of Atlanta and Meleager are entwined physically, we can soar to great heights. We can, by our very being, treatment, and attitude, inspire each other to aspire to our soul's best.

THE POWER OF PARTNERSHIP

We all know of some marriages that diminish one or both of the parties but, luckily, we can also point to others that enhance the individual while creating a vibrant, serviceful whole. Such unions positively affect both the people and institutions upon whom their shadows fall. In these latter marriages, the power of partnership becomes very apparent. These unions make a difference in each partner's life and in the life of the planet. Couples actively working to form dynamic partnerships are committed to moving beyond power struggles *between* them and, consequently, their marriage becomes a powerful ally for themselves and the projects into which they pour their energy.

Part of the ability to expand into sacred partnership comes with the natural maturation process. As we grow in maturity, we have less need to prove ourselves and be considered right all of the time, which naturally shrinks power struggles dramatically. But, no matter how mature the marriage or the marriage partners, more often than not, the penchant for synergistic partnership is the direct outgrowth of the couple's *conscious* commitment to their marriage and their absolute unwillingness to let it slide into mediocrity.

Whether they know it consciously or not, couples enjoying a rewarding one-plus-one-equals-three marriage are probably very good at feeling empowered in their own right and are equally able to help empower their partner. When both parties are empowered—not overpowered or overpowering—it naturally follows that the relationship, itself, will become an empowered and empowering entity.

An easy and often lighthearted measuring stick of relationship empowerment is asking ourselves what "size"—symbolically speaking—is each of us? Is one "big" and the other "little"? The goal of sacred partnership is for both partners to feel, act, and *be* as "big" as possible—to stretch from our birthday suits into our respective "soul suits" and become the embodiment of our potential.

Couples can check the success of that goal by discussing whether the relationship, in the way that it is functioning now, feels enhancing or diminishing. If the "big" and "little" of either partner, or the partnership, is out of balance, it can be righted through good communication and agreeing to work together.

Although sacred partnership encourages us to reach our potential and even beyond, it is important that we are also allowed to be "little" when feelings arise—which they invariably will—that propel us into a vulnerable place. Empowerment actually grows when we can count on being nourished and protected while feeling small and defenseless. If our feelings are allowed to ebb and flow, we will be able to move through most of them constructively, gleaning the learning available from exploring our true emotions. In synergistic partnership, there must be space and encouragement to be real. Being real is an essential part of empowered, heart centered marriage as long as it does not diminish or disempower either partner. Freedom to be real through sharing our wounds and vulnerabilities is *not* freedom to wound in return.

COMPLEMENTARY INTERDEPENDENCE

Complementary interdependence is an ever-evolving process in sacred partnership, an ebb and flow of our ability and desire to complement our partner rather than compete, control, or merely coexist. Science tells us that all life is minutely interconnected and interdependent, each individual life form playing its irreplaceable part in the balanced running of the cosmos. The author of the poem "No Man Is An Island" was aware that we are not isolated islands, cut off from the rest of the world, but integral parts of the same planetary body.

As stated earlier, the miraculous workings of the physical body are a perfect example of differentiation working together in a complementary synergy to create a well-oiled whole. Liver, heart, and brains do their own thing under the umbrella of the entire body system. Each organ's function is vital to the survival of the whole.

Expanding the idea of the physical body to include the less visible but equally viable parts of our make up, we can easily see the need to foster balance and harmony between our body-mind-soul connection by treating ourselves with awed and grateful reverence. For we are inextricably connected within our own body and within the whole body of the universe.

LEARNING FROM THE GEESE

The complementary interdependence of sacred partnership is not a solid, static state of being, but an evolving process of empowerment and support in which partners share decision-making as well as caretaking and caregiving. Respecting each other's cycles of strength and vulnerability, they listen to and inspire each other as they learn to flow with their beautiful and functional soul dance. In exploring this complementary dance of appropriate opposites, we can learn much from the natural instinct for partnership exhibited by wild geese.

The following explanation came from a *Qualife* newsletter several years ago. Not knowing where they found it, I can't quote the source, but I do want to thank the anonymous author for this wonderful lesson from our wild geese friends:

♥ *First Observation:* As each bird flaps its wings, it creates an uplift for the bird following. By flying in a "V" formation, the whole flock adds 71 percent greater flying range than if each bird flies alone. *Message:* People who share a common direction and sense of community can get where they are going more quickly and easily because they are traveling on the thrust of one another.

♥ *Second Observation:* Whenever a goose falls out of formation, it suddenly feels the drag and resistance of trying to fly alone, and quickly gets back into formation to take advantage of the lifting power of the bird immediately in front. *Message:* If we have as much sense as a goose, we will stay in formation with those who are headed where we want to go. We are willing to accept their help and give our help to others.

♥ *Third Observation:* When the lead goose gets tired, it rotates back into the formation, and another goose flies at the point position. *Message:* It pays to take turns doing hard tasks and sharing leadership, each person *interdependent* upon another's unique skills, talents, and gifts.

♥ *Fourth Observation:* The geese in formation honk from behind to encourage those up front to keep up their speed. *Message:* We need to make sure our honking from behind is encouraging, not something less helpful.

♥ *Fifth Observation:* When a goose gets sick, wounded, or shot down, two geese will always drop out of formation and follow him or her to help and protect. They stay with him or her until he or she is either able to fly again or dies. Then they launch out on their own, with another formation or to catch up with their flock. *Message:* If we have as much sense as the geese, we'll stand by each other in difficult times as well as when we're strong.

Like the wild geese, in complementary interdependent partnerships, we need to make sure that our destinations are compatible, conscientiously share the work, and consistently encourage and protect each other, especially during difficult times.

THE PARTNERSHIP JOURNEY

Partnership is a progressive process that goes through several phases of adjustment, growth, and maturation. Each has its own challenges for couples. As with all of life, the following phases are neither tidy nor predictable. More often than not they don't follow a prescribed course. Some couples experience them all, and some couples experience only a few.

PHASE 1: THE FIRST FLUSH OF LOVE

In the first phase of falling in love, we are often blind to our partner's real self and see him or her as the perfect mate. This optical illusion of the heart usually doesn't last that long, but interestingly enough, men often foster the fantasy longer and more enthusiastically than do women. Possibly that is because being in love flings a man into his heart, connecting him with his feelings, perhaps an infrequent and unusual experience for him, whereas we women are more apt to be in touch with our feelings whether in love or not.

Because it had such an impact on me, I can remember exactly where we were when Gene first told me that he thought I was perfect. It scared me to death because I knew he would be disappointed eventually! I had grown pretty realistic about my own frailties, strengths, and human characteristics in general and warned him about my inevitable fall from the pedestal.

Sure enough, the idea of my perfection didn't last very long once we were together full time. The thud of the fall was a jolt for us both, but did allow us to begin relating person to person rather than person to fantasy.

PHASE 2: EMOTIONAL DEPENDENCE

As our relationships deepen and we become more intertwined, it's easy to move into a period of emotional dependence, often referred to as "codependence." I prefer using the term "emotional dependence" as I'm tired of the blame-ideology that so often accompanies what has become the catchall word, "codependence." Actually, emotional dependence can be seen as an immature form of mystical union, a necessary and important part of creating a mature sacred partnership. When we are emotionally dependent, we look to the other person for our happiness, our "self"-concept, and our emotional well-being. We give up what we want and need because we fear rejection, abandonment, or confrontation. Without an awareness of our self, the courage to express who we are, and the willingness to experience the discomfort and exhilaration that follows, we are not truly living. We're existing merely as mirrors, reflecting other people's lives. Until we are able to be our real selves—unique and beautiful or mundane and grumpy—we can't fully love either ourselves or others, and love is what life and relationship is all about.

Long-term, chronic emotional dependence cripples our freedom to be ourselves. However, emotional dependence can be a natural and healthy part of the partnership journey as long as it doesn't persist too long and doesn't diminish one of the partners, most often the woman.

PHASE 3: POWER STRUGGLES

In an effort to overcome emotional dependence, we may embark on the doomed voyage of power struggles by vying for dominance in our marriage. Gene and I were certainly in the choppy waters of power struggle when we had our "top dog, bottom dog" discussion.

Power struggles are no-win situations. If we're indulging in them, it's probably because we want control in some area of the relationship. But since complementary partnership and control cannot coexist, it is very important for us to quickly recognize a power struggle and back off. If feelings are running particularly high, we may need to agree on taking a time-out and return later to finish the discussion. Most importantly, we can gently but firmly examine our own motivations and feelings. Why do we need to win this confrontation or point? What are we afraid of? What patterns of behavior are reflected in this conflict? When we are seriously interested in why we get embroiled in power struggles, and desire to drop them, we will intuitively know any additional questions to ask ourselves. It's important to know that the largest bugaboo keeping us stuck in power struggles is self-righteousness. In order to move beyond the no-win territory of power struggles, we need to honestly exhume and defuse any insidious tendencies toward self-righteous attitudes and behaviors that lurk within us.

PHASE 4: TO HELL WITH 'EM INDEPENDENCE

Either as a direct result of power struggles, or a lack of consistent care and attention in our relationships, we may feel that the only way to be more than a rubber-stamp mate or a disempowered chameleon is for us to become fiercely independent, and "do our own thing." While a certain amount of this behavior might be necessary to get our mate's attention, long-term to-hell-with-'em independence leads to loneliness and isolation from one another. Lengthy inappropriate independence such as this can cause us to be so polarized from each other that an overwhelming chasm develops between us. If this happens, making the journey back toward complementary interdependence is a long and tough, if not impossible, odyssey.

So while it is essential for us to be autonomous and self-reliant, it is equally essential that we not sacrifice our desire for sacred union on the altar of either control or inappropriate independence. Time alone and solitary endeavors that solidify our sense of self and season our souls augment our ability to come together as a complementary couple. On the other hand, independence that emerges from a sense of futility with our marriage or in reaction to power struggles will only act as a division between us, increasing our sense of separateness.

To forestall falling too deeply into the fissure dug by to-hell-with-'em independence, it is important that we keep our eyes, ears, and hearts open for indications that we are drifting, or being thrust, onto divergent, destructive paths. Awareness of where we are headed is essential if we are to continue the relationship journey that our souls have charted for us. For without such awareness, we may well be blown off course.

PHASE 5: ALCHEMICAL CHAOS

Even when we are not emotionally dependent, indulging in power struggles, or stuck in a pattern of inappropriate independence, there will be times when we feel separated, even alienated from one another. That's because although divergent paths can ultimately converge and create expansion and growth, when first embarked on, there is usually an initial time of separation, possibly even chaos. Alchemically, before anything can come together, it must first be totally separated and isolated, because synthesis only takes place after complete disorganization. During fast periods of growth, organisms will totally dismantle, or "separate," themselves before realigning, *always* in a higher form. Likewise, in intimate relationships, we often react similarly when obsessed with a new phase of our relationship or soul's development, separating from our mate as we process the treasures that we're collecting.

PHASE 6: COMPLEMENTARY INTERDEPENDENCE

Our soul's need for separation and space is an alchemical necessity if we are to evolve into our next highest stage of being as individuals and couples. In complementary unions, we can tolerate the separation when we remember that our commitment is from the heart and trust that our beloved will return to us. At these times we must keep the faith that our paths will intersect again, and that when they do, our sacred partnership will be invited to move into its new, and higher, form.

It may be easier and less threatening for us to give each other permission to separate during times of growth and introspection if we remember that the word "alone" is a contraction of "all one." In order to touch into and remember that we are an integral part of the "all one," we must have spaces in our togetherness in which to be "alone."

Just as it is difficult for us to distinguish individual trees when surrounded by a dense forest, it is hard for us to grow and flourish when planted too close to our beloved. We need room for our souls to expand and evolve. In order to stretch toward the light, straight and tall, we must not live in someone else's shadow. As we grow into the serenity of being at peace with both togetherness and solitude, we learn to love the distance between us that makes it possible for us to see each other silhouetted, whole, against the sky.

WHO TAKES OUT THE TRASH?

Because sacred partnership is an ongoing process, the hardest part is often taking the time and making the effort to clarify changing roles, responsibilities, and expectations. Life is change, and heart centered marriage rests, in part, on our willingness, ability, and commitment to change and grow. To ripen into what our souls are calling us to be in each cycle of our life. Roles, to remain viable in the process toward sacred partnership, need to be continually viewed and *re*viewed.

Roles are a collusion between people about who is going to do and be what. Roles can enhance the relationship by fostering growth and freedom or can suffocate synergy and create separateness by becoming too rigid. To avoid becoming stagnant and imprisoning, roles need to be flexible and evolutionary. It's optimal for each couple to create their own definition of "marriage" by letting go of fixed rules and cultural stereotypes and following their hearts about what is uniquely right for them.

This attitude about role flexibility also encompasses the age-old question, "Who takes out the trash?" An equitable division of labor in all areas of our partnership, from the mundane to the esoteric, is a necessary component of living complementary lives. Each couple will need to answer the question of "what trash" their particular relationship needs to share. It doesn't matter how the tasks are divided, only that the division is agreed upon as fair and that each person feels his or her contribution is equally valued.

Some couples solve the task-dispersement challenge by listing each person's areas of expertise and interest and then dividing the work accordingly. Others list things that neither want to do and then alternate doing those tasks or hire someone else to do them. Your solutions will be as distinctive as your marriage itself. As long as each person feels okay about the splitting of chores and responsibilities, it doesn't matter "to whom the trash falls."

In our house, I do all the cooking and Gene does the clean up; I do the washing and he does the folding and we both clean the house. He is the financial manager and I am more the guardian of the emotional climate. It's taken us time and shared history to find a balance in all areas, and we know that both the roles and the chores will probably change hands as we evolve. It isn't so much *what* we do as it is whether or not we *agree upon* who does what and then *do* what we've agreed to do! Not being able to count on our mate to honor his or her agreements can sour the sweetest among us.

DEALING WITH OUR DIFFERENCES

One of the realities in the quest for complementary interdependence is that individuals often grow at different rates and in different directions. One of us may become impassioned by a new spiritual path, for instance, and feel energized and enthralled by fresh insights and divine connection—alive at last! The other half of the couple may think their partner's new track is a waste of time and grieve for "the good old days" of familiar patterns.

In the outdated model of marriage, we often felt that we needed to sacrifice our individual passion for the safety, security, and suffocation of not rocking the boat. In the new scheme of things, we are becoming more and more aware that we can follow our passion *and* also create a vital, growth-producing marriage. We know more about the psychological and developmental realities of the human psyche than we used to. Through our increased knowledge, we are becoming much more tolerant of the singular paths each of us must navigate as we seek to become all that our soul asks us to be.

Since no two people will change, grow, or evolve in the same way or at the same pace, it is extremely important that we hold ourselves and our partners in openhearted hands that acknowledge the reality of our differences. Understanding our own and our partner's ongoing process and current "piece of the road" gives us the ability to encourage us both to follow our bliss, as Joseph Campbell says. With an understanding of our own and our partner's needs, pacing, and style will come the eventual necessity to lovingly make allowances for our differences and to be willing to stretch in response.

For instance, Gene and I have very different security needs. I need to nest and take root wherever we live, while Gene, after ten or so years in one spot, gets the urge to move on to somewhere different. Being in relationship with him has caused me to delve into my insecurities through confronting my need to securely root, and sometimes *rot*, rather than risk the pain of loss and change. In response to my need, Gene has learned to temper his desire to live in fresh locales and find adventure and newness in less uprooting ways. We've both grown (and often, groaned) as a result. Understanding each other helps soften the compromises into loving and caring interdependence. Together, we are becoming more.

GENDER GENEROSITY

Men and women are different. To those of us in intimate relationships with members of the opposite sex, that statement is almost ludicrous in its simplicity. On a daily basis, we experience the differences in both minuscule and monumental ways. Sometimes they're funny, other times terribly frustrating, and almost always challenging. If our goal is creating an alchemy of equality in our partnership, we need to be able to accept the differences between us, using them as catalysts for personal change and the creation of balance.

We *are* different. Denying that, wishing it were not true, rankling against it, and lamenting will not change that reality. We will enjoy much greater peace of mind when we can say, "Ah so! What a mystery . . ." and relax into learning about our differences in order to live gently with them. From a place of acceptance, we can respect and even revel in this mysterious, awesome "other." We can lighten up on ourselves and each other by learning to value each person's contribution to the whole of the partnership.

Remembering the outdated and unreasonable rules that each sex needs to *un*learn will help us extend acceptance to ourselves and our mates. Men need to move beyond and heal from the unspoken admonitions of *"Don't* feel or talk," and *"Do* compete and control," and women need to break the bonds of "Feel for everyone, even though your feelings are not important," along with "Never rock the boat and always seek approval."

While men and women have many inherent and learned differences, we also have many misconceptions that can only be understood through honest communication and the sharing of our authentic inner selves. In order to feel safe sharing at such a deep level, we need to celebrate the differences between us, while extending bottomless generosity toward the gender that baffles and frustrates us, most importantly in the personage of our mate.

But please remember, I said gender *generosity,* not *license.* While the masculine has had—in society and within men individually—the license to disrespect, ignore, devalue, and even kill the feminine for the last few centuries of *his*tory, no more. . . . By letting go of the expression of masculine energy as *the* ideal, we can adopt the ideal of mutual respect and complementary interdependence.

In journeying toward sacred partnership, each gender walks a path littered by rocks from the patriarchal paradigm. Men and women alike will need support, understanding, and a good supply of bandaids along the way. Each of us needs a generous amount of love for ourself and from our mate as we make the journey from separation between the sexes to synergy.

To help us change frustration to understanding, we need to focus clearly on the *soul* of our union and our individual selves. Our souls are integral parts of the Whole, expressed in an infinite variety of ways. There are no cookie cutter souls—we are not little gingerbread people cut from the same pattern with only slightly different spiritual decorations. We are originals, unique and irreplaceable. We are like the millions of varieties of flora and fauna found in the ancient rain forests, all a part of the magnificent whole, yet individual; a fern here, a parrot there, a grub under decaying leaf mulch, or a monkey chattering high in an ivy-laden tree. For the richness of the rain forest to continue, all forms of life are necessary and acceptable. The same is true for the Sacred Whole of our species and planet.

As we bring our whole heart into participating in and encouraging sacred partnership, reclaiming the sacred feminine voice within all of us, we will also be able to move from the seduction of sameness into a deep celebration of diversity. Doing so, we will learn to enjoy the pageantry of opposites rather than insisting on gingerbread replicas of ourselves.

Celebrating gender differences can inspire marriages to thrive through the alchemical convergence of opposite energies and create new ways to nurture and support our soul's evolution. Accepting the differences between us makes it easier for us to give up trying to control our spouse and search instead for what we can learn from them.

While there are myriad differences between men and women, between the connective, relational, receptive, and process-honoring feminine energy and the focused, rational, accomplishing, and goal-oriented masculine energy, we are, *in essence*, complementary and necessary to each other. We must stop the dance of duality and wed our internal King and Queen, Wizard and Wise Woman, in order to create a profound, passionate and tenderhearted new King/Queendom. Doing so will help us stop the damage that duality inflicts, and put us well on the road to the joys and benefits of complementary interdependence.

COMPLEMENTARY DO'S AND DON'TS

The following is a little guide to use as you journey toward complementary interdependence.

COMPLEMENTARY RELATIONSHIPS . . .

DO	DON'T
communicate	*close down*
commit	*carouse*
cooperate	*compete*
connect	*conquer*
have compassion	*control*
co-create	*quell*
celebrate life	*merely coexist*

Look at the list and evaluate how satisfied you feel with each of the "Do's" in terms of your own relationship. Congratulate yourselves. Are there ideas on the "Don't" list that need to be aired through discussion? Hopefully exploring the lists will give you a better understanding of how you both are feeling about the evolution of your relationship.

In using the checklist, do so with the utmost respect and honor for your partner. Compliment each other about the successes and joys of the "Do's," but only share your *own* feelings about the "Don'ts" in the right column. For instance I might say to Gene, "I appreciate your sitting with me here on the porch and talking about our disagreement last night" and, if I needed to discuss a feeling brought up by a member of the "Don't" side, I could say, "It feels to me like you've closed down. I'm feeling alone and sad because of that." When sharing, I need to realize that I may be wrong. He may not feel closed down; I could be feeling closed down and projecting it onto him. If he says that he's not closed down, it's my responsibility to look at my own inner workings.

If the feeling persists, and I'm sure that I'm not projecting, I have every right to gently bring up the subject again at a later time.

OVERLAPPING HARMONIES

Ultimately, in complementary interdependence, our job is to empower, enhance, and augment each partner as we both explore the outer perimeters of our evolution to become who we were meant to be. In doing so, we become overlapping harmonies, attuned to ourselves and each other, while supporting the larger whole that we are animating.

As our relationships ripen into complementary interdependence on both the human and soul planes, we will feel individually honored, encouraged, and valued in the sanctity of our marriage. We will become ever-evolving co-creators of synergistic sacred partnership, co-inheritors of the riches of integrity, respect, and cooperation. We will fly like the geese in a beautiful, supportive pattern of alchemical love. Well, much of the time, anyway.

PILLARS OF THE TEMPLE

Philosopher Kahlil Gibran, in his classic book *The Prophet,* encourages marriage partners to "stand together, yet not too near together: for the pillars of the temple stand apart . . ." In the same passage he urges us to allow spaces in our togetherness in order for the winds of heaven to dance between us. As a person who is committed to complementary partnership and yet requires large amounts of silence and solitude, I've held Gibran's wisdom as a model for my life and marriage.

When I envision a temple in the context of Gibran's quotation, I think of a Greek temple with two main pillars at the entryway and others on all sides. Beautiful, white, carved columns holding up the entire stunning edifice, each equally important to the structural integrity of the whole building. My imagination weaves a slow-motion picture of people in colorful clothing gracefully moving between the pillars, entering the building laughing, singing, and playing ethereal music on exotic instruments. Some visitors take time to appreciate the beauty of the columns, while others are oblivious to them, although grateful for the welcoming shelter of the temple. Still others touch the holy of holies within themselves upon encountering the temple's serenity.

A couple involved in the alchemy of marriage reminds me of the two entryway pillars. Standing together, yet apart. With interlaced hands and hearts, they welcome others into the temple of their marriage, providing sanctuary, solace, and soul growth for those who come. Each partner is strongly and solidly committed to the sacredness of the temple they support. Standing, not in each other's shadow but side by side during the ebb and flow of feelings, they protect the entrance to the interior, whether warmed by sun or ravaged by rain. Over the years, as the winds of heaven dance around and between them, each pillar is polished and honed to its finest essence. Together they become more than two individual columns; they become a gateway to the temple of the Beloved.

Chapter Five

ELEMENTAL WISDOM

*Heart centered loving is an ongoing process
graced by commitment, mutuality, and respect.*

*I*n creating the sacred partnership of alchemical marriage certain basic elements need to be present. Defining the necessary elements is the task of each individual couple, although there are certain essentials we all need: Shared values, respect, complementary purpose and goals, commitment, trust, and clarity of intention, to name the basic ones.

In our search for sacred partnership and communion with the Divine, both within ourselves and with others, the most elemental wisdom for us to keep in our hearts is that partnership—in fact, *life* itself—is a *process*. As with all alchemical processes, we experiment, try and fail at times, redouble our commitment and our awareness, try again, and succeed. Elemental wisdom asks us to relax into the awareness that heart centered marriage is not solid and static like a completed building, but more like the ebb and flow of the ocean.

Relationships are conceived, birthed, and rebirthed continuously. Contrary to what fairy tales would have us believe, we do not effortlessly and automatically get married and "live happily ever after." At least, not often. More likely we get married and "live *interestingly* and *growthfully* ever after." When we can adopt the very feminine outlook of accepting and understanding the ever-changing process of relationship, we will be more able to bypass feelings of failure or discouragement when the waters are rough and growth is painful. Maintaining a loving attitude toward ourselves and a belief in the sacredness of our family is crucial as we journey toward the alchemy of equality and reintegration with the Beloved of our souls.

SHARED VALUES

Sharing similar values with our mate is one of the most important elements of a happy and harmonious love. Looking deeply at values affords us a peek at the human soul; for what we value, we embody. Therefore it makes sense that the basic reason why analogous values are so important in sacred partnership is that we hunger for a soul with matching energy and focus. We long to journey with someone who embodies (or is moving toward embodying) what we, too, are becoming. We yearn for a soul-friend who, from the very depths of his or her being, resonates with our value system. Finding such a match assures us that we are in the presence of a kindred spirit.

Having matching values means that there is agreement between us on basic, fundamental principles. Of course, even in couples with identical values— probably an oxymoron since males and females often see things with a different vision—there will still be disagreements, but not over core issues. Even couples who pursue very different paths in religion or political ideology can resonate deeply on core values.

Georgina and Nick are a good example. During the 1960s, while Georgina was marching in peace rallies in California, Nick was striding up the corporate ladder in the Midwest. Although her radical feminist edges have smoothed and softened over the years, Georgina is still a political liberal with very definite ideas about women's and other human rights. Nick, too, has mellowed, but continues to swim with the corporate sharks and remains true to his conservative views. As a couple, they work on honoring each other's point of view, understanding from where it originated, and agreeing to disagree on many business and political issues. At most elections, they cancel out each other's vote.

Outside of politics, however, their values are very similar. Their family comes first, honesty and integrity are high priorities, and each values spirituality and the growth of the soul. From an inner perspective there are enough value matches to help both feel that their marriage is a sacred partnership, one that helps their souls evolve. So, although to the observer, they may be mismatched, in truth—

deep, profound truth—they are well-suited to each other and the alchemy of marriage.

CLINGING TO THE CORE

When the going gets rough between lovers, it is the epitome of elemental wisdom to rediscover our common core values and cling to them. Being in touch with our likenesses gives us hope and helps us weather the storm. Ideally, it is best to explore our similar values together, but often that's impossible when feelings are acutely uncomfortable. Gene and I are one of those couples who find it difficult to come together to accentuate the positive between us while immersed in the negative of the moment. So I have a little personal ritual that I did a lot during the power-struggle phase of our relationship and still do when the occasion arises.

I write a list of good things inherent to our relationship and ask myself some questions. Being a visual person, seeing something in writing helps me focus on it and believe in it. Some of the questions include:

1. *Why did I choose this person in my quest for sacred partnership?*
2. *If I could move above these current feelings and look at both of us from my heart, what wonderful qualities and characteristics could I see?*
3. *What are my values? What values do we share?*
4. *What do I/we want and need?*
5. *What feels meaningful to me/us?*
6. *What are my/his dreams?*
7. *How can we support each other's dreams?*

I know another woman who lists all the things that she's angry about in the moment, burns the paper and tosses the ashes to the wind while asking to transform and release the feelings as she has the paper. Then she makes a list of all the things that she loves, enjoys, and respects about her husband when she feels good about them as a couple. She says that, although she often grits her teeth over the second list, having acted out her anger and physically released a symbol of it, she is better able to begin the process of reopening her heart to her beloved.

Of course, such exercises require that we move out of a rigid position of righteous indignation, at least in our *actions* if not our *feelings*. Being willing to uncover the core of our similar values, in whatever way works for us, speeds up the process of realigning our hearts and reconnecting with our partners.

GUARDIAN OF RESPECT

No matter how deeply we hunger for it, a true sacred partnership cannot exist without the all-important element of respect. Respecting someone means that we honor and value them while holding them in high esteem. With respect comes consideration of another person's feelings, attitudes, and vulnerabilities. Often, one of the hardest things for us to do is develop a respectful attitude toward ourselves. This seems to go against statements we may have heard as children—"Don't be big-headed. Don't be too sweet on yourself or no one else will like you. Why are you so uppity about yourself? You're no great shakes!" Although most of us were not given such blatant messages, we, nonetheless, gleaned somewhere that respecting ourselves reeked of selfishness and egotistical self-love.

There is no such thing as too much genuine self-love and respect. From the fountain of self-worth, primed by self-respect, flows an ever-ready supply of love for others and for our world. When the Guardian of Respect for ourselves and our families protects the hearth of our home, we are on the road toward the alchemy of connection, moving away from separation to synergy.

Chances are, because we married our partner, we respect him or her—otherwise why would we have chosen that person? Unfortunately, we don't always feel or *act* respectfully. Nowhere is this more blatant than in the "gender wars."

Through frustration and a sense of hopelessness about ever being able to understand each other or connect on a meaningful level, both men and women can be disrespectful about the opposite sex. Countless times I've heard women reduce all men to "little boys" in conversation with each other, and fewer times heard men lament women's overly emotional aspects—which seems to include the predisposition to dumbness—or identify them by their physicality. "*If* only they weren't such *babies*! *If* only she didn't make mountains out of molehills!" There are many more mournful complaints that you can add, I'm sure.

If only . . . I like to think of the word "if" as representing a combination of *ignorance* and *fear*. Often we are ignorant of the differences between the masculine and feminine, and from that ignorance, as well as built-up frustration, we adopt a disrespectful outlook toward those who wear a different body than we do. Ignorance spawns misunderstanding and misunderstanding creates fear. Ignorance and fear cause us to throw up our hands in despair and begin the litany of "If only . . . !"

I believe that gender is one of the devices that our souls use to help them grow and learn. In fact, at a soul level, the "war between the sexes" or the "antagonism of opposites" may merely be an amusing and sometimes baffling morality play. When we can elevate our understanding of gender differences to the status of graduate school soul work, perhaps we will be better able to embrace each other respectfully and joyfully.

Abuse Is NOT Respectful!

In general, it is better to err on the side of too much respect than it is to be stingy and dole it out sparingly. When warranted, we can always retract respect and replace it with wariness, or whatever sentiment is appropriate for the behavior and circumstance. But our society is respect-deficient, not overdosed; therefore, we have a great deal of leeway before we need to be concerned with experiencing over-respectfulness.

This is not the case with blatant abuse. Blatant abuse is easy to spot, but it's not always easy to stop. We *all* have a responsibility to stand up for those who are abused until they can heal into enough self-respect to stand up for themselves! It's a good sign that spousal and child abuse are becoming topics that many people are talking about, but there are still women and children living the reality of abuse who can't speak up. We—their families, neighbors, friends, doctors—need to be their guardians until they can care for themselves.

Of course there are also men who are abused, but the percentage is small because the physical strength and entitlement beliefs perpetuated by the patriarchy have created predominantly male abusers. More often than not, an abuser is acting out of his own fear. Becoming a bully is his way of masking his terror from himself as well as onlookers. The patriarchy is no exception. There is a subterranean terror in the patriarchy—deeply unconscious, especially in the top echelons of the hierarchy—of what they would be if they were required to share their power by *empowering* others. What and who would they become if not deferred to by others?

Those of us committed to sacred partnership are dedicated to transforming relationships of domination to ones of true equality. The work needs to begin with *us*. Where do *we* harbor the need to control and the tendency, however small, to abuse? What little nook or cranny in us still believes that in order to be empowered we must *over*power? We all, men and women alike, have those places, because we have all grown up in the era of power-based, masculine domination.

In our quest for respect, we must look inside. Not only to ferret out erroneous power-based beliefs, but to determine if we allow ourselves to be treated disrespectfully. To a large degree, *we teach others how to treat us;* therefore, it is elemental that we have the wisdom to uncover any reasons, wounds, or underlying beliefs that keep us from respecting ourselves and teaching others to do the same.

If respecting yourself enough is a struggle for you, you may find my book *The Courage To Be Yourself* a great help, for I delve deeply into the issues of fear, emotional dependence, and low self-esteem. If you or your children are threatened physically or your ideas are shot down through apathy or ridicule, or if you even have the tiniest suspicion that your marriage is an agent of destruction rather than a complement to you, please, I urge you, find some help! Very often it is impossible to move out of negative patterns and situations by ourselves. We just don't have the energy or the objectivity to see the real story. It is elemental wisdom to seek help when we need it!

PURPOSE AND GOALS

As a volunteer member of a hospice chaplaincy team, I often talked with people about their idea of spirituality and what they needed spiritually. Most patients, now at the end of their lives, needed to believe that their life had meaning. They often talked about doing a life-review, quietly scrutinizing their lives to ascertain how meaningful they felt it had been. What I noticed, with both hospice patients and clients, is that when they had clearly defined their life's purpose early on and, correspondingly, had lined up their goals to support that purpose, they felt that life had been meaningful and that they had made a contribution.

Many years ago, in a lunch discussion with some therapist colleagues, I first heard articulated the wisdom of finding our purpose and then consciously aligning each of our goals to support and promote that underlying purpose. Purpose is usually defined in sweeping and general terms. (Mine is "to love and to serve.") Goals, on the other hand, can be tiny and minute-by-minute. Making a certain phone call, getting the baby to sleep, clearing up a garbled communication are all examples of goals.

I was so excited by the wisdom and simplicity of the concept of purpose and goals that I could hardly wait to share it with Gene. He came dragging in from work that day, grumbling about how noisy the kids had been in the car both going and coming from school and how horrendous the traffic was. I didn't particularly notice how tired he was because I had a *goal*—we were going to have this great conversation about purpose and meaning. I trailed him into the bedroom, where he collapsed with a sigh, and began my spiel, chatting away excitedly. Eventually pausing, thinking he would add some pithy response to the philosophical nature of the talk, I looked at him expectantly. Gazing at me, he said tersely, "My purpose is to be a *chauffeur!*"

After my silent and angry questions to myself about why in the world I'd ever married this guy in the first place, I had to laugh. Here was a perfect opportunity to line up a current goal with my overall purpose to love and to serve, and I almost blew it! An in-depth heart-to-heart was obviously not going to serve the purpose of being loving to Gene right then, or me, either, in the long run. He was just too pooped to care. What immediate goal would line up with loving and serving? Looking at the situation from that angle, I was able let go of my resentment and say, "We'll talk about it later. How would you like me to massage your head now?"

Goals, needs, and desires evolve. As long as we keep our goals aligned with our primary purpose in life, we will be doing soul work for ourselves and for our marriage. When we were first married, Gene's main purpose was to provide a secure financial base for us, while my way to love and serve was to provide an equally secure emotional sanctuary for all of the family. As we've aged and our children have moved into adulthood, I've become passionate about my career and we've edged more toward center. Although our general purpose remains the same, my way to love and serve has evolved into including more fiscal responsibility, and Gene's goals include much more emotional connection than they once did.

One of the blessings of sacred partnership is that we have as a mate someone who will support our purpose and help us attain our goals. For instance, my minister friend Patti would have been hard pressed to complete her goal of graduating from seminary if not for the support, understanding, and cooperation of her husband, Garret. He was with her every step of the way, sometimes not understanding her draw to the ministry, but never faltering in his willingness to help her fulfill her purpose. Although he didn't share her dream of ministry, he was and is a stalwart champion of her vision. He's now gathering many accolades from her congregation for being a great minister's "wife." After all the hard work for both of them on to the road to the goal, they are more deeply connected to each other than ever before.

ENVISIONING MEANING AND PURPOSE

All of us yearn for purpose in our lives. We want to make a difference, create a wave in the ocean of consciousness, be of service as well as a force for love in the world. Without purpose in our lives, we float, untethered, in a vast and lonely universe. Purpose anchors us in our selves and in our relationships.

We are the architects of our lives. It is up to us to design and build a life that brings beauty to the universe and grows our soul in the way that feels best to us. Sometimes we forget to sit down at the drawing board and *consciously* envision the life structure that feels right to us. A great place to start would be our partnership with our beloved.

Try asking one another the following questions:

> *What meaning do we already feel is inherent to our marriage?*
> *What meaning would we like to infuse into it?*
> *What goals augment and support our purpose?*

These are not light questions. They are, rather, *life* questions. Envisioning the purpose of our relationships is extremely important for several reasons. First, it is so much easier for us to be completely committed to our beloved when we understand the meaning of doing so. Second, we are magnetic beings. What we envision, we will more likely magnetize to us and make a reality.

I'm not saying that we can arbitrarily sit down and say, "Okay, gimme happiness. That's the purpose of this relationship!" Rather, I'm suggesting that we need to open our hearts to the alchemy of our marriage, the meaning and purpose revealed by the ancient wisdom of our soul. Being able to hear the voice of our soul is being able to intuit our sacred feminine voice and hear her message. What gold yearns to be mined from and in our union? We already know. It's really just a matter of trusting that we know and then listening and honoring what we hear.

THE HEART OF COMMITMENT

Purpose is vital to sacred partnership, but without commitment, purpose seems to slip between the cracks of our lives. Commitment anchors itself in a sense of meaning and purpose. Robert Frost said, "Home is the place where, when you have to go there, they have to take you in." The optimal reason that we "have" to take in family members in times of need is that the meaning and purpose of our bond with them is so clear and sacred to us that we *want* to be there for them. They are so deeply etched into our hearts—our commitment to loving them is so all-encompassing, so unconditional—that we would never even consider *not* taking them in. They *are* in, intrinsically embedded into the very essence of our souls.

The entire temple of marriage rests on the cornerstone of commitment, and the strength of our commitment determines the strength and durability of our creation as a couple. Without the commitment to love, honor, and cherish ourselves, each other, and the family we create, sacred partnership cannot exist. Only when shored up by a steadfast commitment to care for each other as much as we care for ourselves can we create a heart-centered, complementary relationship.

The heart of commitment is continuity and consistency. Is it *always* present? Absolutely. But our commitment is essentially meaningless unless it is backed up by behavior, particularly a willingness to do both the inner and outer drudge work, as well as dance the soul dance. As one male friend states, "Commitment means doing the dishes!"

At the end of a poignant long-distance conversation with one of my dearest friends I said, "Words can't describe how much I love you, Bonnie." Her cogent reply was, "No, but your behavior does on a consistent basis." Wasn't that a beautiful response! (She's like that—profound little jewels pop out of her mouth regularly.) That's it, in a succinct little nutshell. In order for commitment to be valid, valuable, and vital, our behavior must match it on a consistent basis. A new rendition of "actions speak louder than words."

Very simply, a good plumb-line for us in checking the heart centeredness of our actions would be to ask if they (either words or behavior) match our commitment to the person or circumstance. If the answer is "yes," go for it. If "no," stop right there. If you are not clear, do nothing for a while. A concise little statement that I try to adhere to is, "When in doubt, don't!" Usually when we ask for clarity and wait patiently for insight, it will come.

REVISING OUR VOWS

In practicing commitment it's good for us to do some spring housecleaning every now and then. What wedding vows did we make that we might like to change or freshen up? Have we slipped into a routine where only the issues that itch the most get scratched or the commitments that cry the loudest get heard? Are we still excited and interested in our love and life together? Regularly reviewing and revising both formal and casual vows made between us will enable us to keep current about our own and our mate's wants and needs.

HOLDING THE VISION

A very important part of our commitment to the process of sacred partnership is that we are able to "hold the vision" of the meaning and purpose of our union in both smooth and difficult times. During periods of despair, disappointment, or anger it's very helpful if each person can hold the vision in their hearts—it needn't be *felt*, just held; that the mutual creation of the marriage is good, strong, and beautiful regardless of the feelings right now. When both partners can hold the vision of the sacred viability of the marriage no matter what the feelings of the moment, the walls of our mutual creation remain firm, solid, and secure. If one person loses the vision during tough times, the perimeter of the marriage sprouts little "energy leaks" and it begins to wobble.

It is natural that there will be times when one of the marriage partners is unable to hold the vision of the partnership as basically sound, and in those instances it is enough for one person to keep the depth of commitment, intention, and sacredness of the union in mind. When one is unable, the other can answer the call to be the "keeper of the connection keys." If this is a once-in-a-while duty, it's no problem, but too often the keeper-of-the-connection role falls only to the feminine.

That's because holding the vision tends to be especially difficult for men, who seem to focus in a narrower band than women do and are often unable to see the whole while immersed in the current. To masculine energy, if the current is stormy and upsetting, so is the whole river. This differing ability to hold the vision is something that Gene and I have had to work through.

For years, Gene, with characteristic masculine focus-on-one-thing-at-a-time tendency, was unable to hold the vision of the essential goodness of our marriage while we were in a hard place. I, on the other hand, was the one who saw it as my responsibility to make the marriage "work." Because the feminine lives in the relationship realm, she will do almost anything to preserve the connection that symbolizes the union, even disempower herself.

There came a time when always being called upon to hold the vision became absolutely wearing for me. I was tired of giving myself away to preserve the union, and knew that we needed to come back into a new balance of each holding the vision.

Both partners need to become aware of the potential good to come from committing to holding the vision *all* the time, even when it is difficult due to hurt feelings or disillusionment. Holding the vision doesn't mean that we have to feel a certain way, it only means that we have the intention to choose to see our union through sacred eyes, even when it feels profane. This will be more difficult for men and also for women who carry the majority of the masculine energy in their relationships. But, because they are good at *doing* what needs to be done, men can commit to holding to the *idea* that the "We" they have created is good, true, beautiful, and strong.

In our case, as soon as Gene decided that he would accept the challenge to hold the vision with me, he did. And that's the beauty of the masculine's dynamic energy: once he decides to focus on and reach a goal, he will do it.

TRUST

Sacred partnership is moored in trust. Trust is built on commitment, congruity, and alignment of action and word. We must be able to trust our beloved to consistently support us, mean what they say, say what they mean, and do what they say they will do.

Trusting our partners allows us to be open to what *is* and authentically express who we *are*. Without trust, we feel the need to defend and protect ourselves. Encased in a shell of protection, our true self is camouflaged and unavailable. Defended we are imprisoned and imprisoning, trusting we are free and genuine. With trust as an integral part of our relationship, we can cup each other in the soft palm of our hand rather than clutch each other in a clenched fist.

Although it's good to be a trusting individual, deep trust develops over the years. Each time we honor an agreement, come home when we say we will, support each other in crisis, or profess our love and follow through on commitments, trust grows and strengthens. One of the biggest reasons why it's so difficult for marriages to survive infidelity it that a sacred trust has been broken and can only be painstakingly repaired one tiny strand at a time.

REESTABLISHING TRUST

If trust has been crushed in your relationship, please don't despair. I've known many couples who have weathered even the storm of infidelity and remade their relationships into heart centered marriages and soul-nourishing partnerships. They used the crisis to reevaluate and redesign themselves and their marriages. Like potters, they picked up the shattered pieces of clay from the original union, reconstituted and reworked them into a new a vessel of love. Not without pain. As Rilke says, "In the difficult are the friendly forces, the hands that work on us." They triumphed because they were willing to move through the difficult times and be worked on by their higher selves.

But practically speaking, how do we reestablish trust if it has been broken? Or even if we fear it may be breached? The first and most important thing to do is to make sure that you can trust yourself to take care of *you* if trust is broken. Second, don't create a framework that sets you up to be lied to and thereby lose trust. Rather, establish an open door policy of truth, an agreement between you that no transgression is too great not to be worked with and, hopefully, through.

To clarify, let me share an example from a client's life. Lilith married Jack, who was a recovering alcoholic. Her greatest fear was that he would revert to drinking and lie to her about it. She shared her fears with him and they agreed that their commitment to each other was so deep that even a drinking relapse would be worked through. Together, they decided on the steps by which they would move toward reestablishing trust should her fears manifest. The steps included immediate couple's therapy and a commitment by Jack to enter a recovery program. Although such a situation would be difficult and painful, knowing that fears had been stated and received honestly and that a game plan was in place allowed both Lilith and Jack to relax into their natural commitment and camaraderie.

CLARITY OF INTENTION

Intention is a close friend of commitment. Without commitment and intention, the Princess would still be alone, and the Prince would be sunning himself on a lily pad. To begin with, the spellbound prince carried a strong *intention* to be free of his frog suit and, toward that end, pursued his goal of the liberating kiss. Of course he got it, for in fairy-tale and myth, the Prince symbolizes our higher inner Masculine who is able to slay dangerous dragons and awaken beautiful princesses who have innocently fallen under a paralyzing spell. Essentially our interior Prince is great at doing what needs to be done, successfully carrying out his intentions.

Our commitment to come from the heart and enter into the process of sacred partnership comes mostly from the feminine energy of our internalized Princess, but, in order to keep the commitment viable and on track, we need the dedication and intention toward the *idea* of sacred partnership that comes from masculine energy. If the masculine *intends* to protect a certain ideal or live by a commitment, he will. It is something to *do*, a goal, a carrot, a way to focus. Because masculine energy is adept and wise in the art of doing, it is a valuable asset in keeping our intentions clear for our journey of sacred partnership.

Intention is also closely tied to purpose and goals. Knowing our purpose helps us formulate our goals. Knowing both helps us set our intention, in both attitude and action, to realize our dreams. For instance, in my relationship with my family, my intentions include:

1. *Being as loving and understanding as I can be while not being run over by any of them;*
2. *Gently, but honestly communicating;*
3. *Being true to myself and my beliefs;*
4. *Providing a safe place for us all to grow, evolve, and express who we really are.*

These are easy for me as long as everything is going smoothly and there isn't a need for confrontation. However, if being true to myself and being honest require that I say something that may create a stir, I have to work on calling in my inner Prince to help me stand up for myself. Being in touch with and expressing my masculine energy is my growing edge, and I'm still a little shaky about doing it, especially with Gene.

Luckily I have a friend who, during my wimpy times, frequently says to me, "What is your intention in saying or doing this? Or *not* saying or doing anything?" If I can truthfully say that my intention is in line with my purpose of loving and serving, first my soul-self and then others, then I can begin gathering up the courage to tackle the difficult agenda before me. But, if my intention is to hide and avoid, or fold, stamp, or mutilate someone, then I'd better pause for however long it takes, center myself in my heart and wait until my action can match my higher intentions.

Commitment and intention are daily, no, minute-by-minute, choices. Having the intention to commit to ourselves, our partner, and our marriage, bringing the sweet fragrance of love to our choices will go far to ensure that our family is a safe island in the turbulent seas of life, a rock from which we can soar and then return to rest and replenish ourselves.

Elemental wisdom realizes that our soul has a purpose in being here. Our task is to be kind to ourselves and others as we stumble and bumble—and sometimes leap—toward realizing our soul's purpose with as much clarity as possible. Opening our hearts in love and allowing the flow of God to dance through us is one of our most sacred intentions. When we do, we create an atmosphere in which spirit is breathed into the dispirited and love softens pain-hardened hearts.

Chapter Six

LIVING TOGETHER
IN BALANCE
AND HARMONY

The diamond of our being sparkles more brilliantly
when all facets are turned toward the light.

To walk the path of sacred partnership with practical feet requires that we bring balance and harmony into our lives. That isn't easy. So often it feels as if we're hopping on one foot and then the other while juggling a multitude of "shoulds" and "have to's" that relish spinning almost out of control. Exhaustion and feelings of being overwhelmed obliterate harmony from our lives and mask our soul's whispered invitation to live in the subtle and sacred inner core of our being. When this happens to us, what is missing? Balance! If our lives are to feel meaningful and sacred, we want and *need* to live in balance and harmony within ourselves, with others, and with circumstances.

AWARENESS FIRST

Although both balance and harmony seem difficult to attain, they *are* possible. As spiritual beings, we have a deep longing to bathe in the renewing waters of God's eternal spring, allowing her to replenish us. Because of this innate yearning, sometimes all we need to begin the process of rebalancing is some information about how to do so and encouragement to try. Becoming aware of our desire for balance is the first important step toward making it a reality. What we focus on and intend to do, we can attain, for "energy flows where attention goes."

Realizing what needs to be balanced in our lives requires a deep commitment. All change takes effort and desire. Bringing equilibrium into our lives through our day-to-day, minute by minute choices will invite the harmony of love and serenity to be a part of our daily experience. It's a simple process, although certainly not easy, and will require consistent commitment.

FIRE AND WATER

Living in balance and harmony sounds great, but how do we do it? First, we need to recognize that balance requires us to create a marvelous braid of energy by weaving together both our feminine and masculine aspects—the yin/yang qualities of being and doing, receiving and giving, feeling and thinking, connection and separation, intuition and logic, softness and firmness—with our unique brand of practicality and spirituality.

Onto our own distinctive alchemical scales we need to place both the inner and the outer worlds, working to attract equal parts of the fire of goal-seeking and the water of receptivity and comparable periods of sound and silence. Too much masculine energy—fire and sound—can consume us. Overwhelmed by it, we burn out. By the same token, too much feminine energy—water and silence—can pull us from the "real" world so far into the depths of the inner world that we may lose touch and drown. Since our culture is vastly over-weighted in the doingness of masculine energy, most of us are in much greater danger of burning out than drowning.

Balance and harmony within ourselves will encourage balance and harmony within our relationships, within society and, ultimately, throughout the world. The gifts of a balanced life—peace of mind, love from our hearts, and grace of spirit—start with one person at a time and swell in strength, resonance, and beauty as each heart, mind, and spirit welcomes the next, and they learn to sing and dance in harmony together. Balanced within ourselves, we will be more able to connect with others through meaningful, transformative love.

OUR INNER ORCHESTRA

Braiding together different energies in order to create a more harmonious whole begins within our own psyche. We all have various internal voices—I call them sub-personalities—that vie for attention. If we are not familiar with our own and our partner's sub-personalities, life can get very chaotic. An easy way to become better acquainted with these voices is to use the analogy of an orchestra.

We've probably all heard the cacophony of an orchestra tuning up before a performance. As each instrument does its own thing there is dissonance, instead of harmony. So often it seems that this is the way the various inner aspects of ourselves play the different music we are given to interpret. When sub-personalities vie with each other for attention and power, or ignore and deride each other, we experience dissonance within. However, we can learn to balance and harmonize our inner instruments, reclaim parts of ourselves that we've abandoned, and transform clamor into the ability to play in concert.

When I speak of the different sub-personalities, I'm describing a very natural and normal way that we *all* operate. Psychology has been talking about facets of our inner orchestras for years. Transactional Analysis introduced us to several of our inner parts when it spoke of the Parent, Adult, and Child voices in each of us. The expanded idea of sub-personalities is the brainchild

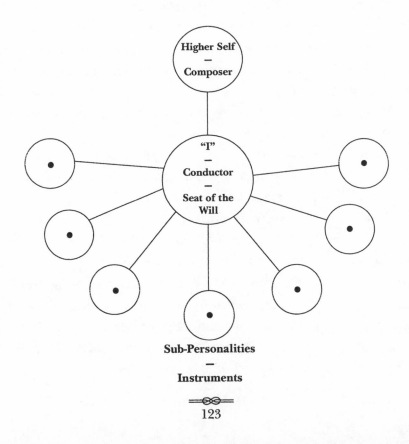

Sub-Personalities

—

Instruments

of Roberto Assagioli, medical doctor and psychiatrist. In the early 1900s, Dr. Assagioli realized the need for a comprehensive psychological method that incorporated the soul, imagination, and will of an individual. His system, called Psychosynthesis, is unified around the awareness of a self at the core of each individual that can direct the harmonious development of all aspects of the personality. In Assagioli's system, the director part of us is synonymous with the orchestra conductor and receives its instructions—the score for our life's music—from the Composer, our Higher Self or God/dess Self. Sub-personalities, then, when welcomed into our inner circle, have the ability to listen to the conductor and Composer and work in concert with their orchestra mates to create a harmonious whole.

Exploring Our Orchestra

There are several particulars about sub-personalities useful to those of us creating sacred partnership. First, sub-personalities are aspects of our being that allow us to express ourselves in the world, and they can almost always be transformed into productive and supportive members of our orchestra. Next, the conductor of our orchestra is the seat of our will, the dispassionate "I," the pivotal part of us that makes decisions without emotional interference. The "I" within can be likened to a railroad switchman who changes tracks to suit each train's destination. We utilize our "I" constantly throughout a normal day. We make choices and decisions to switch back and forth between personalities without even realizing it. Imagine that you are deeply into a sad feeling and crying almost uncontrollably when your child runs crying to you with blood streaming from her hand. What would you do? Ninety-nine times out of a hundred you would switch from your emotionally distraught sub-personality and take care of your child. Your will, the internal "I," observing the situation, makes a rational choice to move to the appropriate caretaker sub-personality.

The "I" within reminds me of the android, Data, on *Star Trek: The Next Generation*. He is programmed to do the right thing without question. But why doesn't the inner "I" always work that way? Because our sub-personalities don't listen to it. They may be so starved for attention that they block out instructions from the "I."

In working with sub-personalities, it's essential to remember that our internal "I" receives its instructions from the Higher Self, the composer in our orchestra analogy. The "I" within needs to be intimately connected to the Higher Self through an open channel of communication in order to interpret our unique musical score. This channel is more readily available to us when we nurture ourselves with quiet time, sincerely *ask* for a connection, and then allow it to happen. The stream of wisdom runs down from the Higher Self, to the "I," and then to our sub-personalities. If the connection is broken between any of those parts of ourselves, balance and harmony will be lost, and we will be disconnected from the fountain of wisdom within us.

TUNING UP

As we practice the fine art of accepting all aspects of ourselves and transforming those that have been hurt and abandoned, one very important thing to remember is that *all* sub-personalities have, at their core, a *quality* worthy of retaining. No matter how destructive or deformed a sub-personality may appear, it has a core quality that is vital to us and can be transformed, through love, into a productive and harmonious part of ourselves. It's our task to look for the virtue within the vices.

For instance, when I was newly emerging from being an emotionally dependent person, looking to everyone *outside* of myself to give me my self-concept, a sub-personality appeared whom I named Brunhilda. She was a huge Norsewoman who brandished a sharpened broadsword and was clothed in metal breast plates and crowned by a metal helmet with large curved horns. She was formidable. Quite the antithesis of my "nice girl" persona. And she scared the absolute daylights out of me! Gene didn't much care for her, either, when she dared to flash a sword tip at him. He was right in realizing that, in her present, intemperate form, Brunhilda was malicious toward men whom she perceived as the enemy, those who devalued and demeaned women.

Luckily, I was involved with a Psychosynthesis class when Brunhilda came to the fore and, with their help, working with her became fun and productive. The quality at Brunhilda's core was the strength to be assertive and stand up for my rights, wants, and needs. Because I hadn't been good at exercising that quality, the aspect of myself characterized by Brunhilda—the warrior archetype, according to Carl Jung—had become absolutely enraged by inattention and had, wisely, exaggerated herself to get my attention. In my inner orchestra, Brunhilda became a clanging cymbal, so loud that I finally had to pay attention.

Our sub-personalities will change over the years. As we integrate them, aspects of ourselves retire, mellow, and change the roles that they once played. Brunhilda has matured out of her early valiant and fiery rebellion into being able to own her own strength and be quietly and gently assertive more often than not. I look back on the "terrible twos" of Brunhilda's emergence with amusement and gratitude.

Adopting Inner Orphans

As well as uncovering the core quality of a sub-personality, it's important to ask it what it needs from us and then to examine our response to its request. Our society has taught us that we are tainted by innumerable unacceptable flaws and circumstances. From that judgmental concept, we have become adept at denying aspects of ourselves who appear unworthy or shameful. Unfortunately, denying parts of ourselves creates imbalance and internal fragmentation. With each part of ourselves that is chastised and exiled, there is less life force available to us.

In order to regain the gift of our entire life force, we need to find inner orphans that we have cast out and adopt them back into the fold. Underdeveloped, undernourished, and wounded, inner orphans carry our fears and our penchant for self-devaluation. The disenfranchised parts of us live in a constant state of low self-esteem and, although longing to be loved, are unable to love in a healthy and mature manner. Remembering Rilke's statement, "All in us that is terrible needs to be loved," we can be reassured that, through love and acceptance, our seemingly terrible inner orphans can be healed, empowered, and set free to augment our life force and become compassionate lovers, beautiful expressions of our soul's luminosity.

Sub-personalities that we have shoved out of our consciousness often scratch and bite in their clamor to be invited into the circle of our inner family. Being under the level of our conscious awareness, they are almost impossible to control. Have you ever wondered why in the world you made a certain comment or acted in an unacceptable way, feeling as if someone else had acted and spoken through you? If so, that was probably an orphaned sub-personality with whom you need to become reacquainted. During the infamous Brunhilda period, my friend Bonnie and I often said to each other, "*Who* said that?" It was a lighthearted way for us to help each other become aware of, heal and integrate our orphaned aspects.

Because we so often deny them, inner orphans are forced to take desperate measures in order to be heard and recognized, much like agitated toddlers may bang their heads against the floor for attention. Often rejected, sub-personalities will take aim at the most handy target, our mate, and sometimes our children. They fire lethal salvos that create destructive echoes that reverberate long after the words end. Being shot at by unbalanced sub-personalities brings discord to a relationship, not harmony.

If we consistently ignore and avoid angry or wounded sub-personalities, it is easy to fall into the Projection Trap and play our vulnerabilities and angers out against the screen of our relationship with our partner. No one likes or deserves to be the blank screen upon which someone else spews their venom. Such projection is one of the most detrimental behaviors that a marriage can experience. The recipient of projection feels frustrated, angry, misunderstood, and hurt. And rightly so. The projec*tor* often does feel judgmental and righteous. These two feelings are usually present when we're trying to place blame or make someone else responsible for our actions, reactions, or feelings. Definitely a lose/lose situation. More often than not only a part of us is prone to projecting; that's why finding the sub-personalities who do project is extremely important.

Not only do unrecognized and unresolved aspects of our being indulge in projecting behavior, they are also totally incapable of creating a relationship based on complementary interdependence. They are too needy and self-centered.

SHARING OUR MANY SELVES

When we reclaim rejected parts of ourselves and encourage them to be a part of our inner family, we will also be better able to see, understand, and accept parts of our beloved that until now may have been mysterious or painful to us. Sharing our varying aspects with each other is wonderfully healing. In allowing another to see the whole of us—vulnerability and all—we feel closer, more transparent, and truly accepted for all we are rather than just who we think we should be.

Introducing *all* of us to our partner allows us to be loved in stereo. It also helps us to understand both the differences and the connections between the two of us, specifically, and the genders, collectively. Culturally, men and women have been influenced to deny different aspects of themselves. Men are applauded for the competition and conquering done by their Warrior sub-personality, while women are chastised, shamed, and often labeled a "bitch" if they allow a powerful part of themselves to stride forward. On the other hand, women are praised for the self-sacrifice and understanding of their Mother sub-personality who nurtures others and creates bridges between people.

Generally speaking, then, a man needs to find, claim, and heal the parts of himself that express his heart and feelings. By making a heart connection, a man's ability to be compassionate and reverent is increased, and he learns to take responsibility for his own emotional nature. Men who have rejected their emotional sub-personalities often look to their wives to *do* their emotional life for them. A huge down side to that arrangement is that a man can begin to feel so dependent on that *one* person that, to compensate, he unconsciously puts his wife down.

At the other end of the spectrum, women need to acknowledge the part of themselves that holds their personal power and not rely on their men to be the only empowered person in a relationship. An empowered sub-personality is a representative of the Goddess, who radiates soft, gentle, *strong* power; a being filled with respect for herself, aware of the wisdom she has, and the contribution that she *needs* to give to society.

Here Comes the Judge

Although many inner orphans, like my Brunhilda, are wisely trying to get our attention in order to help us change limiting patterns or learn lessons that we are fearfully avoiding, there are others, so wounded or ignorant that they are destructive to us. It is especially vital for us to reform and transform them.

One such destructive inner aspect could be named "The Judge." To varying degrees, each of us seems to have a black robed, ferocious entity who judges us mercilessly. The internal judge is probably formed around an admirable quality like "discernment," but has been corrupted by pain or power. More often than is healthy, our inner discernment becomes a harsh and severe critic. Although it's tempting to run from the Judge, we need to get to know him. By finding out what he needs and why he acts the way he does, we can transform him into a *fair* witness for ourselves. A fair witness can be an internal mentor who guides, corrects, and congratulates us in a loving and non-judgmental manner.

Internal judges play havoc with relationships, for they often project their own issues of control, perfectionism, intolerance, and fear of failure outside of themselves. The unlucky recipient is often our partner. If we find that we've disappeared into the realm of righteousness or judgment, it would be very wise of us to check on the whereabouts of The Judge. Is he busy projecting his own unowned stuff onto "them"? If we are heavily invested in changing another, it's a good clue that we *are* projecting. Wanting to change someone else is an act of arrogance. Even more importantly, we're not tending to our *own process* when concentrating on the other person's process. We need to accept responsibility for our own feelings and let others accept responsibility for theirs. Anything else is actually impossible, and is definitely not conducive to sacred partnership. Codependence, yes. Partnership, no.

Two good questions to ask ourselves when feeling judgmental or believing it is our obligation to help someone else "see the light" are: (1) Am I upset at myself about something that I don't want to acknowledge? and (2) Does anything about this person's actions or behavior remind me of something about myself that I loathe or avoid? Answering these questions honestly will help us retract the "projection poison" that taints the harmony of so many marriages and sabotages the complementary interdependence for which we yearn.

Converting The Judge ain't easy! Here's where we can help one another. Just yesterday my inner judge (who has mellowed considerably but still loves to indulge in an occasional bout of perfectionism) was stridently talking long distance to Gene about my commitment to conquer a certain amount of writing by the time he returned home in a couple of days, "even if I have to stay up all night to do it!" With a little chuckle Gene said, "How very masculine of you. Are you being gentle with yourself? Are you having fun?" Hummm, well, no and no. We laughed, but when we hung up I had to have a little chat with The Judge in order to wrestle the gavel from his hand.

VISUALIZING WHO'S WHO IN THE INNER SANCTUM

As well as viewing our sub-personalities as instruments in an orchestra, we can use the analogy of their being actors on stage in the drama of our life. The following visualization uses this metaphor to pull the curtain open on our inner stage and discover what characters are currently active in our lives. You may do this exercise alone or have someone lead you through it. In order to anchor the inner experience in outer reality, it's especially helpful to discuss the personality aspects presented to you by your wise subconscious. You and your spouse might want to guide each other through the visualization, or do it with a group of people, and then share your experiences.

To begin the visualization, find a time when you won't be disturbed for about fifteen minutes. Make yourself comfortable. Lower your eyes and bring your attention to your breathing. For a few moments, allow your mind to float free, continuing to focus on your breath as it moves in and out through your nostrils. Now deepen your breathing. With each inhalation, draw in a sense of peace and safety. With each exhalation, loosen your grip on the cares of the day and let them slip from you. Softly, gently concentrate on simply breathing in and out. Now, with confidence and gratitude, ask your wise inner Self, your Inner Oracle, to give you the information and the experience that you need from this exercise.

Feeling yourself relaxing, imagine that you are seated in a darkened theater. The curtains begin to open revealing the lighted stage. Take some time to notice if the stage is decorated with a set. If so, what is it like? If they are not already there, invite onto the stage the sub-personalities that you need to see at this time. Calmly, with great interest, observe the characters as they move about the stage. They may appear in any form: human, animal, or symbol. It doesn't matter. You may not see anything, but simply sense the presence of your sub-personalities. Anything is fine. There is no wrong way to do the visualization, there is just your experience. Allow yourself to accept whatever happens.

In a leisurely manner, observe the stage and its occupants. When you feel ready, choose one or two characters to talk with. You may choose anyone, remembering that often those who don't appeal to us can offer us very fruitful insights. Start with one character and ask if it is willing to communicate with you. Although it may not speak, per se, you will know its answer in your heart. If it is unwilling, ask it why. If it remains uncommunicative, move on to your next choice. After you've established a sub-personality's willingness to communicate with you, ask it anything that you would like to. Listen carefully, not only to its answers but to your own responses and reactions. How do you feel toward this character? Why?

Some good questions to ask your character:

1. *Are you willing to talk with me?*
2. *What would you like me to call you?*
3. *Why do you act the way you do?*
4. *What do you want from me?*
5. *If it is different, what do you need from me?*

If your character is willing to tell you what it wants and needs from you, are *you* willing and able to give it to him or her? Exploring your willingness or resistance to fulfilling a sub-personality's request will give you a good handle on how much work you have to do in order to wholeheartedly love, forgive, accept, heal, and transform this aspect of your being.

Good questions to ask yourself after the visualization:

1. *Who was on stage? or Who's talking?*
2. *Whom did I choose to relate to? Why?*
3. *How did my sub-personality and I feel about one another?*
4. *What is this sub-personality's growing edge?*
5. *What does it want and need from me?*
6. *What is its core quality?*
7. *Among my cast of characters, who is fighting whom?*

As an example, Brad, a young man in his late twenties, was confused and anxious about a budding romance with a woman who had been a good friend for several months. Tuning into his sub-personalities, he asked to see which one was carrying the most confusion. In response, he saw a character who looked like a tar-baby. Its gooey appearance disgusted him and he wanted to turn away. After some courageous exploration, Brad discovered that "Gollum's" quality was sensitivity and that past love experiences had deformed his sensitivity into guilt and confusion. Gollum wanted acceptance and needed forgiveness from Brad. "No way! How can you forgive yourself when you've hurt people?!" was Brad's initial response.

But he agreed to continue meeting with Gollum. After a time of examining that part of himself, Brad came to a much better understanding of his sensitive sub-personality and was able to befriend it. After Gollum was accepted into Brad's inner family, his confusion dissipated and the guilt melted away. As a result of this clarity, he was able to make the decision to slowly and consciously pursue a relationship with his friend.

As in Brad's case, the redemption of sub-personalities is usually a *process*. With time, commitment, and love, all of our internal characters can become protagonists, and all of the instruments in our inner orchestra can learn to play in concert, complementing and enhancing one another. If you run across a sub-personality that is totally intractable, it could mean that your inner wisdom is telling you to seek help with it. The wound of this aspect of yourself may go so deep that you will need a helping hand during the healing process.

NUTS AND BOLTS OF SUB-PERSONALITY WORK

In addition to the questions asked of your internal cast of characters during the visualization, or when you notice them during the course of a day, the following "work sheets" are helpful for adopting inner orphans and reclaiming all aspects of ourselves as we journey toward holy wholeness.

EXPLORING SUB-PERSONALITIES

Name	Characteristics	Quality	Wants and Needs
_____	_____	_____	_____
_____	_____	_____	_____

1. *Whom do I ignore? Why?*
2. *Whom am I ashamed of? Why?*
3. *Whom do I value? Why?*
4. *Whom do I love? Why?*
5. *Whom am I unaware of? (ask your beloved or a good friend)*

6. If _____ sub-personality was healed and transformed, what quality could it bring to my life?

OTHER WAYS TO WORK WITH SUB-PERSONALITIES

1. *Write their biography . . . invent a mythical history.*
2. *Describe them physically and emotionally.*
3. *Share sub-personalities with trustworthy people.*

MEETING INNER MENTORS

Interestingly, although the orphaned parts of us have a reputation for being dark, wicked, and slimy creatures, they are often exactly the opposite—Emissaries of the Light whom we refuse to recognize and claim within ourselves. We have been so brainwashed by facets of our culture into believing that we are innately sinful and shameful beings that we tend to negate, ignore, and distrust our light-filled, divine selves. So don't be surprised if you meet a Monk or Mystic, a Priest or Priestess, an artist or philosopher, or a gathering of Wisdom Keepers as you explore the depths and heights of your collective sub-personalities. The Light is within us! Our responsibility is to know ourselves, sunbeams and shadows alike. Our alchemical challenge—our "golden" opportunity, if you will—is to transform our shadow material, liberating its life force to become a source of light, vitality, and power. The diamond of our being sparkles more brilliantly when all facets are turned toward the light.

Each of us has secret, undamaged persons within, who retain their innocence and divinity no matter what wounds we may have sustained in this school called life. In our desire for reunion with God through sacred partnership within ourselves and with our beloved, it is our responsibility to free our divine aspects. By adopting inner orphans and reestablishing the sovereignty of our Higher Self (or Soul), we will invite the secret, undamaged divinity within us to dance with the divinity within our beloved.

PLAYING IN CONCERT

A major goal of sub-personality work is to integrate all aspects of ourselves, bringing them into balance and harmony with the whole of our being. Welcoming each facet of ourself home, as it were. Nurturing the growth and evolution of a more balanced and integrated self and then bringing that unfolding self into our marriage will naturally lend itself to creating a more balanced and harmonized partnership.

Sacred partnership is a process enhanced by playing in concert with a committed and loving mate. A partner's loving view reveals us in our radiance and our vulnerability. Through his or her insights, unclear and embryonic parts of ourselves can be redeemed, while those who have perhaps lived in disgrace for years can be reclaimed.

Recently I ran across a long-forgotten twenty-year-old request that I'd written to Gene. In it I described why writing was an important process for me and, yet, how easily I avoided doing it. I asked him to help me remember the writer/mystic in me who was nourished when encouraged to channel divine energy through words. Although both of us had "forgotten" the letter, at some level the commitment was made and remembered, for in our years together he has been, and is still, my staunchest supporter and backer. Without him, my writing career may never have happened.

When I'm in one of my I-can't-do-anything-right or I-don't-have-anything-valuable-to-say vulnerable sub-personalities and have a lousy image of myself, Gene still *sees* me as a writer. During those times, I need to see the reflection of myself in his eyes to regain my own vision. That's one of the boons of sharing sub-personality discoveries with our mates. We can announce who's in charge. For example, in times of writer's anxiety, I might say to Gene, "Well, Ms. Beige Dishrag is in charge and I am boring even myself!" Because he knows "who" is talking, Gene can often cajole Ms. Beige Dishrag out of her mood through humor and hugs.

One of the reasons that I value sub-personality work is that it can easily be seen and experienced as sub-personality *play*. Most of us enjoy going to movies and plays, but we actually have four-star dramas going on within our own heads, hearts, and homes. It's fun to do character studies on our own internal cast and, in turn, it's a wonderful way to get to know the scripts and musical scores that our mates are working/playing from. Although lots of times it's easy to keep our insights light, they're worth their weight in gold for the information and understanding which they provide. Playing in concert with our partner, we can help name and reclaim parts of ourselves, and welcome them back together into our inner families to be transformed through love and acceptance.

A BEAUTIFUL SAFETY NET

By integrating, synthesizing, and appreciating all aspects of our being, we are more able to bring all of ourselves to our beloved while appreciating all aspects of them as well. Of course we also must commit to balancing and harmonizing our external lives as well as our own internal factions by prioritizing and simplifying our lives. Then, from the trust generated by the deep acceptance we feel from our partner and the sense of spaciousness we create in order to be together, we can weave a rich, colorful, warm, and cozy partnership, one that will form a beautiful emotional safety net for each of us and create a service-full entity for others. As we bond in this way, even a little bit, we will bring into the world a new energy for marriage that will add to the balance and harmony—peace and healing—of ourselves, our children, and our planet.

Chapter Seven

THE CRUCIBLE
OF
CRISIS

Safe in the arms of the Sacred Feminine,
our souls, seared by pain, can be sanctified.

$\mathcal{C}$risis is a part of the human cycle. We ascend, flourish, bear fruit, and then, seemingly as an answer to the law of gravity, we arch, hit a plateau, descend, and die to the part of us wounded in crisis. Because feminine energy is deeply aware of and in tune with cycles, crisis is often best handled by the Sacred Feminine within us. She, in her wisdom, knows that crisis is followed by rebirth. When a part of us—an old pattern, an expectation, a role—is washed away in the alchemy of crisis, new parts of our being are conceived and born. Trauma and transformation walk hand in hand.

Grief and loss require a feminine response. Healing is a *process*. It can't be fixed or solved by *doing*, and can only be soothed and healed through *experiencing* the feelings involved.

All of us will have crises of varying proportions in our lives, running the gamut from the simple frustration of being late to a meeting to the excruciating wilderness caused by a devastating illness. Many crises are a reflection of external circumstances, while others are generated internally, often stemming from our sense of separation from God. As Carl Jung said, "A whole person is one who has both walked with God and wrestled with the devil." The Sacred Feminine within knows both God and devil and is able to accept each through her trust in the ultimate balance and harmony of All.

At no time do we need to be clearer about our intention and commitment toward our beloved than in times of crisis. The statistics on the survival rates of marriages when they are subjected to the fire of extreme crisis are discouraging. Sadly, as many as 90 percent of marriages break up after the death of a child or during a life-threatening illness. Partly this happens because men and women deal with crisis differently and, when they most need each other, their differences tend to make them feel the most alone.

When our hearts are bleeding and mangled, it isn't easy to open them to another in unconditional love and acceptance. But that's exactly what we need to do if we are to be close to our mate during crisis rather than distanced and alienated. During my years as a psychotherapist and hospice worker, I've known many couples who forged unbreakable bonds by being lovingly and unconditionally present for each other during crisis. Although it wasn't often easy, they accepted and allowed their differences in dealing with pain and sought help for themselves and their marriage when it was appropriate.

KATHY AND PAUL

Kathy and Paul were paralyzed with grief when their only child was killed in a dirt bike accident. Their thirteen-year-old son had been the light of their life, the strongest bond between them, and the carrier of their dreams. Instantly, he was gone. Not only did they lose their heart-child, they lost their roles as parents.

Kathy came to therapy only three weeks after Kevin had been killed. She was still deeply in shock but beginning to feel the searing pain of her grief. I asked how Paul was and she said she didn't know, that he'd gone back to work immediately after the funeral, worked ten to twelve hours days, and she rarely saw him. Like many men, Paul's response to his grief was to run away and bury himself in *doing* something that was familiar and at which he felt successful. It's easy for women to feel bereft at this response. We feel abandoned and isolated. We begin to wonder if these strange creatures have any feelings at all. In reality, it's *because* they have deep feelings and often haven't the vaguest notion of how to deal with them that men avoid experiencing their emotions. All of us, when faced with unfathomable grief, are afraid that we may be overwhelmed by it if we allow ourselves to feel it. But men are *terrified* of being overwhelmed or out of control, and often deem themselves failures if they succumb to emotional responses.

Also, deeply embedded in a man's psyche is the injunction to *protect* his family. In Paul's case, his son was killed on a bike that he had bought for him. He felt he had failed to protect his only child. In his mind, the best way he could now protect Kathy was to spare her *his* grief, leave her alone to work through hers (not something many women want, but what *he* wanted and *assumed* she would), and provide for her in a generous manner. He was also afraid of appearing weak in front of her and, thereby, diminishing himself in her eyes.

Over the months, Kathy began to heal, but Paul drifted farther and farther from her. Not surprising, since each time he saw her, his unresolved grief writhed in his gut trying to get him to work *through* it, not sit on it. Because she didn't want the marriage to fail and could intuit the pain Paul was hiding from, Kathy finally issued a gentle ultimatum: Go with me to Compassionate Friends—a support organization for parents who have lost children—for at least one month. Grudgingly, he did.

The other men at Compassionate Friends understood what Paul felt and empathized with the way he'd tried to cope with it. They shared their stories, and in "man fashion" challenged him to face his grief and feel it. Hearing what other men felt and how they dealt with it helped Paul open the flood gates in his own heart. Finally he could give himself permission to express his rage at himself and acknowledge the excruciating pain of missing his son.

FIND HANDS TO HOLD

Whatever the crisis that is perpetuating a chasm between us and our beloved, it's good advice to seek help. Out of balance and embroiled in confusing feelings, we can usually find great help from a third compassionate and objective party like a therapist, or a support group such as Compassionate Friends. There are times when we are blinded by anguish and need to hold hands with another to keep from falling into an abyss too deep to climb up from. Hopefully, we can hold each other's hands, but sometimes the best we can do is cling together like drowning people. At those times, we need other, stronger, more objective hands for a while. Seeking help is not weak; it is logical, courageous, and wise.

DARK NIGHT OF THE SOUL

Dark nights of the soul are stretches of time in which we straddle an emotional abyss, a seemingly bottomless chasm of despair, depression, and confusion. Nothing is as it was and we haven't the slightest idea of what is coming next, nor the energy to care about making anything happen. The very foundation of our world no longer feels familiar or comforting. We are in profound crisis.

Crisis, in the Chinese language, is a combination of two characters; one for *danger* and the other for *opportunity*. Dark nights of the soul are crises pregnant with opportunity. We need the dark, fertile, moist soil of crisis to define ourselves. Without struggle, there is no energy to break the shell encasing the seeds of our new self, the soul-Self that we are becoming. As the Sufi poet Rumi says, "Your grief about what you have lost lifts a mirror up to where you are bravely working."

Whether we are suffering from accumulated fatigue brought on by the myriad demands of life, or have been ripped from the very ground of our being and feel as if our roots are laid bare, exposed, and quivering with sorrow and hopelessness, there is opportunity inherent in the crucible of crisis. For, as well as being a severe test or trial, a crucible is also a container made of a substance that can resist great heat: used for melting, fusing, and burning to ashes or powder ores, metal, etc. In other words, a crucible—whether test or container—is an agent of transformation.

In the depths of our darkness, we need to hold fast to the awareness of the sacred opportunity for soul growth in *all* experiences and create a container of our marriage that can withstand the heart-melting agony of loss, change, and trauma and become a sanctuary in which the alchemy of transformation can take place for both partners. This is not easy, and requires deep commitment, courage, friendship, and unconditional love from us to both ourselves and our beloved.

Interestingly, not only individuals, but marriages and relationships also go through dark nights of the soul. In marriage, boredom is our first clue that we have come to a transformation place. We are moving from one level to another with our beloved, evolving to the next stratum in our soul's growth within the partnership. To follow the path of sacred partnership, we need to be aware of the opportunity within the crisis and open our heart to it. What is yearning to be born between us? What radiant spiritual possibility waits in the shadows? What new *we* is longing to be expressed?

"Seldom, or perhaps never, does a marriage develop into an individual relationship smoothly and without crises," Carl Jung reminds us, "There is no coming to consciousness without pain." Would that that were not true, but it usually is.

SPIRITUAL OPTIMISM

If we adhere to the belief that God is vengeful and punishes us for our sins via crisis, trauma, illness, etc., it will be difficult for us to make it through hard times. Not only will we need to carry the pain of our losses, but we'll also shoulder the guilt and blame about how sinful we must be to deserve them. On the other hand, if we are spiritually optimistic and have a strong belief that our pain can be used in the service of higher consciousness, trauma and crisis can lead us deeply into psychological and spiritual healing.

Dark night experiences are a mystery. At times all we can do is surrender to the "not knowing" and make the best choices that we can. Do the best that we can, heal as deeply as possible and learn the most that we can. Surrender is not the same as resignation. Surrendering to the unknowable mystery is a courageous choice, an act of faith, and trust in God and ourselves, whereas resignation to "fate" is often a lapse into victimization.

Not only does spiritual optimism support us in difficult times, but in my view, it also includes the belief that God is good and creates us in his image. As likenesses of God, we must also be spiritual beings and, thereby, good. Spiritual optimism is an upper that creates the natural tranquilizer of endorphins within us, which enhance our immune systems and increase our peace of mind. Being spiritually optimistic, remembering that we are lovable, divine beings, is essential during crisis. Forgetting our divine core magnifies any pain we're feeling a thousand fold.

We have a choice. As an act of will, or as an act of faith and trust, we can choose to be spiritual optimists. We can allow ourselves to rest on the soft bosom of the Mystery, believing that She cares for and consoles us. As an emissary for the Mystery, we can invite our beloved to rest and renew him or herself on the breast of our love. When he or she is weary or filled with shards of sorrow we can decide to offer solace. It is a choice we can easily make when we are in tune with the inner core of our divinity.

CHOOSING HOW TO HANDLE CRISIS

Lisa, a beautiful twenty-two-year-old woman whom I've known from infancy, was injured badly in a terrible car accident. Paramedics at the scene were fearful for her life as they struggled frantically to free her from the wreck. Knowing that she had a better chance for survival if she remained conscious, they urged her to stay awake. She did, but in the ambulance yearned to give in to pain-free unconsciousness. Instead, she asked the ambulance attendant to say the Lord's Prayer with her. He didn't know it, so Lisa chose to handle this crisis by teaching it to him as they raced to the hospital.

What a wonderful choice! What presence of mind and strength of spirit! Not only did Lisa's choice save her life, it has inspired all of us who've heard it. I know that I thought, "Wow, if she could choose to react in such a soul-growing way, maybe I could, too, if the need arose."

We can't always choose what will happen to us, or even *in* us, but we *are* free to choose how we will respond. The choices we make will determine whether our spirits learn and grow through crises or collapse as a result of them. Of course, collapsing for periods of time may actually be essential for our healing and well-being, but I'm talking about the difference between collapsing helplessly into bitterness and defeat and eventually evolving into compassion and increased understanding. It is our choice, and we need to gently assist ourselves, as Lisa did, to choose *life,* as painful as it can be, not death by denial, avoidance, or bitterness.

The Grace of Tears

It's a well-known scientific fact that tears shed in grief, anger, hopelessness, and contrition contain significant toxins, whereas tears shed in joy and awe do not. From these findings, it appears that tears have the capacity to cleanse the body. I believe they can cleanse the soul as well. On occasion we've all probably known—at least women have known—that what we needed was a "good" cry. We can feel the build-up of energy and intuitively know that release can be found in the goodness of tears. If we allow ourselves to have a good cry, we often feel refreshed and revitalized.

There is frequently a stigma attached to crying in the modern Western world, and we avoid the "shame" of tears as much as possible. Although scientists have found the toxin data which may help us give ourselves permission to cry for the "health of it," mystics and other heart-centered beings have known forever about the grace of tears.

Thirteenth-century German mystic, Mechthild of Magdeburg, wrote that "tears are a passing on of the river of grace." She believed that tears were God's divine energy flowing through us. Wouldn't it be wonderful if we could move into the heart of our feelings and let warm, moist tears cleanse our bodies and fertilize our souls? I know that letting myself cry is hard. I hear, ringing in my head, injunctions such as, "Why are you crying and making a mountain out of a molehill?" and "For God's sake, what do *you* have to cry about? Your life is a piece of cake compared to many!" Slowly, and I hope surely, Mechthild and other mystics are helping me believe in the grace and soulfulness of tears.

"Jesus wept" is the shortest verse in the Bible, set off to underscore its significance, I presume. Who was more in the river of grace than the enlightened Christ? A good example for us to follow.

In the crucible of crisis, being able to shed our tears will place us in the flow of divine love and launch us into the river of grace, in which we can absorb solace and be washed free from grief. Whether they flow from a contrite heart in order to punctuate a sincere "I'm sorry" or are shared grief with our beloved, tears establish a flow of divine energy between us and bond us in grace.

There's a little story that suggests God saves each of our tears, turns them into pearls, and presents them to us when we enter heaven. Maybe if we can come to believe that we are not only passing on the river of grace but are adding to a celestial string of pearls, we will be able to anoint ourselves and our beloved with the blessing of tears.

SANCTIFYING OUR PAIN

Mystics and philosophers agree that it is pain that seasons and strengthens our souls. Pain used as an impetus for soul growth and understanding is sanctified as a result. It is natural that staying open to the lessons to be harvested from pain is difficult at the onset of a wound. Our task, when first thrown to the mat, is to gently allow ourselves to grieve the pain and, if we're able, to be willing to open to the soul growth inherent in the experience. Eventually, if we keep our intention clear about soul growth throughout all that life brings us, we will transform our suffering into increased wisdom and awareness.

When initially faced with the knowledge that my first marriage was on the rocks, I was devastated. Grief, disbelief, and rage vied for attention and expression within me. I was obsessed with the searing pain that I felt. At first, if anyone had told me to open to the soul growth in this experience, I would have wanted to punch them out. Over time, with much help from friends, family, and a therapist, I was able to open to the possibility that this was the crucible in which a new and better me would be fired. And that was the turning point.

For me, Jung's statement, "It is through the wounds that light can come in" was absolutely true. In the fire of my pain was born the therapist I became, the spiritual seeker that I still am, and the person I quest to be. Through the wounds of my failed marriage and the resultant rips in my self-concept eventually flowed the light of greater understanding and compassion. I can truthfully say that I feel blessed beyond words by the gifts that emanated from my divorce.

Paradoxically, there are still—and always will be—fragments of sadness to hold side by side with the gratitude. That is the way of life. It's rarely totally black and white. As in the yin/yang symbol, there is a vestige of black in the white and of white in the black. Sanctification of our pain requires that we embrace the paradox and give thanks for both the growth and sadness hidden in the Mystery. By embracing all aspects of the Mystery of crisis, it will be easier to find meaning in our suffering.

REFRAMING CRISIS

We can also *re*form and *re*frame crisis through *re*wording how we think and talk about it. A few simple, but helpful suggestions are:

1. Change "my" and "our" pain to "the" pain. THE pain is less personal and more manageable. We can get very attached to MY and OUR pain and imagine that it will be with us forever. Letting go of THE pain is easier.

2. Replace both the words and attitude of "Isn't it awful!" Instead, learn to say and believe, "That's good." We don't have to believe that something is good right away, but being willing to reframe our reality by remembering to say, "That's good" will help improve our attitude and our resilience. If we just can't bring ourselves to say "That's good," we can pray, "I can't yet see the good in this. Please help my vision clear and my trust return." Both statements foster spiritual optimism and acceptance of the Mystery.

3. We can dis-identify with our feelings by remembering that at the core of ourselves is an indestructible divinity who understands and remains apart from the crucible of crisis (or, at least, remains unscathed and unscarred). This core, our soul-Self, will always be there for us when we reach out, open to receive it. In our darkest hours can come the greatest solace. A phone call, a perfect paragraph, an inner flash, the feel of arms around us.

   We can help ourselves dis-identify with our pain and remember our Self by saying, "I *have* this feeling, but I am *not* this feeling. I am _____." We then fill that space with whatever feels the most healing. I use "a pure child of God" or "a wonderfully strong and wise spiritual being." It varies with my need.

4. Remember, "This, too, shall pass." When this challenge has passed, what growth and insights will we have gleaned?

"This, too, shall pass" is a wonderful sentiment emanating from the depths of the feminine wisdom that trusts in the cycles of life. Crisis and calm, joy and sorrow, clarity and confusion, illumination and darkness all have their place in our lives as well as their own special gifts to bestow upon and within us. Resting in the arms of the Sacred Feminine, our pain can be sanctified. And, we *can* take it with us. Joy, wisdom, truth, love, and the refining of our experience into the gold of understanding and compassion are all things we can take with us through the gates of death. Precious nuggets alchemized from the dross and lead of life into the gold of soul progression.

CREATING CLOSENESS, NOT CHASMS

In dealing with crisis, the most important thing for us to do is to look in our *own* mirror by gently and lovingly accepting responsibility for ourselves. When we realize that we are bravely working on our own evolution, it will be much easier *not* to project the blame onto our beloved.

In the face of the unfathomable and unbearable, it is such a temptation to blame those close to us in an attempt to alleviate some of the pain. Please don't. Driving a blame-wedge between us creates chasms, not closeness, and increases the heat of pain. As the wise old saying goes, "United we stand, divided we fall." This is so true for couples in a crucible experience. Each person needs to find solace separately, and together as a partnership. We need different things in order to heal, but, very importantly, we need *each other!*

In the alchemical furnace of crisis, communication is *all* important! In sacred partnership, we're asked to open our hearts to our beloved at the very time when our hearts are broken and the only thing that feels safe is to tightly close them around our pain. Sharing our feelings and what we need (although it's even difficult to know *what* we need while in extreme pain) allows us to join our pain, embrace, and dance through the agony together. Entering and blending with the pain in a nonresistant way will ensure that we don't isolate ourselves from each other and fall into a chasm of loneliness and separation.

Holding each other and dancing together through the hell of healing can cool flames that otherwise threaten to consume us. Grief is sometimes too deep for words, or even for thought. Collapsing wordlessly into each other's arms and letting our tears blend can be sacred communion of the highest order. Treasure the moments when you are able to share your grief, while also remembering that grief and healing is partially a silent, solitary, inner process to be allowed, encouraged, and revered.

As soon as possible, after the first fierce swords of pain have dulled, we need to share the intention that, together, we can make this crucible of pain an incubator for greater compassion for ourselves and eventually many others.

Pain Is the Incubator of Courage and Compassion

In the crucible of crisis, our courage is fortified and empathy and understanding for others is born within us. For it is from the bleeding heart of our wounds that compassion flows. Having known pain and allowed ourselves to be vulnerable to it, we can truly be present to others who are wounded. From the memory of our own woundings and the soul growth reaped within them flow empathy, compassion, sensitivity, and grace.

Our intention for our own and our partner's healing, growth, and unfoldment will help the fires of trauma and struggle to forge an even stronger vessel of love of our marriage. From the healing and love contained in our commitment to sacred union, we will be able to pour forth onto our sisters and brothers, in this battered world, more compassion and support. Having suffered ourselves, in our presence the wounded can feel secure. Safe in our compassionate warmth, those who mourn can find the courage to tentatively reach toward their own hope and strength.

Part Three

THE ART
OF
MARRIAGE

How do we become artisans in the craft of love?

$\mathcal{W}$e know from explorations of their hieroglyphics that early Egyptians saw relationships as an art form, an invisible picture created by two people, demanding intimacy and commitment from its creators. The same is true today, but in addition we have the privilege of becoming masters in the art and craft of sacred partnership. The most important word in the preceding sentence is *becoming.* None of us start relationships as master craftspersons. We *learn* to sustain and nurture love. Through commitment and practice, we *become* masterful lovers and faithful friends as well as teachers and students of our beloved.

Although relationship is the foundation for individual peace of mind and the ultimate safety and survival of our planet, we have only recently accepted the idea that we must be *taught* the art of relating. Confused by Hollywood, Wall Street, and the infamously inaccurate tag-line of many fairy tales, "And they lived happily ever after," we have had unrealistic expectations about relationships. Thankfully, we are becoming aware that relationships, like *all* art forms, require rudimentary training and then practice, practice, practice.

Although aware of the need to learn relationship skills, we are slow to *accept* the fact and *act* on that need. Deeply embedded in our psyche is the misconception that, if we truly love someone, we should naturally know how to craft a relationship. Like most skills, the craft of relating to others takes time to refine.

As with the ability to master any art form, marriage requires a passionate desire to become proficient in our chosen craft and a high degree of commitment to practice and remain present. Relationship guru Ngakya Chogyam Rinpoche believes that "It's possible to stay in love forever. You just have to *act* like you're in love forever." Simple, but profound. Even as the intensity of our love energy mellows, it is possible to consistently treat our beloved as if we're in love. Making that choice, accepting that commitment, can lead us on one of the highest and most rewarding spiritual paths imaginable.

The old adage "Practice makes perfect" is true. As we bloom into relationship artists, we begin to create a hand-crafted life, knit together with the threads of authenticity, purpose, and love. Grounded in our unique talents, skills, and passions, our marriage will not be dictated by the status quo nor by societal expectations. With practice, we can create support systems that nourish and further spiritual growth and joy through loving and honoring each person's beauty and personal expression. As we continually recreate our art, a vibrant mosaic, enhanced by each family member, will be pieced together, with all individual colors and patterns complementing the others through love. The picture of our marriage and family will emanate grace benefiting those within its immediate circle as well as those outside.

Chapter Eight

LIVING GENTLY
WITH YOURSELF
AND OTHERS

It is always best to be heartful rather than hurtful.

$\mathcal{M}$ahatma Gandhi said, "There is more to life than increasing its speed." Wise words from an equally wise man, but difficult to build into the framework of our lives. From what I can tell, although many people talk about their desire to slow down, relax, and enjoy the finer things of life, few have been able to do so. Why does this matter? One reason that it matters a great deal is that what often gets lost in the hurly-burly rush of our lives is the luxury to cultivate the art of gentleness. When we are frantically trying to abide by a timetable that is at odds with our natural ebb and flow, the ability to consistently breathe deeply and *choose* our reaction before automatically responding to an irritating situation, a thoughtless statement from our beloved or—a supreme temptation for me—a rude driver, is diminished. Another loss inherent to the acceleration of our pace is the loss of desire and time for gently supporting and nurturing ourselves and our loved ones. The loss of graceful, gentle living is quite a price to pay.

Time pressure and the stress of over-commitment is not the only factor in our culture's loss of gentleness. We might still be rough, harsh, or severe if we were invited to spend all the rest of our days under a banyan tree in a tropical paradise with servants catering to our every whim, unless our *intention* were to be gentle. In order to make gentleness an integral part of our lives, we will need to make a strong commitment to live gently and adopt an *attitude* that supports our resolution. As usual, we'll need to start this attitude adjustment by treating *ourselves* gently. What a thought!

When first entertaining the concept of being gentle with myself, the very idea seemed blasphemous. Of course I expected myself to be gentle with others, but wasn't I supposed to be my own hardest taskmaster and severest critic? Wasn't keeping myself in line, pulling myself up by my bootstraps, and never letting on as if anything was bothering me my job? No! In reality, learning to be gentle with ourselves enhances our ability to love, trust, and respect others. Embraced by a nurturing, sensitive *self*, we make better lovers and are much safer friends and family members for others. Treating ourselves harshly bruises our hearts. A bruised heart is more likely to treat others in a bruising way, or at least wish it could.

Most of us really want to choose gentle awareness and action for, inherently, we have gentle hearts. If we don't feel gentle-hearted, it's probably because we have been wounded and are protecting ourselves from the pain of our injuries. The core of our being is filled with the spirit of love and, when we can act from the gentle reality that *is* us, we feel so much better about ourselves, more authentic, more able to express the soul of our true Selves.

I believe that we sincerely want to be gentle, but we often don't know how. Sometimes all we need to cultivate a gentle attitude is some small reminders. For many years I had a 3x5 card on the refrigerator with my business card logo, *Live gently with yourself and others,* written on it. Recently, Gene had it printed on floppy refrigerator magnets. We send them to readers who write to me. It's a little cue to the subconscious, a gentle jolt to help put us back on track when we've lost sight of our commitment to live gently.

What would be a good reminder for you? Maybe a little note by the phone or in your checkbook? Or an agreement with your beloved to ask, "Is that gentle?" when you're hard on yourself or accept too many commitments. As you think about it, you'll know how you can work with each other to welcome the art of gentleness into your relationship and home.

UPDATING CHOICES

Along with gentle reminders, we need to revisit decisions made in the past to determine if they are still a gentle choice for *now*. We make big decisions often and thousands of little ones each day. Some of them might be long forgotten, but still acted on from a subconscious level, and now need to be recalled and revamped. One of mine that comes to mind was made during the intense pain of my divorce. I decided never to be that vulnerable again and, toward that end, proceeded to build a protective wall around my heart. When I fell in love with Gene, I needed to re-decide what was right for me now. Did I want to love him without reservation or honor my earlier decision to keep myself safe? I knew what I wanted to do, but the decision to let myself be vulnerable again was not easy, and I continued to struggle with it even after we'd been together for a while. Still, on occasion, I want to wrap my heart in a protective cloak and hire a loyal dragon to watch the cave door. When that happens, I eventually *re*decide to opt for the freedom of vulnerability.

Many decisions that we made early in our lives were wise at the time, and probably even helped us survive. But they may be out of date now, no longer needed because we have more internal and external resources than we did at the time they were made. Or we have simply outgrown them. Review, revisit, and revise your decisions. What is appropriate now? What will open you to a more heart centered marriage and bring more gentleness into your life? What new decisions will help your soul evolve and express as it longs to do from the very core of your Self? Some of the qualities essential for the art of living gently are patience, presence, kindness, enthusiasm, hope, humor, appreciation, gratitude, prayer, and applause.

COMPASSIONATE PATIENCE

This is a difficult time in history. Change is accelerating at an unfathomable rate. Our roles—our very identities—are in total flux. More is being expected of men in relationships and women in the marketplace. We feel (and actually *are*) pressured to do and be it all. Many of us are scared and confused.

Although we may hide our fear and confusion from all but a few close confidantes, it nonetheless contaminates our ability to live gently with ourselves and others. Because of rapid changes in our society, and the feelings induced by them, we need to surround and protect ourselves and others in an aura of compassionate patience. We're all in the same boat. We're all trying to bring ourselves, our relationships, and our world into the new paradigm of partnership and heart centered love, and we have darn few patterns from which to work.

It's important for women to realize that, although the lack of a surefire road map to the new paradigm of sacred partnership is difficult for us, it is even more difficult for our men. Masculine energy doesn't have as much native ability to move willingly into the unknown as does the feminine. Therefore, we women may need to be even more patient with men than they need to be with us.

Nonetheless, it's optimal for us to lace our expectations and requests with patience for *both* sexes and realize that creating the new paradigm of sacred partnership is like learning to write with our non-dominant hand. At first the message may be awkward, messy, and hard to decipher, but, given practice and *intention*, the meaning will become more fluid and easily understood. We need to "Row, row, row our boats *gently* down the stream. Patiently, patiently, patiently creating what we dream."

God Is Not Finished with Us Yet

Several years ago, our minister passed out buttons to everyone in the congregation. Each read, PBPWMGIFWMY. His sermon, centering on the need for us to be gentle and patient with ourselves and others, explained that the initials meant, *Please be patient with me, God isn't finished with me yet*. This little statement carries a big message. In a very feminine way, it honors the fact that we, and our whole culture, are *in process*. Although we are unfinished, God cares enough to continually mold, shape, and fashion us. Our job is to pay attention and do our part to assist with the process of "growing our soul."

OUR HEARTS ARE WHO WE ARE

We are offspring of the Almighty, filled with divine energy and powerful potential. As we can gently weave the belief of our worth and value into our attitude toward ourselves, we will *become* even more able to access our beautiful soul energy and will also nurture that becomingness within others.

It might help us realize the value of treating ourselves and our loved ones with gentleness if we were to visualize each of our hearts as a delicate treasure, hand-blown from the rarest ethereal glass. A treasure valuable beyond imagining—fragile, irreplaceable, priceless, and ancient. There is *no* other like it—infinitely precious, existing before time and after infinity. In reality, we *were* entrusted with such an inexplicable treasure when we were given the gift of life. Our hearts are who we are. Infinitely strong, vastly vulnerable, deserving and needing the soft, gentle touch of love.

Minute by minute, we can decide to choose gentleness, to accept the sacred charge to express ourselves from the very heart of our tender soul. How we can hold ourselves and our beloved in our hearts can be summed up in the following:

ABCs OF GENTLE LIVING WITH OURSELVES

A   Be AWARE of and ACCEPT who we authentically are.

B   BELIEVE in who we really are and in who we are BECOMING.

C   CHOOSE to act from who we really are—gentle-hearted, soul-full spiritual beings.

C₂   CELEBRATE who we are right now, as is.

BEING PRESENT

Being present is a "present" of gentleness that we give to ourselves and any other person for whom we are fully available and attentive. It means being in the here and now, listening and speaking deeply and staying as honestly aware of our feelings in that moment as we can be. Consciously committing to gently and consistently "plugging into" our partner and our relationship ensures that there will be more harmony between us and in our home. Being present to each other without the need to accomplish a goal or reach a destination comes from the heart of Feminine/Yin energy. Encircled in the protection of presence and compassionate caring, we can more readily open our hearts and allow our souls to grow into their full expression.

Our spirit longs to be visible to our beloved. In my psychotherapy practice, each of my clients, in their unique way, often stated their need to be *seen, heard,* and *held*. Being accepted, valued, and *seen* makes each of us feel safer and more significant. In sacred partnership, it is our gift to be present to our beloved, seeing, hearing, and holding him or her in the ways that he or she needs. Our beloved usually doesn't need our explanations or solutions, but does long for us to be present and gently take in what he or she tells us by listening from our heart and soul rather than from our mind.

Staying conscious to the present moment is simple but not easy. Especially when we've been in a relationship with someone for years, we can almost automatically go unconscious and fall back into old patterns right at the time when the present moment has something important to reveal. Fear, especially, often takes us out of the present. A little motto I like to use to remind myself to stay conscious is *This moment . . . if I don't use it, I lose it!*

CIRCUITOUS ROUTE THROUGH HEAD AND HEART

Being able to stay present when we feel justified in reverting to familiar reactions is a talent of the Sacred Feminine. Because feminine energy is heart centered, it is receptive to feelings evoked in the moment and often able to intuit their meaning. The Feminine knows when something is off key or out of balance between us. As we allow our Sacred Feminine voice to be heard within ourselves, we will be better able to understand, accept, and *live* the present moment.

Even though coming from the heart and being fully present in the moment is a good habit to cultivate and leads to greater harmony between people, in the short run, in may be frustrating. Why? Because the feminine way takes longer. It's a much more circuitous route through the head *and* heart. Feminine energy needs to ponder, sort, and understand, making sure that what is under consideration is good, true, and best for everyone. Masculine energy is interested mainly in the goal, getting the job done, *now*. This, of course, has its place, but in communication with our beloved, we're usually much better off choosing the heartful consciousness of the feminine.

GRACIE ALLEN'S CLOCK AND THE FREEZE-DRIED WIFE

A friend visiting Gracie Allen (the late comedian and wife of George Burns) told her that her electric clock was not running, and she answered, "I only plug it in when I want to know what time it is." Without a commitment to be heartfully present, our marriages may end up like Gracie Allen's clock, disconnected and not receiving the "juice" that they need. If we only plug into our partnership when we need help with a project, a sounding board, or sex, our partner likely will not want to "give us the time of the day."

What we definitely *don't* want is for our beloved to feel taken for granted and devalued in the marriage. A friend, whose husband can get totally absorbed in his work and forget all else for weeks at a time, sadly told me, "Sue, I feel like a freeze-dried wife. My job is to just stay quietly on the shelf until he wants or needs me." Needless to say, when my friend's husband decides that making love would be nice and hasn't first given her some attention other than sexual, she's often still "all dried up" and unable to feel much of anything for him.

Our relationships are kept moist and juicy by "making love" all day long through conversation, presence, attention, and gentle kindness. Without dependable and meaningful connection between us, we dry up. If we have allowed ourselves to freeze dry our mate through inattention or unloving behavior, it will take considerable effort to "reconstitute" our relationship to one of balance, harmony, and gentle love. However, with patience and commitment, it can be done. Our relationships with our beloved, even if they have been allowed to dry out, can become nourishing, rewarding, and reenergized once again through gentle loving, commitment, and attention.

ENERGY FLOWS WHERE ATTENTION GOES

It's well known that what we place our attention on expands and is energized. Therefore if we focus on gently being present to ourselves and to our beloved, energy will flow into increasing our ability to *be* both gentle and present. We will find it easier and easier to hold ourselves and our beloved in the softest and most caring of embraces. Contrarily, if we focus on that which we don't like, that, too, shall increase exponentially. Focusing on what we appreciate creates a welcoming greenhouse of energy where the positives between us can grow and flourish. When we decide to zero in on what *is* working rather than what *isn't*, we're often delighted to discover that there's much more that "ain't broke" than there is that needs fixing. With enough energy flowing to the positive, the good may actually squeeze out the bad; flowers overtaking weeds!

As Mark Twain recommended, "Let us endeavor so to live that when we come to die even the undertaker will be sorry." When we truly care about others and are able to be gently present for them, allowing our energy to accentuate their attributes and values, while staying present to ourselves, even the undertaker will be sorry to see us go, *and* the angels will be joyous at our coming.

HOW TO BE PRESENT

There are a few very simple things we can do to help ourselves master the art of being more present. First, it's important to *know* and *honor* what we want and need. What nurtures us and gives us the strength and energy to be as gentle and loving as possible? What keeps us in balance and harmony with our universe? Make a list of what nourishes you—your soul-food—and then allow yourself to partake of it.

Be *aware* of yourself, how you feel, and what you are saying and doing. I know that sounds obvious, but how many of our precious moments do we lose to apathy, inattention, living in the past, or dwelling on the future? Many. When we become aware of ourselves drifting, we can choose to gently bring ourselves back to right now, right here. Usually those "right" moments are rich and fruitful.

Even if we feel bored standing in the line at the bank, we can decide to really *stand in line*. Try a little experiment and completely *be* someplace that usually seems more like an insignificant interlude rather than a real part of "important" life. Let's use the bank line as an example. Be there. Feel your feet on the floor. Really see (and maybe even smile at) another person. Scan your body and psyche for an awareness of how they really feel: hungry, cranky, joyous, tired, excited, bored? Experiment being fully present and see how you like it. If we can find it fascinating to stand in line, think how much fun we will have when we're fully present during laughter and love making!

The present is the only *real* experience we can have. The past is memory and the future is an enigma. We can *re*live the past or fantasize about the future, but we can only *exist* in the gift called Now. Of course we want to enjoy memories of the past and need to heal wounds inflicted there, and we also need to thoughtfully plan for the future so that we needn't fear it. But it's best to give the majority of our attention to the present, allowing our energy to flow into creating the best possible current moment, the only *real* one ever available. Each moment is ours, and only *we* can choose to live it or lose it.

THE FOUR NOBLE TRUTHS

One way I use to stay in the present is to remember the Four Noble Truths. The wisdom of the four noble truths can be found in many cultures, but I'm sharing knowledge found in The Great Wheel of Life and augmented by anthropologist Angeles Arrien and myself. The Great Wheel of Life is an ancient circular symbol, a mandala, that has been used by native peoples for thousands of years. If we did nothing else but adopt and live these four noble truths, our lives would elevate and improve dramatically.

The Four Noble Truths are:

1. SHOW UP and choose to be present to all that life offers. Be a good model—by walking your talk.

2. PAY ATTENTION to what has heart and meaning for you and resonates with your soul.

3. TELL THE TRUTH without blame or judgment. Say what you mean and mean what you say (Indigenous peoples call this "Speaking with spirit tongue"). Or, KEEP NOBLE SILENCE. From an empowered position, *choose* to remain silent.

4. STAY OPEN, BUT NOT ATTACHED, TO THE OUTCOME. Deeply care, from an objective place. Break old patterns. Practice discernment.

As we incorporate these four wonderful truths into our lives, they will be overlaid with gentleness and grace.

COMMUNICABLE GRACES

We've all heard of communicable diseases, but the truth is that we're equally susceptible to communicable graces. Joy and enthusiasm are just as contagious as doom and depression. In this difficult time on our planet, we need to expose ourselves to as many grace-filled germs as possible, and then make it our mission to infect as many other people as we can.

We can become gentle-joy-spreaders by bestowing on others, for instance, an infectious grin. It's especially fun to transmit the joy-bug to a fellow driver whom you've just annoyed in some way. More often than not, a grin from us, accompanied by a lightheartedly contrite "whoops!" gesture, will elicit an answering smile from a previously frowning, judgmental, and probably harried driver. Maybe it will be the first smile either of you has shared so far that day.

We may decide that our "bug of the day" will be infectious affection. Affection spreads rapidly. Put one hugger in a group and soon the whole group will be passing around healing hugs. As a young woman raised in Missouri, when I first moved to California I was shocked by all the hugging Californians did. But soon I was acutely and chronically infected by the hug-bug, so much so that my license plate read: IM4HUGS.

First, my intimate family circle fell victim to the hug contagion, and then my extended family. As a therapist, I hugged my clients. Hospice bereavement groups became great hug fests. Churches fell under the spell of myself and other dedicated hug-boosters. All this started years ago when hugging was still a new phenomenon. Now, thank God, we know the value of hugging and realize that to be optimally healthy we need at least eight full-body hugs a day. But, maybe, you have a relationship that hasn't become hug-infested yet. Grace it with hugs.

Hugs are *especially* important with our beloved. Being held, no matter how briefly, feeds our hunger for connection, makes us feel special and inoculates us against disease.

In cultivating the *dis-ease* of spreading communicable graces we need to make sure that we infect the person nearest to us—ourselves! Choosing to be kind and gentle to ourselves makes it easier for us to be kind and gentle to others. Love your neighbor *as* (you love) yourself! Self-sacrifice is no better than sacrificing others.

KISS OF KINDNESS

One of the most important communicable graces that we can invite into our lives is the attribute of kindness. When in doubt, choose kindness. There is no situation that will be worsened by a dose of kindness. This was brought home to me dramatically at a little neighborhood restaurant. One day, an employee that I knew slightly seemed surly and not very service oriented. It was uncomfortable just to be in her presence. I asked her if she was okay and her tearful answer was a choked, "No!" The restaurant wasn't busy so I asked her if it would be okay if I gave her a hug. She practically fell into my arms, and the tears began to really flow. During the few seconds that I held her, she said over and over, "I haven't been hugged for so long!" Sad, but true for far too many of us. When I saw her later in the week, she told me how important that hug had been. It was nothing. Just a tiny little kindness, but meaningful to her. We really have no way of knowing how important a simple act of kindness may be to the recipient.

Chinese philosopher Lao Tzu extols the virtues and effects of kindness in this lesson, "Kindness in words creates confidence; kindness in thinking creates profoundness; kindness in feeling creates love." Since the creation of more love is our main task as spiritual beings, learning to kiss ourselves and others with gentle kindness is essential for bringing sacred partnership into our lives.

A climate of appreciation multiplies communicable graces. If your mate or children show a germ of kindness, appreciate it! What is appreciated tends to be repeated. To grow more communicable graces in our lives, we can flood those that do appear with awareness, appreciation, and applause. Soon, all of God's children will be contaminated with kindness. It's a dream that can come true.

Divine Enthusiasm

Enthusiasm comes from the Greek *enthousiasmos* and means having a god within or possessed by a divine spirit. I love that! One of the most enthusiastic people I know is my mentor and soul-mother, Annabelle. Interestingly enough, she is also one of the most spiritual. Because we no longer live in the same state, she is intermittently our house guest. Having her as a guest is magical. Annabelle's enthusiasm backlights areas and attributes of my town that have faded from my sight. I see things brand new through her eyes. It's the same thing that happens when taking a child for a walk. Things that we may have become inured to by seeing them daily are illuminated by the light of a child's enthusiasm and wonder.

Since our enthusiasm is linked to the god within, to our divine spirit, it's incredibly important that, as partners, we endorse rather than drown our beloved's fiery excitement. Many of us have had our enthusiasm dampened as children. Although no one may have purposefully set out to squelch us, it undoubtedly happened, at least on occasion. If we've been silenced, cautioned to "calm down" or, worse yet, put down when enthusiastic, it's even more important for us to "tend the fire" of enthusiasm for both ourselves and our beloved. Doing so will help ignite, or *re*ignite, the divine spark ever present within our souls.

If we have gotten in the habit of raining on our partner's enthusiasm or they ours, we need to question our motives. What fear is evoked by another's enthusiasm? What underlying attitudes come into play when confronted with passion and excitement? What limiting patterns get played out when we smother enthusiasm with obligation or rationalization? Who, in our inner cast of characters, throws cold water on our own or our partner's flame? And why? Finding and eliminating the reasons for being a "wet blanket" can usher energy, excitement, and Eros back into our marriage.

Enthusiasm is incredibly infectious and enlivening. We need to spread it, not deaden it.

Hope Springs (from the) Eternal

Hope is essential to the art of gentle living. Jean Kerr wryly defines hope as "the feeling you have that the feeling you have isn't permanent." Right. There are times when hope is the final refuge of a ravaged spirit. Hope is the quality that keeps us hanging in there when the going gets tough. When beaten down, if we didn't have hope that this, too, would pass, we just couldn't put one foot in front of the other.

Gene and I used to volunteer with a little boy who was severely brain damaged. Once a week we went to Chip's house and helped his mother "pattern" him so that his brain could make new connections. On the wall of their modest living room was a hand-embroidered hanging entitled simply HOPE. Chip's mother told me that some days the only thing that kept her going was reading the message on that wall hanging.

Hope is an excellent companion for *all* parts of our journey. Even on her death bed, my mother was hopeful. She realized that life as we know it was ending for her, but she also believed that life itself would go on. One of the sweetest encounters of my life came when Mother whispered to me that she was afraid she wouldn't find the right place to go after she died. Having that particular fear was disarmingly applicable for Mother, who hated maps and was not good at navigating new areas. I reminded her that, as we'd discussed earlier, she wouldn't have to find her way alone—her guardian angels and probably the spirits of her mother and father would come to guide her. With a soft sigh and a slight smile, she murmured, "Oh, yes, I remember." With fear laid to rest and hope restored, my wonderful mother found her way Home a few hours later.

Of all the communicable graces, hope may be the most important, for without its grace, life could often be too crushing. A soul assignment for us may very well be to transmit hope to all those with whom we come in contact. If we are in a period of time when hope eludes us, then we need to seek out people who reinforce our natural tendency toward it. I have a theory that many people who commit suicide do so during an interlude in which hope has disappeared from their view and they have no one with them who can hold the vision.

Hope is a kissing cousin of Trust. As heart centered, complementary partnership evolves, and the renaissance of the soul becomes firmly rooted in our consciousness, hope *will* spring eternal. When we are in touch with our soul voice, we will not lose hope, for it springs from our awareness of the eternalness of All. Aware of and expressing our own god-spark, while reinforcing and encouraging the spiritual aspects of our beloveds, we will be in blessed *re-union* with the Divine, whom we can trust explicitly. From that eternal spring, all communicable graces, including trust and hope, flow freely.

CHOOSING A SACRED ATTITUDE

Sacred attitude is the gentle ability to look at ourselves, others, our relationships, and the world around us with an overflowing sense of awe. Wow! Ahhh! The sharp intake of breath when seeing a fall tree silhouetted against the sun or a baby smiling, the feeling of pressure as our breasts swell in gratitude. That is sacred attitude. More subtly, sacred attitude is a decision. A decision to choose to decorate our hearts with green boughs rather than dried, dead twigs.

If we have control over nothing else in our lives, we still have the ability to *choose* our attitude. We are free to view things through the vista of an open heart or see them merely from our heads. It's our choice, and only ours.

Of course we won't always *feel* loving or desire to live gently with each other since we are human beings infused with foibles and lacerated by wounds, as are our mates. But we *can* maintain a commitment toward an *attitude* of loving acceptance, which will help us regain the corresponding feeling relatively quickly.

Remembering how it felt to be newly in love can help us regain a sacred attitude toward our beloved. When newly in love, we personify love. It's as if being in love calls forth the love in us, but it doesn't have to stop when the honeymoon ends. Making a commitment to maintain a high level of sacred attitude in our marriage, choosing to act as if we're freshly in love, will allow love to deepen. When we choose to act in a gentle manner, think lovingly, and bathe ourselves and our beloved in the water of sacred attitude, our hearts can more easily stay open, thereby allowing love to flow freely through us. In this flow, the mysteries, magic, and secrets of sacred partnership will be unveiled.

It is always best to be heartful rather than hurtful! Although we are strong, wise, and wonderful, we are also tremendously vulnerable, especially in our love relationships. The bond between us, no matter how secure and solid, is also fragile. A harsh word, a thoughtless action, a judgmental attitude can wound us and snap the bond, if not for good, at least for a while. We don't want that, for we are lovers, nurturers, and friends to our beloved. It is our sacred charge to bring an attitude of love (or at the very least, an *intention* toward loving) to all of our encounters.

That doesn't mean that we hang a "Wipe Your Feet Here" sign around our necks. Quite the contrary, a big part of real loving is honesty, but honesty with *kindness*, a loving attitude, and a continual awareness of our beloved as a magnificent spiritual being. Imagine what a difference it would make, no matter how we felt in the moment, if we looked at our beloved and said silently, "This is a child of God speaking to me." or even, "This is a child of God annoying me." Choosing to look at someone in this light, even if they are being particularly difficult, can soften and resacralize our attitudes and our hearts.

THE OIL OF APPRECIATION

We've all heard about pouring oil on troubled waters, and when we generously pour the oil of appreciation on our beloved, there will *be* fewer troubled waters in our relationship. Everyone needs the fuel of appreciation, but in my years as a therapist, a wife, and a mother of men, I've learned that men not only need appreciation, they *crave* it. Men like appreciation almost as much as they do sex. Women also want and need appreciation, but men seem to be the original "appreciation sponges." It's very important that we women accept and honor what they need. They'll love us for it. For men and women alike, knowing that we're valued, recognized, and admired gives us the energy to do and be more.

One of the best ways to build our appreciation muscles is to bless everything and everyone. As often as I can remember, I do this when I run across someone and my judgment button is automatically activated. For instance, if I find my mind reciting such things as, "Yuck! He looks horrible" or "How could she possibly say such a thoughtless and tacky thing!" I try to make the choice to change that opinion by replacing my comment with a blessing such as, "Bless that person, dear God, and forgive my automatic condemnation" or "Please bless both the speaker and the hearer of that statement and may understanding be the result." If I'm particularly centered I also send a little, impersonal love dart to the person whom I've just judged. Even when I indulge in judgment and forget to replace it with a blessing, if I remember the incident later, I put out a blessing then. Whenever, whatever, whomever . . . *No* blessing is ever wasted as our world is definitely *under*-blessed! Appreciation is a wonderful blessing that all of us can give as we become more artful in living gently with ourselves and others.

NICE WEARS WELL

Niceness is one of the finer graces of gentle living, per se, and one thing is sure, *Nice wears well!* In counseling, I always ask couples if they are consistently nice to each other. Many qualities and characteristics of partners can wear thin over the years, but being nice always wears well and *never* wears out.

Being able to count on living in a nice, supportive environment is like a warm, welcoming bath followed by a cozy nap under a down comforter. Being the recipient of "not nice" behavior is more like taking a scalding shower and then being scorched by a branding iron. Not nice sears our soul and damages our psyche, wounds that not only take a while to scab over but often leave scars.

I was gratified to read that my simple, homey philosophy about the indispensability of niceness is now being upheld by scientific research. The Family Formation Project, led by John Gottman, has found, from twenty years of extensive research and tests with thousands of couples, a very simple reality about the endurance of marriage. In their book *Why Marriages Succeed or Fail,* they share their conclusion: Couples who stay together are simply *nice* to each other more often than not! Gottman asserts that, "Satisfied couples maintain a five-to-one ratio of positive to negative moments in their relationship," while couples in danger of divorcing slip below one-to-one.

Those of us aspiring to sacred partnership will need to raise the ratio of positive to negative dramatically. There is really no reason why a mature, loving person, one who is aspiring to spiritual growth, can't be nice *all* the time. I'm not claiming that we will always *feel* nice, but I am saying that we can choose to *act* nice. If we clearly can't, then it's wise to take a time-out until we cool down and can act nicely.

BECOMING RE-ENCHANTED

In my hospice work, I have been privileged to walk with many couples during the last few miles of their relationship on this plane. The majority of them hungrily value each precious moment left to them, appreciating and savoring the tiniest flicker of connection still apparent between them and their mates. "He smiled at me today, and we talked a few minutes about our wedding day. It was such a blessing," one wife excitedly told me. She was thrilled and totally appreciative of the effort he had made. The awareness of his approaching death had re-enchanted them with each other.

We can re-enchant ourselves with our beloved before death stands beckoning on the threshold by looking for ways in which we can be happy with him or her. A few suggestions for what we might do:

1. *Pretend we are meeting for the first time and look*
   at each other with new eyes.
2. *Talk with each other about what enchanted us when*
   love was fresh.
3. *List all of the things that we would desperately miss*
   if our partner were gone tomorrow.
4. *Listen to music that awakens sweet memories.*
5. *Pour over our wedding album together. Reminisce.*

Get creative and have fun making up re-enchantment exercises of your own. Becoming re-enchanted with our beloved sprinkles our relationship with fairy-dust. Sprinkled with the fairy-dust of enchantment, appreciation, and laughter, our hearts can experience the effervescence of love energy dancing between us.

STANDING OVATIONS

In the center ring of sacred partnership, we are each other's most intimate audience and closest cheerleader. Our stature as Chief Encourager and Most Appreciative Audience grants us the sacred privilege of congratulating, supporting, and encouraging our beloved. This doesn't mean that we make up things to applaud, but that we honestly and earnestly tune our awareness to actions, feelings, statements, etc. worthy of applause and then give a standing ovation.

Standing ovations can come in many forms. On the day that I finished writing my third chapter for *Heart Centered Marriage,* Gene came home with three beautifully delicate roses, with a "Congratulations!" card attached, to celebrate the number of finished chapters. It was so wonderful to have him notice and acknowledge my progress. For days, as those three little flowers unfolded, I was reminded of his "blooming" ovation and his appreciation. The gesture was especially meaningful for me because Gene knew better than anyone the struggle that I had sitting down to begin this book. By getting the flowers, Gene not only congratulated me, he said in effect, "I *know* you can do it!" At that point, I needed someone else's belief in me to buoy and bolster my own.

HUMOR HELIUM

Another great way to make sure that our relationships sparkle with fairy-dust is to sprinkle them liberally with humor. Humor is the leaven and helium of life. Laughter and humor lighten us. Without them things can get pretty heavy and leaden. Humor helps us float up from the depths of hurt and hardship.

Laughter is good medicine. Because of that, it behooves us to elevate our own humor level and help our loved ones up theirs also. Starting with Norman Cousins, who laughed himself free from a rare and usually fatal disease, science has become more and more aware of the healing power of laughter and lightness. Laughter, it turns out, not only lightens our moods but also enlivens our bodies by exercising our innards and flooding them with endorphins. Since our bodies, minds, and spirits are so intricately linked, laughter and a "lightened up" attitude actually acts as a buoyant for all levels of our being. Humor magnifies the magic of family and fun.

A few years ago, several hundred single people were asked in a poll what qualities they hoped to find in a mate. An overwhelming majority listed "sense of humor" in their top three desired qualities. The good news is that almost everyone has the capacity for a sense of humor. Often, all that people need for their sense of humor to blossom, bringing delight to themselves and others, is some positive response and encouragement. A sense of humor is like a sponge in that it expands as it soaks up recognition and responsive laughter.

Gene and I were both adequately humorous when we met, but our humor quotient has risen significantly over the years that we've been together. I believe that's because we egg each other on by our appreciation for each other's witticisms. In a group, each of us is often the only one who catches the other's joke, and we laugh at them whether anyone else is laughing or not. It's been an evolving process, and we made a commitment to consciously increase the laughter and humor in our lives. By our commitment, we're creating sort of a humor greenhouse. It's fun. It's healthy. And it's infectious.

But it took elbow grease and commitment to oil our humor mechanisms. When Gene and I first met, the six of us (we each had two kids) didn't just come together as the ideal step-family, and immediately and always yuck it up. In the early years, we worked constantly and *hard!* I always have to smile at the term "blended family" because, during much of the early bonding time in our family, I felt as if my guts had been thrown in a Cuisinart and were being "blended" beyond repair!

One of the major ingredients that sustained us through the really rough times was our appreciation of each person's unique sense of humor. Now when together, our family laughs a lot. Thank goodness!

THE GRACE OF GRATITUDE

Gratitude is an attitude. As with any attitude, it can be nurtured, cultivated, and changed if need be. Gratitude, like laughter and humor, lifts our spirits and hearts. It makes us thankful for the incredible gift of life that we've been given, and appreciative of the wonderful people who have chosen to share it with us.

We've all experienced times when we've misplaced our sense of gratitude. Without it, doesn't the world seem to diminish and darken as if a narrow furrow of complaint, criticism, and limitation is closing over us? In the shadow of ingratitude, our eyes are blinded to the light above and focus only on the dingy, trampled dirt of our trench.

When we get caught up in the darker aspects of life—and no one denies that they are there—we need to be especially gentle with ourselves. We are human. Our hearts hurt at times, and we forget to be grateful. When I'm experiencing a time like that, it helps me to remember a quote from the Sufi poet and sage, Rumi, "If you put a little dab of vinegar on a mound of sugar, what does it matter?" What Rumi softly says to me with that statement is, "It's okay, Sue, so what? Now, if you want, you can make a different choice. No big deal."

Another valuable process I've learned for dark times is to say "Thank you!" even when doing so seems phoney and hollow. The intention toward gratitude and the energy inherent even to an apathetic "thank you" seems to resonate within the very core of our spiritual being and is a helpful agent for soothing our hearts.

Gratitude gentles even the roughest roads and gives wings to the heart. When we can buoy ourselves with gratitude, we can sail over most situations while keeping a healthy, and even joyful, perspective of the landscape of our lives. Gratitude is communion with God. Gratitude graces our relationships with a high and holy soul-communion. Gratitude is meditation. Gratitude is the single most powerful medicine for physical, mental, and spiritual health for us individually and for our planet as a whole.

POWER OF PRAYER

Although we don't often realize it, attitudes—both conscious and unconscious—are powerful prayers that can make a miraculous difference in our lives. With an attitude of gratitude, the quality of our lives and love relationships is enhanced dramatically. On the other hand, attitudes of hopelessness, fear, or futility can dramatically depress us and even deplete our immune systems.

While religion and psychology have long recognized the power of prayer to affect our energy, attitude, and healing, science is now hopping on the band wagon. Larry Dossey, medical doctor and author, defines prayer as the action of non-local mind. He and other scientists have conducted experiments to test the scientific impact of prayer. My favorite study was done at Spindrift Institute, where seeds were soaked in salt water to keep them from germinating. Volunteers agreed to pray for the seeds, which were divided into three groups. The first group of seeds was not prayed for at all. The second group was prayed for using directed prayer such as, "Please help these seeds germinate." The third group was the recipient of non-directed prayer that included such statements as, "Thy will be done" or visualizing the seeds whole and perfect and able to germinate if it is the right outworking for them in God's eyes. Interestingly, none of the seeds from the first group sprouted. Although some of the ones in the directed prayer group did germinate, *two to four* times as many seeds sprouted when they were prayed for in a non-directive way!

What that experiment says to me is that God knows best and our soul task is to believe that and stop directing her. When I was in the process of divorcing but still longing to be with my first husband, I prayed, "Please bring me the perfect, right partner in *Your* eyes." But, then, lacking trust, I would add an addendum, "P. S. You know who." Only after I really could rest trustingly in God's love and accept the realization that the perfect, right partner in God's eyes might be no one, was I healed enough to welcome Gene into my life.

It's so important, in our practice of gentle living, that we use non-directed prayer for the people we love. To do so, we may need to overcome the idea that *we* know what is best for their happiness. Actually, we're very rarely able to penetrate deeply into the verity of their soul needs. God and their guardian angels *are* able, and we can use the power of prayer to call on them.

Learning to use non-directed prayer is an evolving process. When my seven-year-old son was wasting away from an undiagnosable illness, you better believe that I clawed at God like a rabid cat, begging, "Please make him *well!*" I might do the same thing again if the need arose, even though my son is now thirty. But, for the most part, I trust God enough to let her handle the specifics. My usual prayers include asking for the best outcome for the souls of all concerned, sending light and love, seeing a person whole and perfect and asking for their angels to be with them in their perfect, healing way.

PASSION FOR THE POSSIBLE

Psychologist Eric Fromm, noted for his wonderful attitude, talks about a "passion for the possible." Being able to envision the possible for ourselves, other people, and situations engenders within us a deep respect for all, and an enduring hope in our evolution. As the saying goes, possibilities are endless. Being passionate about possibilities ensures that we will maintain our enthusiasm for the mysteries and joys of life, and have enough energy to successfully handle the tasks and trials.

When we bring our passion to the possibility of sacred partnership, it *will* happen. It *is* happening. By listening to the messages emanating from our souls, we are bringing the elemental wisdom of gentle, heart centered love to our relationships. Through our soul's deep hunger for union with our beloved and the Beloved, anything is possible!

Chapter Nine

THE FOUNTAIN
OF
FRIENDSHIP

Friendship gives Love its wings.

$\mathcal{S}$everal years ago Gene gave me a little plaque that reads *Happiness is being married to your best friend*. So true, and even sweeter because our friendship is the fruit of our commitment. Although we were immediately attracted to each other when we met, our friendship has deepened and widened over time, through intention, gentle cultivation, and just plain hard work.

Not only is friendship between lovers the result of intention and work, it is also one of the blessings of sacred partnership, a wellspring of grace and goodness. Friendship is the single most important element in the art of creating sacred partnership. Lord Byron said that, "Friendship is Love without his wings." But I believe that *Friendship gives Love its wings!*

The idea of a wellspring is fitting, for a fountain is an apt metaphor for friendship. A fountain is a natural spring of water, the source or beginning of a stream, as well as the source of anything, such as a fountain of wisdom. Friendship too, at its finest, can be the origin of much beauty and growth.

In a letter to her mother, writer Anaïs Nin shared her idea of a friend: "Each friend represents a world in us, a world possibly not born until they arrive, and it is only by this meeting that a new world is born." We certainly need a new and improved world, a world of peace, love, and cooperation. We can begin the needed changes by concentrating on making a new world of our marriages. Befriending ourselves, our beloved, and our children—supporting each person's soul growth—will give birth to a fresh, new world, with complementary equality between all persons.

Our first step is to create a fountain of friendship and gentle beauty within our own heart and the sacred hearth of our family. As we allow peace and love to grow within the microcosm, we will be guided in the right ways to move out, by example and action, into the larger arena. The Talmud tells us that each blade of grass has its own angel bending over it whispering, "Grow, grow." In the same way, our intention and commitment to expand loving friendship in the world will be honored by our angels and the still small voice of our Inner Oracle will coach us about how to take the next step.

MYSTERY OF FOUNTAINS

In nature, fountains combine the feminine elements of water and earth with the masculine elements of rock and directed power. The goal of water, as it leaves the womb of earth, is to return to its source, and it lets nothing deter it from its goal. The paradox in this is that water, the most feminine of all elements, exhibits strong masculine energy and determination in its desire to re-unite with its source. This is a wonderful example of masculine and feminine energy working in concert. So it is with us as we create a loving friendship with our mate by combining the flow of the feminine spirit with the goal-oriented determination of the masculine drive.

We can become a soul-soother for both our beloved and ourselves as we sculpt our marriage into a fountain of friendship. Bathed in the water of love and supported by the granite of commitment, we'll become marriage artists, artists able to feed the souls of our families while renewing and replenishing the very earth.

FILTER OF FRIENDSHIP

Love is a decision that springs from our choice to see the best in people. When we embrace the attitude that everyone is a spiritual being, here for a sacred purpose—bumbling and stumbling though we may be—we will more easily be able to view those around us through a filter of friendship.

The filter of friendship is gentle, compassionate, and patient. A friendship filter adopts the rose-colored glasses approach by focusing more intently on the good, true, and beautiful in a beloved than it does on his or her negative aspects. We often use it with our children and grandchildren. We see their best. That doesn't mean that we deny the darkness or put our heads in the sand, it merely means that we *choose love.*

Choosing to see the light in ourselves and in others actually serves us well. Our hearts open more readily when we choose to focus on what we like rather than on what we don't like, and on what we appreciate rather than on what we disparage.

Thomas Hughes spoke wisely when he said, "Blessed are they who have the gift of making friends, for it is one of God's best gifts. It involves many things, but above all, the power of going out of one's self, and appreciating whatever is noble and loving in another." To practice the art of love is to be happy with whatever is noble and loving in ourselves and another. There is nobility and lovability in everyone, for we are all sparks of the Divine.

RIPENING OF FRIENDSHIP

Samuel Taylor Coleridge says, "Friendship is a sheltering tree." As with trees, friendships start from little seeds and, with care and nourishment, flower into safe and sheltering havens. Our friendships ripen as they mature, but not without consistent love and attention. As we become masters in the art of marriage, we create an inner space in which "being in love" ripens into sacred, heart centered, enduring love and friendship.

Ideally marriage partners are linked together in the common purpose of creating more love in the world, and committed to carrying out that purpose from the seed bed of their own relationship. Because we, like seedlings, are both strong and vulnerable, we must treat each other gently if we are to grow into our full potential. We must be willing to shower an abundance of light and love on ourselves and our beloveds while watching patiently and enthusiastically as they, and we, slowly grow into bearing the fruit of our souls.

Friendship infuses our partnership with a fine golden mesh of safety and defuses difficulties and disillusionment. Friendship with our beloved sustains us and fills our marriage with angel energy that encourages us to Keep it Light, Fly High, and Bless Everything.

TENDING THE GARDEN OF FRIENDSHIP

Loving friendship does not grow when untended. It needs to be tenderly cared for and cultivated. Anne Morrow Lindbergh described this beautifully,

> *There is no harvest for the heart alone;*
> *The seed of love must be*
> *Eternally*
> *Resown.*

One exercise that I've found helpful for keeping the garden of friendship growing is to make a list of the things that make us feel really loved. We might title such a list, "How I want to *be* loved by my beloved." Such a list serves several purposes. It lets our partner know what we appreciate and how he or she can show us love. It also allows us to ask for what we want and need in a positive, non-demanding way.

Gene's list usually includes quiet snuggling sessions, especially while watching late night TV, and mine states how nourishing it feels to have my feet rubbed. My list is heavy on talking and touching and Gene's is filled with his desire for appreciation for what he does and provides. Sometimes there will be surprises on our beloved's list, for they will be yearning to receive love in a new and different way. Because we want to become masterful lovers, knowing what our partner wants and appreciates is a wonderful gift. The more we receive the kind of love we long for, the more our hearts will open and be able to resonate with the melody of the divine.

Wellspring of Affection

True friends are affectionate with one another. Their delight in each other expresses itself through appreciation, attention, and physical affection. Some of us have been taught that displaying affection is weak, makes us too vulnerable, or is a private thing only indulged in behind closed doors. Men especially have been given the message that public displays of affection, particularly with other men, can give the wrong impression. As well as being concerned about how it may look to others, we sometimes feel that any affection given must be returned in like measure. Thinking that can dam up the flow of love in marriage since, generally speaking, men are socialized to be less demonstrative than women. Therefore, if we believe in a "hug for a hug" or a "pat for a pat" both of us may end up affection-deprived.

If given as a gift and not as a barter for sex or reassurance, affection can go a long way to creating friendship between lovers. Establishing an atmosphere in which affection is freely given and received is usually the domain of the feminine. In marriage, it's important that we women teach those we love the art of affection. We can do that most effectively by generously giving what we wish to receive.

Perhaps because we feel personally slighted, the most affectionate person in a pair sometimes balks at teaching affection, believing it's a waste of time and energy. In reality, affection is never wasted. The integral connection between affection and the fountain of friendship was stated beautifully by Henry Wadsworth Longfellow in his poem *Evangeline*,

> *Talk not of wasted affection! Affection never*
> *   was wasted;*
> *If it enrich not the heart of another, its*
> *   waters, returning*
> *Back to their springs, like the rain, shall fill*
> *   them full of refreshment:*
> *That which the fountain sends forth returns*
> *   again to the fountain.*

Just as love blesses the lover and is multiplied when shared, affection—given freely, from an overflowing heart—refreshes and restores the giver no matter how it is received. If our beloved is not in the habit of being affectionate, we can still be true to our own nature by creating a climate in which affection grows naturally. I was not comfortable with much physical affection until I was in my late twenties. But by the time Gene entered my life, I was an avid hugger. Neither he nor his two little daughters were. But it didn't take long for them to warm to the wonders of physical affection and become great huggers themselves.

We all need to be touched. For mental, physical, and emotional health, we need to physically connect with those whom we care about. Wrapped in the warm comforter of affection, icy, stuck places within us are able to thaw and allow the fountain of friendship and love to flow through us.

LOVE IS NOT A LEDGER

All relationships include both giving and receiving, but love is not a ledger. Of course, if there is an imbalance in our partnership, we need to address that in an up front, honest way. But in general, ledger keeping is more like storing ammunition than it is honestly exploring and discussing a perceived problem. If you notice yourself adding up how much you do, or how many times you compliment, or how often you support and then feel angry, hurt, or resentful by your tally, it's time to have an honest talk with your partner. Not in an accusatory way but in a "Let's work this out through better understanding and cooperation" way.

When a partnership is complementary and harmonious, love flows, imbalances naturally right themselves, and each person feels okay about the way things are going. The fountain of friendship is already muddied if we feel the need to keep score. Enemies tally, friends talk. So if you are keeping a ledger and the score is Love-Nothing, it's a good idea to look at why you feel the need to keep track. From that realization, resolution can take the place of blame and judgment.

SOARING ON THE WINGS OF SAFETY

Safety is the wind beneath the wings of love and friendship. Only in the presence of physical and emotional safety are we free to unveil the person we truly are and become the person we are destined to be.

We all know when we're not safe in a relationship, and react by protecting our back. We can do that in several ways, either by withholding our truth in order to keep the peace or by becoming aggressive in an attempt to gain control of the relationship. Neither of these responses is going to lead us to the peace and joy of heart centered partnership. They will, instead, isolate us from each other and from the free and creative being whom we are at our core. Feeling safe in a relationship, we can *act*; feeling unsafe, we can only *react*.

A safe relationship is a springboard from which we can leap to our highest potential. In the event that we crash to the ground, a safe relationship is also equipped with the heavy duty safety nets of compassion, encouragement, and solace. The safety of Gene's love and support allows me to venture out into new and scary territory, such as television interviews and talks in front of what seems like a billion people. When I fall flat on my face—and I do—he is there to encourage me. Sometimes he does that by holding me or pointing out what went well. Occasionally, when it's warranted, he'll join me in a bitch-and-moan session about the set-up or circumstances leading to the belly flop. Often we end up laughing by taking the setback to comic and catastrophic extremes.

In safety-based partnerships, we aren't forced to watch our backs; instead, we watch each *other's* backs. A woman whom I'll call Mary was telling me about her forty-year marriage. She said that throughout all of the sorrows and celebrations of raising seven children, she and her husband had always been each other's best friend. They are in the midst of a family crisis now, and she told me that she said to her husband, "It's just you and me, Wayne, and we're gonna get creamed!" And then they laughed, maybe a little ruefully, but a heart-to-heart laugh, nonetheless.

A SAFE HARBOR

Mary and Wayne have created a safe harbor in their marriage. Intuitively, they have known throughout the years that their partnership is the sacred ground of their being. Like Mary and Wayne, we all need sanctuaries, safe harbors into which we can retreat, confident that no torpedo will blow us out of the water.

The most important thing for us to do in order to create a safe harbor is to continually stand by our mate and believe in them whether they are soaring or sinking. Knowing that our beloved is *with* us, never against us, surrounds us with an invaluable aura of safety. We will all stumble and fall, every one of us. That's why it's such a comfort to walk hand in hand.

Because none of us is perfect, we often have to suffer through the pain of unwittingly gunning down our beloved when he or she enters the marriage harbor. As long as we admit and learn from our mistakes, our relationships can return to being the safe harbors we need.

CHARACTERISTICS OF A SAFE HARBOR

- ♥ safety
- ♥ approval
- ♥ respect
- ♥ kindness and consideration
- ♥ ability to be heard
- ♥ to be valued as we are, not as we *should* be
- ♥ emotional, physical, mental, and spiritual support

In marriages that offer a safe harbor for the partners, we do *not* have to be

- ♥ smarter or quicker than
- ♥ same as
- ♥ careful of our every word
- ♥ wary of attack or criticism
- ♥ invisible

♥ invulnerable
♥ perfect, or even close

FEAR CASTS OUT LOVE

Fear is the major stumbling block for safety in love and friendship. The genesis of almost all unloving behavior, whether expressed as anger, judgment, criticism, or any other "negative" feeling, is fear. Fear casts a shadow over all of our naturally loving tendencies and causes us to act from our lower, insecure nature rather than from our hearts. Therefore, our job is to find the basis of our fears in order to heal and transform them. All of us wearing human bodies have pockets of fear that can erupt and take us by surprise. When we can ferret out the nebula of fear embedded within us, contaminating our attitudes and beliefs, we will be able to free ourselves from slipping unconsciously into a fearful place. The first step in healing our fear is to understand how it is generated:

1. *First, we* interpret, *in a negative way, actions, statements, or body language that we believe are directed at us. Often it is not what actually happened, but what we* assume *has happened.*

2. *Second, an internal litany of, "This is terrible. I'm in danger," begins in response to our interpretations and assumptions. Fear wells within us.*

3. *From this ferment of interpretation and fearful inner dialogue spring all "bad" feelings, including the defensive feelings of anger and judgment.*

In order to rid ourselves of fears that limit the true expression of our heart centered self, we can transform them in the following way:

1. *Questioning our automatic interpretations: Are they real? Are they based on fact or an old habitual reaction, often one formed in childhood? In most cases, with awareness and desire, we can choose our interpretations. If not immediately, at least eventually.*

2. *By monitoring our fear-inducing inner dialogue and changing it to something more positive. Create a positive affirmation out of a negative statement. For instance, instead of saying to myself, "I don't have anything to say to this sophisticated audience," I have an affirmation I repeat, "I'm glad that I'm here. I'm glad the audience is here, and I know that I know!"*

3. *Very importantly, we need to comfort, not chastise, our fearful self. By treating ourselves as a gentle and loving mother would treat a fearful child, we create a safe climate in which we can move through our fear more quickly.*

Becoming aware of our interpretations and taming the fears they induce will change the quality of the energy in our partnerships and make us better lovers. Bringing our fears into the light of love and awareness helps us build a bridge from the insecurity of fear to the safety of a loving heart. For, if fear casts out love, the opposite is even more true. Bathed in the light of love, fear cannot exist.

SUPPORTED, WE FLY . . . SHAMED, WE DIE

One of the biggest boulders damming up the fountain of friendship is allowing shame to enter the picture. When we feel supported by ourselves and our beloved, both our bodies and our minds are healthier. In a safe, nurturing environment, our brains create "feel good" endorphins that give us a lift. Conversely, when we criticize ourselves or receive criticism from others, we become weaker.

Criticism is attacking someone's personality or character rather than making a specific request or complaint about his or her behavior. "I wish you had bought more gas after you used my car" is a request, whereas, "You're so thoughtless! You *never* put gas in my car when you use it!" is an attack. Being criticized generally evokes shame in us. With shame comes blame. When we castigate ourselves for real and imagined faults, our brain seems to interpret the message by saying, "Oh, oh! You're bad. You're not worth the effort. I don't need to create 'feel goods' for you!"

Shame swamps us with weakness, fear, and feelings of low self-esteem. In fact, research psychologists at the Family Formation Project at the University of Washington in Seattle have discovered that women are made physically sick by a consistently unresponsive or emotionally contemptuous husband. After studying thousands of couples, researchers can even predict how many infectious diseases women in non-supportive relationships will contract over a four-year period. To be fully functional our immune system relies on our emotional well-being. That's no surprise to many of us nonscientists, who have known for years that we're much more susceptible to colds and flu when our "esteem system" is depressed.

If you'd like to experience the reality of this premise, stand up and raise your arm out to your side. Think of the thing that you like the *most* about yourself and congratulate yourself about it. When you have that inner dialogue firmly in mind, ask your partner to try and push your arm down to your side. How strong are you? Okay, now raise your arm out to the side again but this time think of the thing you *least* like about yourself. Criticize yourself for it. If you're like most of us, you'll probably have a few standard admonitions readily available. When you've thoroughly criticized yourself, have your partner push your arm down again. How strong are you this time?

The majority of us are much weaker after criticizing ourselves. Our arms flop down as if made of string. Interestingly, the same weakness also happens when we criticize someone else. Given this example, we can graphically see that criticism and shame damage our vigor and vitality and also wound——sometimes fatally—the good, true, and beautiful within us. Therefore, in relating to ourselves and others, we need to take to heart the advice given by nineteenth century writer, Dinah Mulock Craik, in her essay "Friendship." She said, "Keep what is worth keeping, and with the breath of kindness, blow the rest away."

NEVER IS HEARD A DISCOURAGING WORD

Our assignment, in sacred partnership, is to *en*courage our beloved (assisting them to live *in* courage), not *dis*courage them. Of course, discouragement is likely to be a part of our journey together. One of us may become discouraged by obstacles in our path, or we might experience times when the world doesn't seem to be turning on its axis in the right way. We may be discouraged by health problems, or we may even become discouraged by the direction our relationship is taking.

In times like these, it's important to share our discouragement with our beloved. But, if we are both discouraged and don't have the energy or desire to encourage each other, it's perfectly acceptable just to admit that, as kindly and gently as possible.

In mastering the art of friendship in marriage, we need to be gently honest with ourselves while examining whether feedback that we want to give our partners is criticism and discouragement disguised as love and support. If we stop and think before we speak, *pause* and become aware of any temptation to spout fear-provoked comments or actions, we will know intuitively if we are coming from our hearts or not.

Being able to soar on the wings of safety in our relationships is more likely when we act only out of pockets of clarity. If confused, wait! Ponder quietly until your head is in sync with your heart. To help access the sacred feminine voice of our intuition, it's always good to ask God or our Inner Oracle for assistance.

PROTECTING, TOUCHING, GREETING

My favorite poet, Rainer Maria Rilke, gives a definition of love that resonates deeply with my personal philosophy. He says, "Love consists in this, that two solitudes protect and touch and greet each other." I'd never really thought about the importance of "greeting" my beloved until I read Rilke's definition of love.

With delight I read the dictionary definition of the word *greet:* "to speak or write to with expressions of friendliness, respect, pleasure, and so on. " Wouldn't our partnerships be love fests if each day we enthusiastically greeted our beloved with friendliness, respect, niceness, and *pleasure!* Even though we are "solitudes," and will never be able to know either ourselves or our beloveds entirely, we *can* become beautifully intertwined by protecting, touching, and greeting each other in love.

Security Sustains a Woman

Vulnerability and a willingness to risk are necessary ingredients for sacred partnership. In order to connect on a heart level with the essence of another, we must feel free to expose the soft underbelly of our own essence. To do so requires safety and security.

Although a secure environment is sustaining for us all, security is particularly essential for women. A woman's sense of well-being is directly proportional to her sense of security. Maybe this need was imprinted onto the very cells of our psyches long ago, when fierce saber-tooth tigers waited hungrily for defenseless human morsels. Whatever the cause, be it fear of saber-tooth saliva giving us a really bad hair day or, more likely, an instinctive need to provide protection for our babies, we women *need* security to a far greater extent than do our men.

Sustained by a sense of security within herself as well as in her partner's commitment to her and to their marriage, a woman can personify love and gentle nurturance. On the other hand, if she doesn't feel secure, a woman can descend into the shadow aspects of herself and become manipulative, controlling, demanding, dependent, bitchy, or sick. These shadowy behaviors don't make things any better. I know. I tried them all in my first marriage without realizing the origin of my dark discontent until later.

For a woman, being insecure in her relationships is like swinging from a branch that is sawed half through. We're always wary and waiting for the fall.

Riddled with anxiety, we are not candidates for either sacred partnership *or* friendship.

We women need to emphasize to our men how incredibly important security is to us. Correspondingly, men need to hear, absorb, honor, and act on their wife's need for security, whether it makes sense to them or not. It's just one of those things that both sexes must acknowledge, accept, and say "Okay" to. Only when she is truly secure can a woman reclaim and speak from her sacred feminine voice and love unconditionally.

One of my favorite passages in *Winnie the Pooh* is:

> *Piglet sidled up to Pooh from behind. "Pooh!" he whispered.*
> *"Yes, Piglet?"*
> *"Nothing," said Piglet, taking Pooh's paw.*
> *"I just wanted to be sure of you."*

Men, we women-Piglets need to be sure of you. When we are, we will fill your lives "with the pastel colors of warmth, understanding, and sensitivity" and "paint your vision with excitement," as Gene wrote to me early in our romance.

SECURITY LETS US SOAR

As friendship and love grow between us, our heart-bond becomes more elastic. Secure in our bond, we can move farther afield. Supported by a committed love, we can risk the dangers of being vulnerable and stretch the limits of our creativity. In order to grow our souls to their full potential it's important for us to unfurl our wings and fly in new directions. This is *so* much easier to do when we feel safe and know that our beloved is committed to being there for us. I've always thought of Gene as the rock from which I can fly and to which I can safely return.

There's another reason for us to expand our horizons. We hate to talk about it and don't even want to think about it, but we need to. No matter how committed we are to our beloved and he or she is to us, no matter how safe we are with each other, one day one of us will be left without the other. In the eight years that I facilitated bereavement groups for a hospice program, I saw many widows and widowers courageously coping with the loss of their beloved. For those whose mate had been not only a fountain of friendship but the *only* source—the fountainhead, the single stream, the entire ocean of their emotional fulfillment—healing was close to impossible. On the other hand, people whose beloved had been their main, but not only, source of sustenance had the strength and resources to heal much faster.

For optimum health and adaptability, we need an expanding and elastic circle of love sources, both for giving and receiving. As our spiritual maturity grows and security deepens, we will naturally develop a supple, flexible, and powerful bond between ourselves, our beloved, and the Beloved.

CREATING AN INTENTIONAL OASIS

Wouldn't it be wonderful if our friendship with our beloved were as welcoming and nurturing as the cool water of an oasis is to a weary traveler on a sweltering day? Given the hectic pace of our lives, in order for our relationship to be an oasis, we will need to stubbornly stick by our intention to make it one.

There are times, I know, when we're drained so dry that it's even hard to think. At such times, the idea of creating an oasis with our mate may seem like yet another obligation. But this is when we most need to be rejuvenated through drinking from the well of our love. A refreshing respite with our beloved doesn't have to take a long time. A glistening dew drop of tenderness here, a gentle shower of appreciation there. . . . It's the heart connection and the undivided attention given to being with each other that continues the greening process, not the time elapsed.

A head or foot-rub can take only five or ten minutes. A short conversation, *with* eye contact, a shared joke or idea, a silent time just resting in each other's arms, gazing at a sleeping child together, a little note showing appreciation, or a full-body hug: each of these can be badly needed and greatly cherished oases that help our relationships continue to grow into beautiful, fruitful friendships.

RE-CREATIONAL WORLD

There are physical, as well as emotional, reasons why regularly resting in an oasis is also important to our individual well-being. We live in a *re*-creational world that is in a constant state of re-creating itself. As a part of this world, we, too, re-create ourselves continually. The very cells in our bodies and organs change. Depending on the part of the body we're talking about, they change slowly or at an incredibly speedy rate. In the space of a few weeks or months, we have an entirely new skin, a new liver, or even a brand new skeletal structure to name just a few. Our astonishing body, including our brain, recreates itself *by* itself, providing we don't frustrate and thwart it too much. One of the best ways that we can assist our body/mind in its continual recreation is to allow ourselves the delight of *re-c*reation. Luxuriating in the oasis of recreation inspires our body, mind, and spirit to replenish, regenerate, rebuild, renew, and recharge themselves. Revitalized through rest and relaxation, we become more creative, more loving, and more in tune with the melody of the divine. Imagination and creativity need noodling—long, inefficient, happy idling, dawdling, and puttering, says writer Brenda Ueland. If we don't have the luxury of extended noodling, we can "mini" noodle.

Rest, relaxation, and recreation are not optional, they're necessary! Without them we become dry and brittle, and cannot be wonderfully, fluidly alive or loving.

NATURE NURTURE

One of the most important friendships that we can cultivate is with nature, for nature is a healing medicine. Perhaps that is because nature is the quintessential model of feminine energy: *Mother* Nature! To separate ourselves from the mother is to separate us from our innate feminine energy. Because we are so overbalanced in masculine energy, being immersed in the feminine force of nature helps bring us into balance and harmony within ourselves. Touched by sun, lulled by bird song and leaf rustling, kissed by breezes, invigorated by rain and awed by panoramic vistas, we dance to the melody of Sacred Feminine music and open our hearts to her wisdom. In nature, we remember, as Hildegard tells us, that, "We are co-creators with God, tending the Cosmic tree."

Most of us are aware of the healing balm of nature and attempt to reconnect with her at least irregularly, but Native peoples lived in harmony with her constantly and seemed to be very aware of their co-creatorship. One Native American legend states,

> *Take time to listen to the winds . . .*
> *To search the skies . . .*
> *To feel the snow.*
> *For in being one with nature*
> *We become closer*
> *To the Great Spirit.*

A therapist I know who specializes in marital counseling sends couples out for an hour's walk in nature. Their assignment is to *silently* hold hands for the first half hour—no matter how they feel about each other at the time—and choose three things in nature that symbolized something about themselves, their mate, or their marriage. The symbol about one's mate must be positive. For the second half hour, still walking and holding hands, they are to share the significance of their symbols.

One couple who took the nature walk had been alienated for years. They had not made love for more than five years, and could think of nothing nice to say about each other when they were in the therapist's office. Miracles happened on their walk. Just being willing to hold hands was a big step, but the most significant breakthrough occurred when the man found a rock. In tears, he explained to his wife that it symbolized his heart and how it had hardened over the years. Also in tears, his wife listened, seeing a part of her husband that she hadn't dared believe still existed. From that moment, this couple began to re-create their marriage.

There is something about the familiarity of nature that is soothing to us. Maybe we recognize, in her predictable cycles, a kinship and reconnection with our own. Going out in nature with those we love moves us out of our heads and into our hearts and bodies. It connects us to the earth, to Gaia, our source. Reconnected with the sacred feminine voice, we are more in tune with our own feminine qualities of intuition, love, grace, compassion, and creativity.

After an afternoon of skiing on a windy but beautiful Colorado day, Gene and I were walking across the parking lot to our car when he reached down and held my hand (an unusual gesture for him since he's not a dedicated hand-holder). Right after he took my hand, I slipped on the ice and would have crashed to the cement had it not been for his support. Catching my breath, I asked him why he'd taken my hand. "I don't know," he replied, "something just said, 'Take Susie's hand *now*' so I did." I firmly believe that, having played on the white bosom of Mother Earth for the afternoon, Gene was deeply tuned to his feminine nature and thereby able to hear her intuitive whisper.

THE POSITIVE POWER OF PLAY

Play is a leavening agent that makes us lighter, relieves tension and stress, and raises our energy level. Play changes us. During play, our body produces healing and restorative chemicals in the form of those wonderful endorphins, the natural tranquilizers overflowing from a happy body/mind.

Playing with our beloved is essential, for play catapults us into the child-like aspects of ourselves which are uncorrupted by circumstances, forever innocent, and naturally connected to the Divine. The child in us is a natural friend and enthusiastic lover. One interpretation of what Christ meant when he told his disciples, "Truly I say to you, unless you change and become like little children, you shall not enter into the kingdom of heaven," is that by keeping our childlike qualities of spontaneity, trust, awe, and wonder, we will intuitively know how to live in the kingdom of continual love and acceptance. Our eternal inner child is perpetually united with the Divine Mother. Therefore, it's not only fun to play, it is also spiritually illuminating. And a great tonic for marriage.

Philosopher and mystic Meister Eckhart says that God created the Universe from ebullience. In other words, God was *playing*, and he created the Universe out of an overflow of his joy; as a toy, his fabulous, fantastic beach ball. Therefore, we as residents of this favored, water-blessed planet are sparks of the Divine fire, brought to birth through exuberance and zest. Playing is our origin, our innate birthright, an inheritance from the very Source of our being.

If God truly was playing when he created the universe, then joy is our legacy. That being the case, how better to reflect God in our lives than to allow ourselves the freedom and joy of spontaneous, childlike, loving play? Individually and as a couple!

One of my favorite Christmas letters came from a woman in California who has started a snowshoe trekking business. Her motto is "When is the last time you did something for the *first* time?" That sure made me stop and think. When *was* the last time I was adventurous enough—childlike enough—to do something for the first time? Unfortunately, it had been a while.

INTIMACY INSTANTS

All of us have the little private instants of intimacy that help us form heart-bonds with our beloved. A wink, a shared laugh, a spontaneous hug, an understanding shoulder, a protective gesture. . . . We can enhance and increase these memorable moments by paying attention, acknowledging, and appreciating them as they happen. In order to instill intimacy-instants in our memory banks, we need to punctuate our playful or tender moments.

Many of these come from the "couple codes" that spring up between us over the years, the private patter that does so much to enhance and underscore our bond. These shortcuts in communication and understanding become a part of the myriad little heart strings securing us to our beloved.

Here's just one example from my life. Because I absolutely hate to, Gene balances my checkbook for me. One day he brought it to me with a puzzled expression and said, "Who is this Vera Steller whom you wrote that big check to?" My handwriting was so bad that "Versa Teller"—our instant cash machine—had looked like the mysterious, Vera Steller. To this day we both write "Vera" in our checkbooks when we get cash from the machine. It's a tiny thing, but it's *our* thing and that's what makes it special!

Whether it's our attitude, the security we create between us or the intimacy-instants we savor, all efforts to enhance our friendship with our partner will help give our love wings. Because the world can bruise both our illusions and our bodies, we need an oasis: a green, moist, alive sanctuary where we *know* that we are safe with ourselves and with our mate, who is, hopefully, our dearest friend. When the fountain of friendship runs freely and clearly, the ground of our being and of our sacred partnership will, in return, be green, sustaining, and fertile.

Chapter Ten

THE POWER

OF

FORGIVENESS

The fragrance of forgiveness permeates
heart centered relationships.

$\mathcal{F}$orgiveness is a powerful agent in our lives. Without it, unconditional love cannot thrive. Unconditional love is not predicated on conditions or expectations, but is the kind of love that makes sacred partnership possible. Unconditional love is the force of God flowing continually and naturally through us, unless we dam it with our own fears and attitudes. An intrinsic grace and gift of our higher Self, unconditional love is an eternal reflection of God within us. Unconditional love is the very essence of Light, while fear is the essence of darkness.

Light is more powerful than darkness. When we open the door to a darkened room from a lighted hall, the darkness does not flow out to fill the hall; rather, the light rushes in to illuminate the dark room. So it is with us. Darkness that we carry in the form of wounds, anger, ignorance, or intolerance is washed clean in the light of forgiveness. A love-filled heart casts out darkness from even the deepest, most shadowy chasm.

If we are to keep the unconditional love of the Source streaming through our hearts and out to our beloved, forgiving ourselves and our mate for not living up to our expectations is an essential art of marriage. The Essene *Code of Conduct* has a wonderful concept of forgiveness that evolved from their psychological and spiritual acumen. The Code states: "To forgive is to cancel all demands, conditions, and expectations held in your mind that block the Attitude of Love; that is to say, to cancel the conditions, demands, and expectations which prevent the mind from maintaining the Attitude of Love."

In other words, in order to forgive, we let go of the expectation or requirement that a person needs to act in a certain way. Of course the same is true in forgiving ourselves. We drop all demands, conditions, and expectations that keep us from allowing love and positive regard to flow through us to ourselves or to others. This doesn't mean that we condone, overlook, or deny unloving actions or errors—actually excellent learning tools. Rather, it means that no one or nothing—not ourselves, nor God, nor circumstances—has to live up to our expectations in order to receive love from us.

Forgiveness is an inside job! Other people, frozen in their positions or behaviors, don't have to change for us to forgive them. The more we forgive ourselves for falling short of internal and external demands, the more we can disentangle from anyone who has hurt us. Not forgiving binds us to our tormentor and to old fears and reactions. To be free, we must forgive.

THE LIFE-FORCE OF FORGIVENESS

While forgiveness generates light and love, non-forgiveness creates a barrenness within us, an impassable wilderness in which we are cut off from ourselves and from whomever we need to forgive. Locked in an unforgiving attitude, ruled by unreasonable expectations and conditions, our hearts close and freeze the life-force energy at the moment of the wound. Without forgiveness we are truly "stuck."

I experienced this stuckness after my first husband fell in love with my "good" friend. I had expected to be loved and taken care of. In fact, one of the major conditions that I placed on my ability to feel good about myself was that I create a happy, secure family. I was so wounded and disappointed in my "failure" that I didn't know if I'd ever be willing to forgive. I circled my wound like an obsessed buzzard, pecking and pulling at it constantly. I thought about it, talked about it, and dreamt about it. And I was getting nowhere in my healing process since my life-force was trapped in a tight little orbit around my feelings of betrayal, rage, and fear.

Because I was so resistant to letting go, I needed to take tiny little baby steps toward my goal. Finally I was able to decide to try to be willing to forgive. I really didn't feel like doing it, but was aware that my lack of forgiveness was injuring me. I began with the affirmation, "I am willing to be willing to forgive *him*, *her*, and *me*." I repeated this hundreds of times during the day. Often my inner response was, "Yeah, sure!" but I persisted.

An absolutely essential adjunct to the affirmation was taking good care of my wounded self. I worked at uncovering and cancelling both conscious and subconscious expectations that made me "bad" in my own eyes. Very importantly, I allowed myself to walk through the dark terror of the pain and rage, and, to the best of my ability, was kind, loving, and protective to myself. If I was totally down on myself, I asked for help from friends and family.

It took quite a while, but with therapy and help from people who loved me, eventually I moved into a space where I was truly *willing* to forgive and then on to forgiveness itself. And it was a good thing I did, for non-forgiveness had *dis*connected me from myself and from my Source, making my life arid and unproductive.

One of the most basic reasons for practicing forgiveness is that old stuff, old pains and wounds—no matter how far in the past—still feel fresh and create the same responses in the body/mind when we hold on to the feelings. I know a woman who is holding on to a fifteen-year-old wound from her divorce. Her inability to let go of unfulfilled expectations made it extremely difficult for her to joyfully participate in her daughter's wedding. Being in close proximity to her former husband and his wife activated feelings as intense as if the divorce had just happened. Her body/mind, stuck in the past, reexperienced the past. Sad both for her and for her daughter.

The ability to let go of regrets, resentments, and the tendency to be critical is at the heart of our physical and emotional well-being and healing. Holding on to negative, pessimistic, or painful feelings puts a crimp in the flow of our life-force, damming it from coursing through us as effectively as we can stop water from flowing through a hose by stepping on it. The Buddha sums this up nicely by saying, "When one person hates another, it is the hater who falls ill—physically, emotionally, and spiritually. When he loves, it is he who becomes whole. Hatred kills, love heals." As the Buddha knew, "just for the health of it" we need to become proficient in the art of forgiveness. Forgiveness *recon*nects us to the life flow of God through us.

WHEN WE WOUND OUR BELOVED

If we have inadvertently wounded someone's heart, it is up to us to seek forgiveness and recreate a climate of safety between us. According to couples workshop leader Gary Smalley, we need to do four specific things:

1. *Get very soft and tender.*
2. *Ask exactly why they are feeling wounded and then try with all our might to understand.*
3. *Apologize and admit when we've been wrong.*
4. *Gently and lovingly touch them and ask for forgiveness.*

All of these four are wise suggestions. I would like to add to them with a reminder that reconnection with someone who has been hurt is often neither a quick nor an easy process. It's not as if we can offend—attack through anger—then become aware of what's happened, softly apologize, and voilá, all's well and we're auto-*magically*, energetically, and emotionally reconnected. Not often.

Resolution is usually not that neat and spontaneous. First of all, we, as the offender, will need to move from our position of righteousness and then not become defensive when we discover that our actions have closed our beloved's heart. Not only will we need to maneuver around our own tendency to be defensive, but we'll need to admit we're wrong—and that is very difficult for some of us. Also, closed hearts and spirits don't often spring brightly back to full bloom once they've been bruised. We will need to be patient with the time it takes for the rupture between us to heal. One of the main reasons that it's hard to be patient with the time and space between wounding and resolution is that our own guilt at having caused pain in the first place nags at us until our beloved seems to be okay.

In order to help ourselves be patient and provide a climate in which our beloved feels safe enough to reopen his or her heart, we need to remain open toward ourselves. Even though (*especially* because) we've made a mistake, we need to concentrate on allowing our heart energy to flow toward *both* ourselves and our beloved, even if they don't forgive us immediately. Reconnecting is a process, and one that becomes easier as we practice and have some successes under our belt that we can trust.

POISON OF PERFECTIONISM

Forgiveness comes more easily when we haven't been poisoned by perfectionism. So much of our unwillingness to love ourselves as we are and to forgive our shortcomings stems from a need to be perfect. We can make allowances for others far more easily than we can for ourselves. Author Jessamyn West says, "It is very easy to forgive others their mistakes. It takes more gut and gumption to forgive them for having witnessed your own." A good explanation of why it's often hard to forgive those closest to us.

One of the most vicious piranhas of perfectionism is the ego's sometimes desperate need to be right. *Having* to be right is a tremendous burden for those afflicted and those with whom they are in relationship. Our ego's need to be seen as perfect can lead to much "wronger" responses, when confronted, than the original slight imperfection warrants. Such a response may consist of defensiveness, attack, withdrawal, put downs, judgment, inflexibility, martyrdom, and righteousness, all of which usually stem from a flood of shame-based feelings about not doing or being enough.

Being a perfectionist poisons sacred partnership by obliterating safety. Being overly vulnerable to our own perceived limitations and lacks causes us to be hypersensitive to anything seen as criticism, and at times, that can be almost anything said or intimated. Our overreactions to "criticism" cause our family to walk on egg shells around us, curtailing their spontaneity and making them wary of uncovering another molehill and watching it explode into Mount Everest.

Perfectionism is the function of an immature ego. An immature ego can only feel valuable and worthwhile when it believes it is *earning* the right to be valuable and worthwhile. Without being bolstered by a commitment to love unconditionally and a belief in our Self's intrinsic goodness and worth, the ego becomes insecure and tries to prove itself. Insecurity drives the ego to define itself by its actions, and they must be perfect to be acceptable.

Antidote for Perfectionism

The only real antidote for the poison of perfectionism is love and acceptance of ourselves and our beloved. As we are, right now! We may have some perfect experiences, and do a few things perfectly, but we'll never be *all* perfect. It's not what we signed up for. We agreed to take the course called "Living as a Human," and a requirement is experiencing imperfection. As we learn to love and accept ourselves no matter whether we're falling short or in the flow, we also learn how to love and accept the other less-than-perfect people in our sphere.

Sacred partnership is a union between two imperfect humans moving toward reunion with the ultimate and, yes, perfect All. Part of the trip is learning to gracefully and graciously navigate our own and others' imperfections.

Befriending ourselves and our beloved means accepting who we are in the moment, wheat and chaff alike, and continually forgiving and understanding to the best of our ability. Rooted as we are in the mud of our Mother Earth, we can expect to have a little dirt under our emotional nails, if not always, at least occasionally. Remember, perfection is not a prerequisite for lovability or love-ability.

When we have the courage, insight, and compassion to forgive ourselves and others for all our errors, including the ego's impossible need to be perfect, we will release ourselves from an emotional straitjacket and be free to risk, create, feel deeply, and love unconditionally from the very core of our God-given, and Godlike, heart center.

EXCELLENCE INCORPORATES MISTAKES

Perfection does not tolerate mistakes; excellence, on the other hand, incorporates mistakes and learns from them. We're here to learn. With just a small tilt in attitude, moving from the need to appear perfect to the willingness to see mistakes as opportunities for great growth and learning, we can make our lives so much more serene and fun. Deciding to commit to excellence instead of perfection, we can welcome our mistakes with a lighter attitude and let them shed light on our path and our progress. We can "Lighten up!" as one of the most profound colloquialisms of our day encourages.

GETTING OVER GUILT

One great place to start lightening up is in the guilt department. Like alcohol, a little bit of guilt goes a long way, and it's easy to get addicted to it. Guilt is useful if it points us in the right direction, but not when it bogs down our process. If we use guilt as a bludgeon, it will knock us for a loop. But if we use it as a stop sign or warning sign, it provides useful messages such as, "Wait! Stop here and pause to think. Warning, wrong turn! Time to quietly consider which direction is best, which road is the soul road."

The ideal time to feel a twinge of guilt is in the "yellow light" phase, just seconds before we do or say something for which we'll be sorry. Catching ourselves at the first little tummy-tug of preliminary guilt allows us to choose our actions and reactions rather than respond automatically. Learning to heed yellow light guilt pangs can save us from lengthy and painful guilt trips.

One concrete rule of thumb for sacred partnership is: Never attempt to make another feel guilty. Guilt drives a tremendous wedge between us. The "guilty" wants to be as far from the "guilt-giver" as possible.

DISSOLVING BLAME AND JUDGMENT

Each of us needs to take responsibility for our *own* part in what goes on in our lives and relationships. That means not blaming one another.

Blame destroys safety in a relationship. Because of that it's good to ban it altogether. If we absolutely must scream and yell, blame and judge—which is healthy if done correctly and in small doses—then we need to go for a walk and use the trees and grass as an audience, or beat the couch, or call a totally trustworthy friend and vent to her or him. After dissipating the blaming energy, we can talk to our beloved, from a more open-hearted space, without singeing their eyebrows or closing their hearts in the process.

Blame and judgment often are the result of feeling let down or disappointed. Expectations again. . . . A very important thing to know when desiring to let go of blame and judgment is that the things that irritate us the most about other people are probably examples of a stage of development that we just left behind. Our psyches have a natural aversion to what we are trying to outgrow.

That makes a lot of sense to me. I can picture myself walking away from old patterns of behavior but still tenuously attached by a few slender filaments. Of course I'm going to be wary of similar behavior in others. At some level I'm afraid of being pulled back into my worn-out position. Also, if I've just barely moved beyond some behavior, I've yet to distance from it enough to be compassionate and objective about it. Even glancing back over my shoulder, I can still feel embarrassed or ashamed of it. Later, when my new position is firm and I have forgiven myself for ever acting in the old way, I can tolerate and accept the same behavior in others. Until then, it's wise to realize the origin of my feelings and reassure myself that I can remain on my new path. Eventually I will feel magnanimous toward my old self. Thus reassured, I can dissolve blame and judgment and accept others' behaviors that remind me of my own.

Remembering that we're all going up the same mountain, just using different trails, can help us let go of the desire to blame when faced with faults that irritate us. Psychology professor Deborah Bowman says, "The psyche, much like the earth, is constantly moving, especially along its own fault line." In our progress toward soul growth we all move along our fault lines! They are our growing edges. As we become more comfortable with our soul's progress, we will become less rigid in our definitions of acceptable behavior in our mate. Letting go of the more inflexible "shoulds" and "oughts" will give us permission to stop defending our position, for defensiveness leads to blame and judgment.

FRAGRANCE OF THE VIOLET

In the end it all comes back to forgiveness. Forgiveness originally meant to "return good treatment for ill usage," which reminds me of a beautiful quote, the origin of which I've forgotten: "Forgiveness is the fragrance the violet sheds on the hand that has crushed it."

We are all susceptible to human failings. We've all pointed the finger of blame and have trotted out Ms. or Mr. Perfection to bludgeon ourselves and our loved ones. We will, or have, crushed the delicate violet of another's feelings and have had ours crushed also.

The beauty of such cliches as "To err is human, to forgive, divine" is that, without the immutable truth embedded in their core, they would never have become cliches. We do err. And, because we are so closely connected to them and so vulnerable to their feelings and failures, our intimate partners are often the recipients of our errors and our highest expectations. When we forgive, we invite the divine fragrance of the Beloved to flow through us, bestowing blessings.

Our souls are no strangers to forgiveness, for they have basked in the benediction of God's forgiveness for eternity. Difficulty in forgiving means that we have slipped from the heart of God into our human heads or guts and are no longer centered in the ground of our being, which is unconditional love.

By becoming aware of the skid away from our higher self, we can move back into our hearts. Even though it may sound simplistic, we *can* return to our hearts and revitalize our commitment to become a personification of love by merely asking to do so and accepting that it is done. Remembering to, first, pour the fragrance of God's love and acceptance upon ourselves will set the stage for our ability to forgive the hands that occasionally crush us.

We *are* spiritual beings and, therefore, we are innately love. When we forget, or are enticed into the temporal for a while, God remains, waiting patiently for us to ask how we can best reflect her love in our family and in this adventure of life. When we do remember to climb on God's ever available lap, she will give us a bouquet of violets.

Chapter Eleven

THE VESSEL
OF
COMMUNICATION

Speak and listen from the gentle center of your soul.

Communication is the heart of love, the sacred vessel from which we pour the wine of our souls. When we communicate, we are *communing* with the soul of another. Communing is talking together intimately, sharing our thoughts and feelings, disclosing the very fabric of our being. Artful communication connects us to each other, bonds us together through strands of energy, actions, and words. We need to ask ourselves if these strands are made up of kind and gentle pearls or prickly, thoughtless barbs. Do they bond rather than bind, heal rather than wound, connect rather than divide, and attune rather than alienate?

Mastering the craft of communication is our single most important quest as we engage in the art of marriage. In the following passage, Kahlil Gibran reminds us to keep spirit and soul at the center of our communication: "When you meet your friend on the roadside or in the marketplace, let the spirit in you move your lips and direct your tongue. Let the voice within your voice speak to the ear of his ear; For his soul will keep the truth of your heart as the taste of the wine is remembered when the color is forgotten and the vessel is no more."

CONSCIOUS COMMUNING

We are constantly, intuitively, and innately communicating. But do we *consciously* communicate? To communicate from our hearts and souls, we need to commit ourselves to being aware of how and why, and even when, we communicate. Learning to consciously communicate will help us understand what our intention is during any particular encounter, especially during times of intense emotion and vulnerability. If our intention is to *win,* or to be right, we'd better pause until we can change that to a desire for better understanding and more connection. Needing to win and be right doesn't come from our hearts and souls, and only evokes shame and defensiveness in others. A *no*-win situation.

Consciously communicating means that we want to know if what we're saying enhances feelings of affinity, safety, and sacredness in our relationships. If the answer is consistently a "yes," you are a valuable teacher and model for sacred partnership, and I am thankful for you and all others like you!

Most of us communicate consciously sometimes, but because we and our partners are emotionally fragile, we need to learn to be conscious of the intent of, and attitude in, our communication most, if not all, of the time.

SWEETNESS OF A RESPONSIVE SOUL

Conscious communication comes from the heart of the sacred feminine, the part of us that abounds in responsive, accepting, nurturing, compassionate, and inclusive energy. For our intimate relationships to be laced with deep understanding and grounded in soul-safety, our communication must emanate from the sweet feminine aspects within both men and women.

All that we do and say communicates what we feel and believe. And, interestingly enough, how we communicate deeply influences how we feel. Our state of mind, as well as our immune system, is affected when we are subjected to negative, argumentative communication. Psychiatry professor Janice Klecolt-Glaser and her husband, immunologist Ronald Glaser at the Ohio State University Medical Center, monitored the hearts and blood pressure of ninety happy, newly married couples for twenty-four hours. The couples were interviewed about areas of conflict and asked to spend thirty minutes together trying to solve them. The results showed that, although both sexes had elevated blood pressure and weakened immune responses when negative communication, such as sarcasm, excuses, put downs, and interruptions, was experienced, the women showed greater immunological changes. Preliminary research on ten couples married more than forty-two years shows similar results.

In order to have optimum mental and physical health, it appears that our communication needs to be good, kind, and gentle, emanating from the sweetness of a responsive soul. When our commitment is to communicate from the center of our hearts, we can become an agent for healing and, in the process, deepen our union with our beloved.

THE MIRACLE OF LISTENING

To the Sacred Feminine voice, listening is a sacred art. Deep listening is miraculous for both listener and speaker. When someone receives us with open-hearted, non-judging, intensely interested listening, our spirits expand. New thoughts, unexpected wisdom, and witticisms begin to bubble from the "little creative fountain," within us, as writer Brenda Ueland calls it. Deep listening inspires us to unveil the miracle of our Self, to live from the center of our authentic creativity rather than circle the periphery. Deep listening is a gift and a blessing. The company who named their hearing aid "The Miracle Ear" knew what they were talking about!

As a plant shrivels without sun and water, we are dying in spirit for lack of deep listening. So many of us only listen long enough to form our counter-argument. We feel compelled to get our "two cents worth" into the conversation. In our need to be *heard*, we fail to hear the heart of those we love. We talk *at* each other rather than *to* and *with* each other. The result of not hearing one another in a meaningful way is a profound and poignant loneliness.

OPEN HEART, ACCEPTING EARS

One of the best ways to help ourselves become artful listeners is to give up any *expectations* about what is required of us as we listen. We are all programmed to be "fixers." Intent on our task of fixing, we're too busy rummaging in our minds for solutions to be able to hear the soul in what another person is saying.

We don't need to fix someone through our listening, we simply need to open our hearts and *be* there with accepting ears. *Nothing* else is required.

Although listening with accepting ears seems too simple to be effective, it is powerful medicine. The energy emanating from a listening heart is wonderfully healing and empowering to both speaker and listener. So, while listening may appear to be doing very little, it is, in fact, one of the most powerfully healing things we can do.

John Gray, author of *Men Are from Mars, Women Are from Venus,* tells husbands, "Listening to her helps a woman remember what a great guy you are." Expanding that, I would say that, "Listening to each other with open hearts and accepting ears allows us to remember what great people we are and what a great team we make."

LEVELS OF LISTENING

In deep, heart centered listening, we're being gifted by a person's willingness to show us several levels of him or herself. These levels are:

- ♥ *Words:* What is actually said?
- ♥ *Feeling/emotion:* What feelings or emotions is he or she attempting to express?
- ♥ *Soul/spiritual:* What is the essence and higher meaning of this communication?

Often the feeling and soul levels are not consciously known to either the speaker or the listener. Being open to all levels of a person through openhearted listening, we create a climate in which he or she can become more aware of himself or herself and, therefore, access more of his or her unique excellence.

A wonderful way to become better at listening to all levels is to simply and sincerely say, "Tell me more." Most of us, when encouraged to tell more, will be thrilled to do so. Our souls are thirsty for the balm of a listening heart in whose presence we can flower.

WHO'S LISTENING?

If we find we're not able to open our ears to be fully present when trying to listen to another, we might ask, "Who's trying to listen? Who in my inner cast is having a difficult time really *being* here?" The answer may surprise us, and is sure to be illuminating.

When I caught myself one day not being able to listen to a young woman in crisis, it was my inner Rescuer who was terrified that this darling young person would kill herself. Fear took over and it rendered me deaf for several minutes. I got caught in my own expectation that I *should* be able to *fix* her pain.

During emotionally charged exchanges, we may find a frightened inner child when we ask "Who's listening?" It's okay to tell our partner that we can't listen right now because one of our sub-personalities is having an anxiety attack and needs to be comforted. We can take a break. Or we can share who's trying to listen and ask for what they need. Whatever feels the most open-hearted is the thing to do when we discover a sub-personality who is having a hard time being a good listener.

For Julia, a fifty-two-year-old divorcee who is just starting a new relationship, quietly continuing to listen was the most gentle way to care for herself in a recent encounter. While listening to her friend talk about his business ventures, she began to be extremely uncomfortable. In answer to the question, "Who's listening?" she realized she had begun to feel old feelings of inadequacy that had plagued her ten years ago during her divorce. Her fear was whispering, "You don't know how to talk to a man. He will think you're dull. You don't understand this business stuff, and you'll bore him." Because the relationship is so new, it was wise for Julia to comfort her sub-personality herself and then call a woman friend for backup reassurance and a listening ear.

Another internal character whom I encounter frequently—especially if I'm on a deadline—is my Compulsive Impatient Person (CIP). She can't listen worth a toot because she has Very Important Business to attend to. So, when I realize that I'm listening from the very-harried personage of CIP, I either need to honor her feeling of time pressure and make a date to listen at a different time or *decide* to listen now and *choose* to do so. Not always an easy choice.

WHO'S TALKING?

An equally important question is "Who's talking?" If your beloved is upset or confused and, consequently, so are you, it's a good idea to calmly—either silently or aloud—ask, "Who in you is talking right now?" It's always better to have agreed to use that technique with each other *before* you spring it on someone who is upset in the moment. If our partner isn't interested in, or able to, ferret out inner voices, intuitively, we may need to make an educated guess about who inside is speaking. With that awareness, we can listen from a more open heart.

When Gene spoke to me abruptly one day, telling me that I hadn't let him know what I wanted during a conversation, and that had made him feel uncomfortable and responsible, I could pretty well guess that he was speaking with the voice of the young boy who overheard his father tell a friend that Gene would never be as good as his older brothers. Knowing that, I didn't need to feel so attacked, but could respond to that young boy within Gene with reassurance and appreciation, and a difficult place was smoothed. If I didn't know about Gene's background and vulnerability, I might get pretty huffy when confronted by curt comments.

By the way, I want to acknowledge right here and now how much I appreciate Gene's willingness to let me use us as examples. That's courageous, and I thank him!

Sometimes just realizing what voice we're speaking from helps illuminate patches of darkness within us and gives us a handle on what we need to do or say to move into the light.

PAUSE AND PONDER

To become adept at the art of conscious communication, we must not only learn how to listen, but in the words of Don Quixote, to "Think before thou speakest." We need to adopt the maturity and wisdom to *PAUSE* and *PONDER*. Doing so gives us the time and emotional space to be able to move to our hearts in order to discern what is the most loving and compassionate thing to say. If we pause consistently, we will never again say that which we wish we could retrieve. If we simply can't pause and ponder, we can—and should— remove ourselves from the situation for a while, to take time to cool off.

BEING RIGHT OR BEING HAPPY?

The Course in Miracles has two little sayings that have been absolutely essential in my own cultivation of conscious communication. The first is, "Would I rather be right or would I rather be happy?" When first confronted by this statement I thought that I would be happy if I could just be seen as right. And sometimes I was. But, if being right meant that someone else needed to be wrong, I wasn't happy at all, and neither were they. I'm learning to determine what is important and how to agree to disagree without feeling that either of us is wrong or bad. More often than not, when asking myself to choose between being right and being happy, I'll take happy.

The second important statement is a little tougher to really act from: "In my defenselessness, my safety lies." What!? All sorts of inner objections arose with that one: I've felt defenseless and am not about to do *that* again. . . . What a wimpy thing to do. . . . I'm just now feeling strong, and *now* this dumb course asks me to be weak!?

After first being totally defensive about defenselessness, I pondered just what it might mean and began to see it in a different light. Flexible, flowing, responsive, receptive, willowlike, thoughtful, open-minded, and slow to anger were qualities that came to the surface. Inspired by these feminine images of defenselessness, I decided to try it. Unfortunately, I chose a very difficult person to try it on first, and my attempt was a miserable flop. In fact, after a few minutes of patiently and oh-so-defenselessly explaining to the manager of the office I was renting—for the umpteenth time—how important it was for a therapist's office to be soundproof, I lost my temper and actually swore at him. So much for that test.

I'm happy to say that subsequent forays into the land of safe defenselessness have been overwhelmingly positive and rewarding. When I can remain absolutely safe within myself, bend like the willow and be quietly receptive to, but unharmed by, harsh winds coming toward me, it's amazing how agitation diminishes. What I've discovered is that being defended accelerates attack, whereas moving aside and remaining open-minded and flexible invites eventual understanding and augments my ability to find common ground.

Another thing that helps when caught up in the battle to be right is to remember that while we *assume* a lot and *believe* even more, we *know* very little. Incarnation pulls the veil between us and Spirit, and so we "see through a glass darkly." The intricacy of the soul is infinitely complex. We can drive ourselves crazy if we have an insatiable need for *the* answer, and drive others batty when we believe we have found *the* answer. What resonates with our hearts, in any given moment—that is our answer *now*. It may also be *an* answer for others, but none of us has *the* answer.

DO NO HARM

Following directly on the heels of saying that no one has *the* answer, I'll leap right on one of the few soap boxes where I resolutely and stubbornly stand, unwilling to budge one tiny little iota. I believe that there is never an excuse to *consciously* say or do anything harmful to another living soul! Now, that doesn't mean that others won't sometimes be hurt by what we say or do because they will interpret our statements through the lens of their own vulnerabilities. We can't control others' responses. But, as persons old enough—and hopefully wise enough—to have agreed to the responsibilities and blessings of marriage, we *can* consciously do no harm.

The words we speak are indelible, tattoos on the psyche and spirit. Permanent, forever, non-erasable. Oh, sure, we may forgive and forget actual words, but the energy lingers on. A popular quote from *The Little Prince* reads, "Where you tend a rose, my lad, a thistle cannot grow." Also true is this statement, "Where a thistle pricks, my lad, a scar may also grow." We do not want to scar anyone with whom we communicate, not even ourselves. In order not to tattoo ourselves and our beloved with verbal scars, our vessel of communication needs to be a constructive container.

As you can imagine, I don't buy excuses such as, "I was so angry I couldn't stop myself!" or "I didn't know what I was saying!" and "I didn't mean it, I was just upset!" Tattoo, tattoo, tattoo. Permanent, forever, non-erasable energetic scars. Communication laced with such excuses is not conducive to sacred partnership.

Of course, we're not going to communicate perfectly and lovingly all the time, but we can *stop* speaking and acting in hurtful ways *right now*. It's a matter of deciding to stop, committing to do so, and then doing it.

It isn't my cup of tea, but some couples actually enjoy arguing, "Tossing minor metaphorical rocks," as one man put it. If you are one of those couples who find it stimulating to argue, that's great, as long as the "rocks" are made of foam and neither of you emerges from verbal skirmishes feeling bruised in any way. We're all different, and each marriage will be unique and tailor-made for the individual couple. However, in an arguing partnership, it's very important that *both* of you like it *and* want it to continue.

THE NO-NOS

Sometimes it helps to be reminded of the things we should not do. What is NOT gentle in communication is:

- ♥ teasing
- ♥ put downs
- ♥ "shoulding"

- ♥ projection
- ♥ verbal or physical abuse
- ♥ not listening

- ♥ judging
- ♥ righteousness
- ♥ ignoring
- ♥ preaching or lecturing
- ♥ holding a grudge
- ♥ defensiveness

TIMING

Timing is an essential ingredient in constructive communication. Before we embark on an important conversation about emotional issues, it's good to set a specific time. The person most invested in talking asks for uninterrupted time for sharing within the next twenty-four hours (each couple can set the time they're comfortable with). For instance, I might say to Gene, "Honey, I need to talk (four words that originally struck terror in his heart) to you sometime within the next twenty-four hours. It's about something you said earlier that upset me. On a scale from 1 to 10, it's a 7 for me." A request framed in this way doesn't ambush him or demand his immediate attention. He can now choose a time that's acceptable to him. He can prepare emotionally and doesn't feel bushwhacked.

When we first started making appointments for a talk many moons ago, I had to remind Gene at twenty-three hours and fifty-seven minutes that we still needed to have that talk. But, over the years, a sense of safety has been established between us. Now, he may very well answer such a request with, "Let me have twenty minutes to finish this and then I'm available" or, rarely, he may be the one to ask for a talking time.

COMMON GROUND AND MATCHING ENERGY

Especially during confrontation it is important to come from our authentic Self, to remember our higher purpose and act in a way that lines up with our soul's ideal. Any type of encounter or communication is going to go more smoothly and lovingly if we establish common ground and matching energy before we begin. Inherent to the process is that we talk about our *own* feelings and invite the other person to also stay with his or her feelings. This minimizes defensiveness and helps foster understanding of each other. A process I have found helpful in creating common ground has the following seven steps:

1. *Tell your partner two things that you love and respect about him or her.*

2. *Hold hands, make eye contact, and center yourselves in your hearts in whatever way works for you. (Breathing in unison is good, consciously sending a love flow between your hearts works, praying for the perfect, right understanding to come from your talk is excellent.)*

3. *Clearly state your own feelings (having, hopefully, blown off your searing steam elsewhere).*

4. *Have the person with the issue state what he or she wants—and needs—from the other. "I want you to just listen," or "I hope we can come to a compromise that works for us both," or "I need you to hold me," or "I don't know what I want right now, so please just let me talk."*

5. *Both of you share your purpose for the interchange.*

6. *The listener drops any defensiveness and becomes as clear a receptacle as possible, and honestly assesses whether he can authentically do what is requested of him.*

7. *Realize that communication filled with heart and feeling is usually not speedy communication. Unlike goal-oriented talk, it has many pauses and "feeling breaks."*

"I" MESSAGES ENNOBLE; "YOU" MESSAGES DEMEAN

Ennobling the spirit of our beloved is one of the essential arts of marriage. We want to underscore the nobility of his or her spirit and, therefore, enhance it. Ennobling others doesn't mean that we idealize, deny, or overlook that which is less than noble. It does mean, however, that we consciously hold on to the awareness that his or her spirit is noble, irrespective of less-than-wonderful human behaviors.

Telling our truth without blame or judgment ennobles us by making us visible and honest, not vindictive or submerged in denial. Honest clarity expressed lovingly ennobles our beloved by putting the ball in his court and trusting he'll know what to do with it. Presented with a non-judgmental "I" message, we can choose how to handle situations in ways that best promote soul growth and intimacy. We ennoble another's spirit by giving them the chance to do, redo, make restitution, etc., in ways that are right for them.

The formula for an "I" message is: "When you do/say_____, I feel _____." The idea is to express *real feelings,* not judgments or accusations. Use one or two words at most to describe a real feeling. Examples of feelings: hurt, confused, tired, loved, joyful, grateful, abandoned, sexually excited, withdrawn, discouraged, encouraged. Feelings describe what's happening to *you,* rather than expressing a judgment about whatever the other person is doing. Here are two examples of clear "I" messages: "When you walk away while I'm talking, I feel rejected and angry," and "When you talk openly about your feelings, I feel sexually attracted to you." As you can see by the examples, "I" messages are not limited to expressing difficult emotions.

By contrast, "You" messages point fingers, make judgments, criticize personally, interpret, and demean. The above "I" messages could have been sent as "You" messages: "When you walk away while I'm talking, you're sure not exhibiting much soul growth!" or "You make me angry when you walk away. You hurt me!" The silent tag line at the end of a negative "You" message is, You bastard, you! If we say, "When you talk openly about your feelings, you make me horny," it may end with a much sweeter epitaph, but nonetheless assumes that the other person is responsible for *our* feelings. They're not. Only *we* are responsible for how we feel. It is our responsibility to tell our beloved, honestly and without judgment, how we feel, because unexpressed feelings color our attitude toward them. But they don't *make* us feel certain ways, we do.

"I" messages *inform* and *ennoble.* "You" messages *attack* and *demean.*

HONORING SATURATION POINTS

In general, men and women have different saturation points during emotionally charged communication. The more solution-oriented male often has little patience for the process of talking things through and wants to get to the "bottom line" and solve the problem. Gene used to tell me that I "beat a dead horse" by reiterating points. I, of course, thought I wouldn't have to beat the horse if he hadn't fallen over deaf and dead after the first few sentences. We were at an impasse. Both of us were *right*. Wrong! We needed to get some distance from that belief, move to our hearts, and see how we could both get what we wanted and needed.

To be very honest, it was I who did the adjusting, because Gene was the one who was most uncomfortable with in-depth communication. I know that we women often get upset by the reality that we are the ones in the relationship who make allowances. As I've said, because of our wise feminine energy, we are generally the person best equipped to mentor our beloved into intimacy and communication from the heart. It's our comfort zone, not theirs. Women can resist and resent that truth, but it's simpler and more loving to all concerned to gently encourage and teach about the safety and rewards of intimacy through *being* a gentle and encouraging teacher. If we push and judge, neither of us will get the sacred partnership for which he or she hungers.

After I moved through my rebellion about Gene's inability to talk intimately for long stretches at a time, I could more openly ask him to help me understand his point of view. As we talked, he explained that he literally felt nauseated after about ten minutes and then stopped being present except in body. Recent research has discovered that Gene is not unique in this response. Scientists have discovered that men respond to confrontation with far more physical discomfort than do women. Because of that, they withdraw or run away. Who can blame them?

Gene and I made an agreement. He would tell me when he was five minutes from his saturation point and I would wrap up what I was saying. And, it *was* usually I who was talking. I've since learned that's not unusual.

Gary Smalley says that women speak an average of 25,000 words per day and men speak less than half that many. My part of the bargain was that I *would* stop talking within the five minutes, and then we would agree on a time during the next twenty-four hours when we could resume.

Stopping and then regrouping was frustrating at first and I had to increase my tolerance for feeling separated from him during the time when issues were unresolved. But, learning to honor his saturation point and my need for eventual understanding and completion were probably two of the most important things that we ever did to eventually facilitate intimate communication.

WITHDRAWAL, A NEW IDEA

Realizing that I sometimes used anger and irritability to push Gene away and create the solitude that I either felt ashamed of needing or didn't realize that I needed, I reexamined the phenomenon of withdrawal. Withdrawal has traditionally been a man's prerogative and women, driven nuts by it, have seen men's withdrawal as avoidance of their emotions or as a lack of love and commitment.

I began to wonder if withdrawal wasn't sometimes an indication that we needed solitude, rather than a sign that our marriage was shaky. Maybe part of women's adverse reaction to withdrawal pivots on the fact that we don't allow ourselves the luxury of ebbing into it ourselves. We must always be in the flow of love and be flowing toward those whom we love. Because of our "discomfort with disconnect," I think women have overlooked the advantages of withdrawal.

To be sure, it's constructive to move away from our partner when exploring and clarifying intense feelings within ourselves (unless our mate can willingly and comfortably be a sounding board). But what about withdrawal to nurture the soul? Support of our soul and spirit, filling our inner well, is very rarely addressed, let alone honored, in Western society.

Maybe we can free withdrawal from the bad rap it has as being either neurosis, lack of caring, or irresponsibility if we look at it as a *symbol* for the need to formally and honestly retreat to care for our spirit. Refilling our inner well-spring can happen so much more easily if we are alone with the Source. Re-framed as a nudge from the soul rather than a tightly defended position, we can welcome withdrawal as positive and hopefully not have to pick fights to get time alone.

SHARING, NOT SOLVING

Another common area of gender conflict in communication revolves around sharing a problem versus solving it. I need to share my process when I'm working something through because then I feel connected to Gene. But he's sometimes uncomfortable sharing my process because he doesn't know what to *do,* what is *expected* of him. Without having a clear idea of what I need while talking, he automatically jumps into "solve the problem" mode and quickly lists several things I *should* do to work out the perceived problem. Usually that's not what I want, but if I don't tell Gene what I *do* want, then he will do what comes naturally to him.

We need to be specific about our needs when we're sharing with our beloved. Not knowing how to respond can create feelings of helplessness and impotence, which propel us into "shoulding, fixing, advising, and judging." None of those bring us closer together unless they are the specifics requested. So it helps, if you want to just share something, to start out saying something like, "I'm not asking you to solve this, I just want to tell you about it."

CLARITY FORESTALLS ASSUMING AND INTERPRETING

In order to create a constructive container for communication, we need to be clear about what we feel and what we want and need. Clarity of feeling helps us avert the communication gremlins of assuming and interpreting. Because we yearn to know and understand our mate, we will "fill in the blanks" with our own assumptions when faced with confusing messages, body language, and conversation. Lots of misunderstandings result when we assume we know why another person is acting or speaking a certain way and then interpret why he or she is doing it. No matter how much we feel to the contrary, partnership is *not* an exercise in telepathy; the statement, "If he loved me, he would. . ." is unfair and serves only to leave us disconnected.

Here's an example of how to be clear. It drives me crazy to lose things. So if I'm frustrated by not being able to find something, I may say to Gene, "I've lost my glasses and I'm feeling crazed about it. Would you please help me look?" or I might say, "I've lost my glasses again and I'm feeling old, ugly, and senile. I need you to hug me and tell me I'm gorgeous and brilliant." Unless he's in a super horrible place himself, he's happy to do as I ask. He loves knowing how he can love and support me "right"! We all do.

ARGUMENT AND AIKIDO

Living with another person almost guarantees that there will be at least a few flurries of arguments although, hopefully, no full fledged storms of devastating fights. That's why the ability to resolve conflicts in a win-win way ranks second only to being nice to our partner as a predictor of satisfaction in marriage.

Unfortunately, we have very little training in conflict resolution. Especially when communication is chock full of emotion and reeks of confrontation, it's easy for us to fall back into destructive and defensive patterns. Most of us, when challenged by other people, fight back, flee, or freeze, depending on our conditioning and our fears. But another, more constructive communication option is becoming increasingly available in our Western culture, an approach that's embodied in the Japanese martial art called *aikido,* a word that literally translates as "the way of harmony of energy."

Aikido differs from other martial arts in that it stresses the feminine values of meeting attacks and challenges with cooperation rather than competition. Aikido is described by some practitioners as the essence of love and the art of reconciliation. Rather than becoming defensive or warding off attacks, aikido practitioners try to see what's coming at them as an energy to be danced with.

They learn to gracefully blend with an attacker's energy and redirect it, neutralizing it in the process—and to do so without harming the attacker. In aikido, if you fight, you've broken your connection with the universe. It's the classic difference between the flexible willow tree, dancing with strong winds, and the oak resisting them.

How wonderful if we could learn to retain the connection between ourselves and our mate during conflict and neutralize negative energy by dancing with it!

THE MYTHS OF CONFLICT

Before we can adopt an aikido attitude, we need to let go of two prevalent myths about conflict.

Myth #1: Conflict is a contest that must be won, and the person with whom we're in conflict is an opponent to subdue and/or persuade. Actually, conflict provides us with great opportunities for growth and our "opponents" are usually friends, family members, and co-workers with whom we want to live in harmony. Using aikido strategies, we can learn to harmonize our energies and cooperate and complement each other.

Myth #2: Conflict is negative. "If we love each other, there will be no conflict" is a myth that keeps us resistant to working *through* conflict. *Because* our lives and emotions are deeply entwined, there is bound to be some conflict. When handled well, conflict is an excellent way to stir up static energy and allow much-needed change to happen. Acknowledging, accepting, and embracing conflict, we can use it as the oyster uses a grain of sand. Take an irritant, dance with it, cooperate with it until a beautiful pearl of growth and change is created.

TURNING CONFLICT INTO COOPERATION

Okay, sounds great. But how? According to aikido experts here's how we can use the principles of aikido to turn conflict into cooperation:

1. CENTER

Remembering that energy flows where attention goes, when faced with conflict, get your attention off the other person and back on yourself, if only for a few seconds. Doing so will help you move from "being beside yourself" with anger, or a kindred emotion, to being "inside" yourself, and therefore, in a position of strength. Take a few deep breaths. Bring your awareness into your body. Feel yourself sitting in the chair. Become aware of your feet on the floor. Consciously relax any areas of tension. Put one hand over your heart and lightly rest the other just below your navel and breathe deeply into both places.

Aikido views the center of our body, the belly, as our power source. By breathing into our belly we come to a "centered" state, and are more readily in touch with our inner strength and better able to choose well. Breathing into our hearts reminds us to allow divine compassion to flow through us.

2. ENTER

Once we are centered and feeling our strength we need to practice moving *toward* the conflict with openhearted interest rather than running in fear. It's very difficult to do this until we adopt the aikido attitude that conflict can be constructive and positive, an impetus for better understanding and closer connection with our beloved. Instead of resisting the conflict by becoming defensive and fearful, we can move *with* the energy of our loved one. *Engaging* with him or her, rather than battling or retreating.

Entering a conflict might sound something like this: "We've disagreed about this before, and I really want to work it out so that we don't have to fight about this. Can you tell me more about how you feel about this problem?" We clearly state what we want and then ask for more clarification from our beloved. We neither capitulate nor challenge. Rather, we move with the energy, hopefully, toward better and deeper understanding.

3. BLEND

In aikido training, students are taught to blend with an attacker's energy by shifting positions so that they are facing the same direction as he is. Failing to meet rigid, face-to-face resistance, an assailant is thrown off balance and even a tiny woman can guide him in a new direction—such as toward the ground. The concept of blending helps us understand Sufi Pir Vilayat Inayat Khan's statement, *"Turn the other cheek* is absolutely irrational, but makes the ultimate sense."

In a verbal dispute, how do we put those principles to work for us? We try to embrace the view of the attacker. What is his point of view? How does he see the situation? Sincerely explore his perspective with the intent to better understand where he is coming from. Blending with another in this way—really and truly listening and understanding—may just melt any aggression and make it easier for our loved one to, in turn, appreciate our point of view. Encouraged to *tell us more* rather than fend off counterattacks, our beloved will be better able to let down his guard and we can, therefore, get to the *heart* of the matter.

4. ATTACK CLEANLY

Aikido instructors often have a hard time getting women to play the role of the attacker. Women have been trained to be "nice girls," and to hint and manipulate rather than directly state what they want and need. In communication, attacking cleanly simply means that we honestly, passionately, and openly state our needs and our feelings without subterfuge or blame. "I" messages, used correctly, are perfect examples of a clean attack.

Once when my mother criticized me for allowing my son to go to bed without a bath, I bit back my desire to defend myself and protect my son. Breathing deeply and centering, I moved over to her side and said, "It's hard for me to say this to you because I value your opinion so much, and it scares me to confront you. But it hurts when you seem critical of my parenting." Mom replied, "Well, he *shouldn't* go to bed dirty." Another deep breath and a reminder to myself that "I" messages sometimes are not heard the first time, I replied, "Mom, I'm feeling like I'm a bad girl. I feel hurt when you criticize my decision about the bath." I could literally feel her relax, and she assured me that she thought I was a good parent, but *she* could never have let me go to bed dirty. I said that I understood, and that we were different in that respect. The confrontation passed. No hard feelings and no lingering resentment from not sharing my feelings.

5. LEARN TO FALL

This is *so* important! In aikido, falling is an art. Students are taught to relax into a fall so that they don't get hurt and can use the energy of it to roll up again. Resisting a fall wastes energy and makes it more painful when we hit the floor. Ah! If we could all learn that wisdom. We'll all fall. We won't communicate perfectly all of the time. Even though we yearn to share the most precious wine from our souls while communing with our beloved, we *will* falter and fall. When we can really accept the okayness of falling—perceived as failure by so many of us—we will also be better able to apologize when appropriate and love more freely and joyfully without worrying if we're "doing it right enough."

Following the five principles of aikido in our communication will likely lead to better understanding and an openhearted acceptance of the ebb and flow of energy between us. Conflict can become cooperative, productive, and evolutionary. Thomas Crum, aikido instructor and author of *The Magic of Conflict*, says, "Conflict is nature's primary motivator for change. It's the catalyst that forces a system to evolve."

CONFLICT'S NEVER COMFY

Learning to resolve conflict in a cooperative way leads us into more complementary lives. As our son Brett says, "It's almost always better to put on the kid gloves rather than the boxing gloves." Entering conflict gently, intending that it will be constructive, allows us to drop our defenses and be open to both ourselves and our beloved. Centered in our own secure flexibility, we can say, "What do *I* need to learn from this? What can I learn about myself and my beloved?" rather than "What do I need to do or say to be right and get my way?"

Choosing to resolve conflict in a container of caring means that we will train ourselves to align our behaviors with our intention and desire for sacred partnership, and not with the feelings of the moment. Anaïs Nin warns, "Beware of allowing a tactless word, a rebuttai, a rejection to obliterate the whole sky." Aligned in intention we can avoid obliterating the whole sky by blowing our conflicts out of proportion.

By identifying each person's needs, desires, and concerns, we can find a win-win, gentle way to work things through. After each person has been able to express his or her basic needs in a conflict, we are free to brainstorm for complementary solutions. The goal is not the solution, itself. It is the connection and understanding that arises between us from having listened and heard each other that is important.

Also important to remember is that love means having the guts to say you're sorry!

BEFRIENDING ANGER

Many of us were taught that expressing anger of any kind was unacceptable. The trouble with non-expression is that our passivity is likely to turn into "pissivity" and we become resentful and grumpy. The Buddha said, "The grudge you hold on to is like a hot coal that you intend to throw at somebody else, but you're the one who gets burned." Resisting authentic anger magnifies it into resentment and feelings of victimization, both of which can burn you *and* your partner.

One of the best things we can do to ensure that mismanaged anger doesn't drive a wedge between us and our beloved is to learn to befriend our own anger. Especially for women, anger is verboten. We can neither have it nor express it without being labeled a bitch by society, and, more importantly, by ourselves. But we do have anger. No matter how successfully we repress it, anger lurks in the darkened caverns of our minds and hearts, and waits for a chance to break free and be seen and heard. Like an earthquake fault, suppressed anger waits until the pressure is too great to resist and then explodes, shaking the very foundations of our lives, sometimes with disastrous results.

Expressed cleanly and clearly, anger is a friend. Anger can be a flare of intuitive wisdom saying, "Anger Alert! What is going awry here?" Anger is a warning bell, the first step in a journey of increased self discovery. Anger is a many-layered thing; when activated, there is usually sadness, grief, frustration, need, yearning, or fear beneath the surface.

Clean anger is examined anger. It comes from our ability to allow our own anger without shame and judgment—not *acting out* anger, but exploring and understanding its origins, genesis, the whys—and then expressing it clearly. Using the aikido techniques to share clean anger bridges the space between us, bonds us more closely, and assists our marriage to evolve into increased intimacy and understanding.

WHO IS FEELING WHAT?

Emotions are momentary. Accepted and explored, their energy will flow *through* us and pass. Stopped by shame or fear or repression or judgment, emotions congeal into frozen energy, obstructing health and well-being. These frozen emotions are carried by our various sub-personalities.

In the midst of conflict, it's especially important to know *who* is reacting, talking, fighting, frightened, cowering, defensive, withdrawing, sniveling. Who's in charge? By discovering which sub-personality is in charge, we can go with its energy instead of fighting a murky current, which is counterproductive.

When faced by emotions that are difficult to understand, it's often helpful to ask, "Who is feeling what?" Become quiet and go inside, asking for help from your wise intuition or inner oracle. What character in your inner cast is filled with these troublesome feelings? Can you understand why that aspect of yourself is upset, threatened, or fearful? What quality does this part of you carry that you can now call on for help?

Becoming acquainted with who is carrying the bulk of the feeling, you can find out what they want and need from you and then increase their safety and well-being by giving it to them. Befriending our anger and fear requires that we befriend, accept, and love the parts of us who carry it.

Being able to tell our beloved who in us is experiencing the feelings gives him or her the chance to know us more deeply and be with us in the ways that we most cherish. Knowing who in our inner cast of characters is in the lead helps both ourselves and our mates engage in the appropriate dance of intimacy for the situation.

INTIMACY AND AIKIDO

Bringing the essence of aikido—love and the harmonization of energy—into the art of our communication will help us flow through difficult times with our beloved. Even if we learn to accept conflict, assume responsibility for understanding our own emotions, blend energies, cleanly state our feelings after pausing, pondering, and clarifying them, we'll still be thrown to the mat on occasion. Having been thrown, it's okay to relax into the realization that this is one of those times, as my dear friend Bonnie puts it, "that you just breathe in and out and watch the sun come up and go down and know that this will pass."

VESSEL OF COMMUNICATION

How we communicate is, in essence, how we love. When our vessel of communication brims with the nectar of openness, honesty, deep acceptance, and gentle understanding, it emanates from our heart and provides enduring sustenance. Sacred partnership, anchored in the bedrock of caring, intimate communication, is a sweet soul-filled mystery of love—both a blessing and a gift.

Part Four

The Gifts

of

Marriage

What gifts does sacred partnership bestow
upon individuals and the greater whole?

$\mathcal{S}$acred partnership feeds our deep hunger to recognize and revitalize our soul-self, whose essence is love. Because it is conceived and born in a matrix of love and soul-growth, sacred partnership bestows upon us *many* gifts of the spirit.

All realms of our lives are touched by the gifts of love. Love is source; from it flows openhearted trust, service, honor, awe, humor, compassion, commitment, and pristine joy. This sounds esoteric and highfalutin', but it's simply a matter of energy. We all know how energized we feel when love is flowing freely in our lives and, in contrast, how stymied we feel when love is blocked or frozen. Why? Because, when love is freely flowing, we are in tune with the energy of our soul-self. When love is blocked we are cut off from it.

The ultimate gift of sacred partnership is energy—an exorbitant, lavish, luxurious profusion of energy. That energy becomes a creative fountain, a font of well-being from which we can not only revitalize ourselves and others, but tackle projects that serve the greater whole.

When I'm "in the love-flow" with God, myself, Gene, the kids, and other important persons in my life, I feel energized and have incredible stamina. But if my love-flow is sidetracked or stymied, I feel droopy, cut off, and out of steam. Our commitment to living from the heart and creating sacred partnership infuses us with the energy of love, and there is no greater or more efficient fuel. Being sparked by love—self-love and love of others—ignites us into heartfelt service to those who need our care and attention.

In his book, *First Things First,* Stephen R. Covey states that, "The main thing is to keep the main thing the main thing." The main thing for those of us who yearn for sacred partnership is our commitment to creating a secure foundation of love within the microcosm of our selves and our families, a foundation upon which the world can rest and be revived. As men and women *co*-create sacred partnership, with an emphasis on soul-growth for each partner, we will *re*-create our world in a way that reflects the love, honor, esteem, and respect we hold for one another.

Chapter Twelve

TEMPLE OF LOVE

*Nowhere is the sweet balm of Sacred Feminine Energy
more needed than in the bedroom.*

$\mathcal{S}$ex. . . Nothing in our culture has been more maligned, misunderstood, or misused than sex. We in the West have eliminated the feminine face of God as an aspect of the Divine worthy of our devotion, and thus negate Feminine Energy, the receptive, soft, flowing aspect of the Divine. Is it any wonder, then, that we have difficulty surrendering in sacred joy and abandon to our beloved during sex?

Many Eastern cultures have held the belief that sexuality mirrors the creative life force of the universe. In those cultures, women are honored as embodiments of divine feminine energy. Sex is seen as a way for men to merge with that energy, and the genitals of both men and women are seen as sacred symbols of the God and Goddess, respectively.

We in the West have moved away from that awareness. Most of the sex education that we received as kids was minimal and biologically oriented at best, or abusive and shame-provoking at worst.

I think my exposure was fairly typical. The extent of my early sexual training was a trip to the YWCA with my mother to pick up some little brochures about menstruation and how babies were made. There was very little talk about the mechanics of "the curse," as many people referred to menstruation at the time, and none at all about the emotional and spiritual facets of sexuality. It wasn't our parents' fault; they undoubtedly were hamstrung by embarrassment, having received even less instruction as they were growing up than we did.

I really don't know where I gleaned the idea that sex was "a necessary evil." Maybe it was church, maybe it was just the Midwestern atmosphere, I don't know. But I do know that I felt absolutely comfortable writing love poetry to God as a kid, but paradoxically felt deep shame at both my sexual curiosity and my physical explorations. I remember devoutly hoping that God was too busy to notice my "sin." Of course, I didn't automatically just drop that shame and inhibition at the altar when I said "I do" the first time.

Gene fared better. Although he says that you "could round up to zero" the amount of instruction he was given about sex, he was unscathed by shame as a kid and remained very interested, although totally ignorant about what all the fuss was about.

Like Gene and I, most of us need to heal the wounds inflicted on our sexuality through ignorance or malice in order to have a sex life as beautiful and bonding as it can be. We also need to *re*educate ourselves and *re*form our attitudes about sexuality. We need to undo the damage author Andrew Harvey underscores when he says, "Our refusal of the divine life force has shown itself most disastrously in the religious hatred of sexuality."

An extremely important aspect of heart centered marriage is to bring the love energy—the sacred heart exchange—back to the act of making love. Part of our healing will be learning to love our bodies as temples housing the Divine, and realizing that sex is God-inspired, and therefore sacred. Perhaps when we can approach sexuality as the temple of love, our shame and shyness will be washed clean in the fountain of the Mystery.

Although we may all have mislearned the function and philosophy of sex, I believe that at the deep core of our soul-selves, we have never lost our knowingness about the sacredness of sexuality. Out of that buried awareness springs our longing for the ecstatic sexual communion possible within sacred partnership.

SEXUAL ENERGY IS DIVINE ENERGY

Anyone who has shared a tender sexual encounter has known something of that divine love energy and, basking in it, has made a sweet ascent to the temple of love. Those experiences make such an impression on us that their fragrance lingers in our memory for years, maybe a lifetime. Why? Because our hearts are opened, our souls are touched, and we experience true *union*. At a deep level, we intuit that this union with our beloved hints of what we can hope for from reunion with *The* Beloved, and we are infused with grace. No wonder this sacred and soulful intercourse is memorable, for our souls yearn for such graceful remembering and reconnection.

In reality, like a fish in water, we are constantly swimming in the love-energy of God/dess. The Divine is in the very air we breathe. She is everywhere, always, and in all ways. As we reclaim the Sacred Feminine voice within us and return to our hearts, we will once more know that sexuality is a noble, healing, and wondrous celebration of the creative Life Force. Sex is one of the original gifts from the Source.

Unfortunately, because it's an area of great vulnerability and massive ignorance, sexuality can become the bag into which we throw all our unfinished business—our hidden wounds, our insecurities, our perceived failures, as well as our guilt, shame, and chagrin. If sex has become your dirty clothes hamper, please find a trusted friend or therapist—it may very well be your beloved—who will gently, willingly, and non-judgmentally help you sort, cull, and heal what has been stuffed away.

SEX AS POETRY

Those of us questing for sacred partnership need to reclaim the lost art of sex as poetry. In our deep desire for union, we need to regain our inheritance of sex as a gift from Spirit and a temple of replenishing, renewing love.

Although poets write endless verses on love, it's so often nonphysical love—head love, like my childhood poetry—not love emanating from and incorporating both our hearts and bodies. But physical love is also poetry, or it *can* be when engaged in with open hearts and an awareness of sacred sexual communion. Sanctified by love, sex can become the highest, closest, and deepest exchange of energy between two people. Sacred sex can be communion, blessed intercourse, an expression of profound caring from our heart through our body.

At its highest, sex can be a communion so profound that it removes us from common time and space, allowing us to fall into the sacred void together. In the void, we touch the Divine.

RESACRALIZATION OF SEXUAL LOVE

Mystical union through sacred sexuality can be every bit as transformational as any heartfelt, meditative experience of spiritual union. In its sacred form, sexual bonding is meant to be a harmonization of masculine and feminine energy, an impregnating and intermingling of opposites. Making love—entering the temple of love—is the intimate physical symbol of sacred marriage between complementary energies, a necessary and holy partnership between beloved opposites.

Viewing sex as the Temple of Love within our relationships, we need to understand how best to ascend the steps to the temple doors. In a nutshell, we can best begin our ascent by taking our beloved by the hand gently and, with great awe and reverence, start the climb together. As we begin, it's extremely important to remember how vulnerable we are in the sexual area. Some of our temples have been vandalized, not sacralized; the doors battered down by religious, societal, and personal brutes who felt they had the right to ravage. The more vulnerable we are, the more gentle compassion is called for.

Those of us who are aware of our holy hunger for heart centered marriage have been entrusted with the task of resacralizing sexuality. We will be the ones to rescue the precious jewel of sex from the dung heap of disrespect and degradation and return it to its place as a sacrament between lovers. We can. And we'll have fun doing it!

ANNIVERSARY PRESENT, THE PRESENCE OF THE GODDESS

Six weeks before our twentieth anniversary, Gene and I followed the advice of a dear friend and went to a weekend workshop entitled "Tantra; the Art of Conscious Loving" with Charles and Caroline Muir, authors of a book by the same title. I had a vague notion that Tantra was connected with Yoga, was Hindu in origin and erotic in nature, but that's as far as my knowledge went. Thinking that it would be a fun way to celebrate our anniversary and good research for this book, we signed up with few, if any, expectations.

Fun, yes! I've rarely laughed so much or so hard, but I've also hardly ever experienced the grace of that many tears either. A blurb about the workshop in the Esalen catalog reads, "Tantra can transform sex into a loving meditation, putting more consciousness, energy, intimacy, joy, and love into sexual exchanges." True, but that sentence barely scratches the surface of the life-changing effect the weekend had on both Gene and me.

Although we've always enjoyed sex, and sometimes making love felt sacred and divinely connective, the teachings and insights received through learning about Tantra have enhanced our connection immeasurably. Learning about ancient wisdom in which sexuality is envisioned as a sacred, healing gift, as well as listening to other people's stories and experiencing healing rituals, encouraged us to absorb, at a deep soul level, a whole new attitude regarding ourselves and our relationship. An attitude that allows us to sink and soar into the depths and heights of making love from a totally different perspective— one that honors both the masculine and feminine as divine sparks of love.

As a wife and lover, I am thrilled by the increased intimacy between Gene and myself. As a writer, I am overjoyed to have my almost-wordless feelings and philosophies concerning the resacralization of love and sex articulated through an ancient spiritual source. As a Western "lay" person (pun definitely intended), I can't illuminate you on the intricacies of Tantra; I can, however, share with you how my yearning for more sacredness in sexuality has been affirmed through our experience. If you wish to find out about this issue in more depth, other sources for sexual healing and enhancement are listed in the back of the book, and I strongly encourage you to explore them.

Reuniting and Honoring God and Goddess Energy

In essence, Charles and Caroline Muir's Tantra work is the same as mine. All three of us are teaching the essential need for reclaiming the Sacred Feminine voice. This work is not about ignoring masculine energy, but rather reinstating the Divine Feminine as lover and esteemed partner of the Divine Masculine, reuniting the God with the Goddess internally, in our marriages, and in our world. Lovemaking is the closest we come, physically, emotionally, and spiritually to a true integration of masculine and feminine. We are united, in and of one another, blending the sweet nectars created by our God-given bodies.

Gene's comment, when we were talking with our son about the effect of the Tantra seminar on our lives, was, "It does feel life-changing to me. I know that I honor women more than I ever have." I definitely *feel* his increased honoring and bask in it, and also sense an expanded willingness to be transparent, openhearted, and softer in Gene.

To honor means to show great respect or high regard for and to treat with deference, courtesy, and high esteem. In learning to honor both the feminine and masculine as divine, we can consign the same respect and reverence to each other. I, like all women, have experienced, at an often wordless level, the shame and frustration of not being honored, as well as actually being devalued and disrespected. Maybe not in an overt or hostile way, but a woman's second-class citizenship has permeated our culture and religion for centuries. Honoring each other creates a much safer and more nurturing environment, and, as a result, intimacy can evolve in beautiful ways.

As a bonus to elevating the feminine aspects of healing, nurturing, and honoring into a more prominent place, our lovemaking has become much more meaningful and precious to both Gene and me. Resacralizing our sexual relationship by concentrating on holding each other in an attitude of honor and awe has not diminished physical gratification. Quite the contrary, it has been enhanced—sweetened and sparked up!

FROM RUDE TO REVERENT

Before we can give our sexuality the honor and respect that it deserves, we must move from the rudeness and crudeness with which sex is portrayed in our culture into a realm of reverence for the preciousness of this gift between lovers.

Sex, as our connection with and emulation of the Divine Life Force, is too often deformed into the divine life *farce*. We make fun of it and use it to gain power. We bludgeon, wound, and abuse others, using sex as the weapon. At worst, sex can be a tragedy of shame and disconnection, instead of the tender solace and communion that I believe God means it to be.

For males, especially, sex has been misguidedly motivated by conquest and control. Charles Muir says his early sex education was the injunction to "Get it up. Get it in. Get it off," espoused by a street buddy. Make the conquest, notch the belt, or just plain relieve the tension. Not very connecting.

On the other hand, we females were taught that nice girls didn't "do it," and, if we did, sure as hell didn't enjoy it. Instead of being awed by the power of sex and the mystery of love, women often learn to be mortified by their own bodies and desires. A setup for low self-esteem and lack of self-worth, both of which make us less able to connect at a heart level with anyone, let alone a man who may want to acquire and control us by "doing it."

No matter how and why sexuality has been desecrated, its emergence from degradation needs to be honored and assisted. Credit for doing so can go to persons like Rabbi Zalman Schachter-Shalomi, who tells his Bar Mitzvah classes to feel free to masturbate on the Sabbath as well as any other day, and to not leave God out of it. Rabbi Schachter advises his boys to invite God to all sexual encounters, even those with themselves. I can't even fathom having heard such a statement from the clergy when I was twelve! Rabbi Schachter further encourages not only his Bar Mitzvah boys but all of us to become masters of "fore-pray," by which he means to bless all sexual experiences and enjoy the "holy sparks of sexuality."

Along that same line, one of the participants in the Tantra weekend shared that he and his wife were making love when their three-year-old daughter came in, concerned about the noises she was hearing. Rather than embarrassedly shooing her away, Pete opened his arms to his daughter and said, "Mommy and I are loving each other, and this is how it sounds," to reassure his little girl. My heart sings with the awareness that some children, at least, are being blessed by learning of the sanctification of sex from respected elders.

As exemplified by Pete and Rabbi Schachter, the misuse and abuse of sexuality can be transformed. We are fully capable, and deeply desirous of, evolving from rude to reverent in our attitude toward sex. Doing so is a precious legacy we can bestow upon our children.

What's In a Name?

William Shakespeare asked, "What's in a name? That which we call a rose by any other name would smell as sweet." I disagree with the bard on this one. Names do make a difference. I, for one, don't find it as sweet a turn-on to be asked, "Wanna screw!?" as I do hearing, "I would love to enter your sacred Temple of Love." I know. I winced with embarrassment, too, when first moving from the familiarity of crude sexual language to more lyrical expressions of desire. It takes a while to get accustomed to being reverent in our sexual language, but it's certainly worth the effort. Renaming can change our entire outlook.

Our language mirrors our attitudes. We, in the West, are notoriously crass, non-romantic, and disrespectful when speaking about physical love. Our jargon is filled with smirking words such as *screwing, fucking,* and *humping*—none of which engender an attitude of reverence nor make most women's hearts go pitty-pat. As a culture, we are still in the middle-school, boy's restroom, tittering and giggling at what we, in the secret recesses of our Victorian attics, still feel is "dirty."

Other cultures, older and wiser in the fine *art* of lovemaking, speak of sex in poetic terms. As you read this, I'm sure you can come up with several less-than-poetic slang names for penis or male genitalia. In lieu of those epithets, some ancient, Eastern terms for penis include: *Jade Scepter, Wand of Light, Lingam, Jewel, Jade Stalk, Healing Wand, Arrow of Love, Scepter of Love, and Pillar of the Temple.*

Female genitalia are similarly honored in the East. Examples of terms for the vagina and vulva are: *Jade Gate, Golden Furrow, Honey Pot, Sacred Lotus, Yoni, Cave of Warmth, Garden of Delights, and Temple of Light.* Artful, beautiful, graceful, poetic names such as these create a sexual ambience that sanctifies both lovemaking and lovemakers.

With just a slight tilt in perspective and a few name changes, our lovemaking now reflects Gene's and my more sacred attitude. Moving from rude to reverent has helped us make sexual love a sacrament. As a result, we both feel more cherished, nurtured, honored, and energized.

THE ALCHEMY OF AWE

In order to make our physical love a temple of renewal and soul bonding, we need to embrace each other with awe and appreciation. The simple commitment to speak about sex reverently will bring us into a more awe-welcoming awareness. Reverence begets reverence.

Awe is an important ingredient for a healthy life. We need the uplift of an awe-filled attitude. One of my teachers, Evan Hodkins, explains that, "Where awe is missing, anxiety—counterfeit awe—rushes in to fill the void. Anxiety is hothouse awe. Awe without the stars."

His ideas resonate with my heart. The energy, or the "buzz," of awe and anxiety are similar. They both energize us, but in totally different ways. Awe alchemizes and expands our energy into reverence, inspiration, and honor, while anxiety can severely limit our possibilities. The people I know who are the most immune to awe are also the most anxious, yet those for whom the first crocus of spring is a joyful, heart-opening, awesome discovery are seldom felled by anxiety. So for a happier, more sacred life, choose to live with awe, awareness, and appreciation!

REMEMBER THE MAGIC

A scene I return to in order to reconnect with the awe of love is one that I witnessed at our daughter's wedding. Her groom, who had been in love with her for five years before she thought of him as more than a dear friend, had a look of such awed and thankful love in his tear-filled eyes as she walked down the aisle that I get teary eyed just thinking about it. He was so catapulted out of time and space by the extent of his feelings that he forgot to come down from the altar to take her hand from Gene's. Only our daughter's whispered urgings to, "Come get me, Honey!" shook him from his bedazzled reverie.

If only we could keep a lively memory of a similar mysterious wonder that *we* have felt at some time since committing to our mate! How easily we would keep our chalice of love full and overflowing then! What memories can you return to that make your heart swell with tenderness? Take a moment right now to allow your mind to float back in time and retrieve a sweet memory of feeling the magic of awe in your relationship with your partner. Savor the feeling. Soak it in. And bring the feeling into your next lovemaking, so that you can see your beloved with soft, sacred eyes and touch her or him with awe-struck hands.

Such reverence is the domain of the Sacred Feminine and helps awaken within both partners the magnificent shakti energy of the Goddess.

AWAKENING SHAKTI ENERGY

Throughout history, the Goddess has been known by various names. The Greeks called her *Psyche*, in Gnostic and Old Testament literature she was *Sophia*, to mystic Cabalists her name was *Shekina*, the Romans referred to her as *Anima* and Carl Jung respectfully called her "My Lady Soul." The Tantric title of the Great Goddess is *Shakti*. The word *shakti* is translatable to "cosmic energy," and implies power, ability, intuition, strength, receptivity, poetic genius, healing and restorative powers, among other things. In mythology, Shakti is seen as the animating soul and active power of male deities. She is regarded as a god's consort and queen. Without his shakti, a god was powerless to act.

What a retreat women have needed to make during the patriarchal paradigm!

However, the power is still within us. Most mothers, when faced with possible harm to their children, know that their shakti power can rear up on its hind legs and attack the danger mercilessly and fearlessly. Also, many women have intuitively retained the softer side of shakti energy that shows itself in their capacity to heal with compassion and awareness, inspire through wisdom, and love unsparingly.

For the most part, however, over the last several hundred years, sexual shakti/Goddess energy has been locked in the dungeon. Because she is fluid, she seeped out on occasion but was often dirtied and exhausted by the effort it took to be acknowledged and valued. For many women, their sexual shakti energy made the wise choice to retreat into unconsciousness.

Now, thank God/dess, reverence is beginning to replace disrespect and shakti energy—in *both* men and women—is beginning to awaken, slowly. The Prince of Sacred Partnership is coming to the temple to kiss Sleeping Beauty ever so gently to consciousness.

ASCENDING THE TEMPLE STEPS

We have all, on occasion, raced up the steps of the temple of love, disregarding the sanctity of sex in our haste for gratification or fear of not performing well. Ascending the steps of the temple in order to unlock the mysteries of sacred sex takes time, patience, and *consciousness.*

Men, who have basically been trained in the "Get it up. Get it in. Get it off" school of sexual conquest, often have only a dim awareness of the nurturing and sacred aspects of sex. They are unlikely to know of their spiritual need to access the nourishing energy of the Divine Mother through union with their mate. Physical and emotional satisfaction, yes. Spiritual communion, probably not.

Women, also ignorant of the awesome healing energy of the Goddess that is potentially their gift, often use sex as gold stars or punishment, or to ensure their security by keeping their men at home. Who can blame us? Few of us have been deeply understood by our mates, let alone patiently, reverently, and *safely* awakened from our sexual slumber.

It's very important for women to understand that deciding to put our shakti energy to sleep was a wisdom-response from the Goddess-Self. In the face of disrespect, dishonor, and danger, it was better that the consciousness carried within our temple of love retreated behind the veil, into the mists of safety. Honoring the wisdom of that slumber, we can now honor the wisdom of awakening. For the emergence of shakti energy is essential to the sacred unfolding of heart centered marriage.

Together, reverently and humbly, hand in hand, women and men can ascend the temple steps and enter the sanctuary *together.* It will be a long climb, and we will stumble and slip on the ancient, mildewed feelings of fear and shame embedded in us. We may also sit down stubbornly and refuse to move when faced by the continued somnolence of the Goddess within us both. Please be gentle with yourself and your beloved! Please continue patiently to *invite* the sacred shakti energy to awaken in you both, remembering that it has been bludgeoned continually for centuries and is wise to be cautious. As we gently speak to the heart of the feminine, eventually the jade gate guarding the doors to the Temple will gratefully glide open.

There are, of course, techniques that enhance our ability to ascend the temple steps, and they have been described eloquently and in great detail in such books as *Tantra, the Art of Conscious Loving, Sexual Secrets: The Alchemy of Ecstasy,* and *The Art of Sexual Ecstasy.* My desire here is to concentrate on the sacred *attitudes* essential for supporting and augmenting the beautiful techniques outlined elsewhere.

A NOTE TO MEN

Men, you especially, need to be patient kind, and reverent with your beloved as you ascend the temple steps toward sexual awakening of shakti energy. Your sexual energy has not so much been asleep as it has been unaware of the spiritual significance of union with your feminine counterpart.

Because of your physicality, you're ready and rarin' to go quickly, as exemplified by Gary Smalley's analogy that men are like microwaves and women are more like crockpots. It takes a woman longer to warm up and "get cookin'." Over-enthusiasm can cause the feminine to beat a hasty retreat. In your ardor, you may not even notice her withdrawal, except for a little hollow feeling at the root of your consciousness, a murmur of "Is this all there is to this?" Be aware of nuances. Ask your beloved to tell you what she wants and needs. Be gentle. Be respectful. Be conscious.

Attitudes and habits don't change easily, so you'll need to be gently vigilant about old attitudes that, in the heat of passion, want to thunder through the temple gates without either asking permission or wiping the dirt off of their boots.

You can became a gentle, reverent, *and* highly satisfied lover. Because your beautiful masculine energy allows you to *do* what you *decide* and *choose* to do. The ability to get the job done is one of the jewels in the masculine crown. And, believe me, when you choose to come to your beloved's temple gently and enter reverently—and only if invited—the rewards for both of you will be great!

The Goddess/Shakti energy longs to open to you, enfold and embrace you in her moist, soft strength. She yearns to welcome, heal, and play with you. She loves you and has missed the dance of intimacy—deformed for centuries into the dance of intimidation—between you. As you come to her with consistent gentle patience, tiptoeing into her slumbering presence bearing gifts of respect and acceptance, flowers of honor and awe, she will awaken. And safe within the embrace of your beloved, eagerly welcomed into the warmth and healing of the Temple of Love, fully accepted and honored, you will be awakened to your feeling nature. In this sanctuary of love, both of you can heal any rifts between you and come to wholeness.

THE HOLY OF HOLIES

The flames of our soul-self burn brightly when soul and sex are invited to share the same sacred circle. From the act of love comes the most fiery holy of holies, the creation of *life!* But the creation of life is not only the creation of babies—wondrous as that is—but also the exchange of nurturing healing energy between ourselves and our beloved. Sexual union, communion of love between those who care deeply for each other's souls, is entering the holy of holies and begetting Life in many magical forms.

THE POWER OF LOVE

Shakti energy, the quintessential elixir of love, is revitalizing and creative. When free to flow between partners, shakti energy is amazingly empowering and stimulating to our physical, emotional, and spiritual systems.

Although there are many ways of sharing the power of love with our beloved, making love is one of the most important, because it is the single thing that we share with no one else. Sexuality is a sacrament of relatedness. Sacred sexual union enhances both partners by infusing them with healing energy and filling their marriage with a sense of security, well-being, and connectedness. Loving our partner in a conscious, reverent, and respectful way creates a power base of energy between us.

Concentrating on the spiritual and meditative exchange of energy builds the power and rescues sexual connection from the hard-edged, hard-on, goal-oriented need to perform that often colors encounters aimed solely at orgasm. Sexual union, as meditation, can be as simple as holding hands, consciously. We can also become lightning rods of love. All it takes to become a wonderful conductor of love is to open our hearts and *consciously* send out the energy of love.

Exchanging Love Energy

When we exchange love energy with each other, we tend the sparks of awe, appreciation, and joy. Adding a beloved's energy to our own augments and enhances our ability to take in and savor life to the fullest. By sharing energy with each other, we more naturally connect with the fiery, passionate joy of being alive.

A way to view love energy exchange is to use the analogy of the "cookie exchange" popular around Christmas time. People gather together around the theme of "bring some and get some." It's a great help in the holiday rush to take our single recipe of a few dozen cookies to the party, taste the fruits of others' labor, and come home laden with a beautiful variety of tasty treats. In cookie exchanges, shared effort and expertise lead to a richer selection of "goodies" to offer our family and friends.

Although formal cookie exchanges are popular, mostly around the holidays, *energy* exchanges are going on each and every minute of our days and nights both with those we love and with those we meet only casually. Looking at it this way, it's important to ask ourselves if our way of exchanging energy is as sweet and fruitful as a cookie exchange. Are we in the habit of sharing energy that is more nectar than vinegar? When most of our energy exchanges with our beloved are sweet and tasty, they will satiate and satisfy our deep hunger for sacred relationship.

Consistently coming from our hearts during encounters with others and, very importantly, with ourselves, will multiply the energy between us as well as the energy available to each of us individually. In other words, being nice, kind, and gentle will allow us to share many new, exotic, and nurturing emotional and spiritual cookies with each other.

Making love is a great cookie exchange, but we also need leaven for the ordinary day-to-day bread of life. Exchanging nurturing, nonsexual energy with our beloved helps us get up in the morning and put one foot in front of the other. Sharing pleasure and, even more importantly, sharing gentle, healing touch can bring solace with sensuality and help us rise to whatever the occasion calls for.

What are some of the simple, wonderful, *conscious* ways that we can share powerful love energy with our beloved and others? The most important ingredient for sharing love is an open heart. Just as a tiny amount of yeast is enough to make bread rise, our intention toward being openhearted literally expands our hearts. When I want to increase my heart energy, it also helps me to open my arms wide and feel my chest expanding and imagine my heart unfolding inside it. Breathing deeply into our heart centers also encourages them to awaken and open.

NON-SEXUAL ENERGY EXCHANGES

Non-sexual energy exchanges are best done daily. They don't take much time and their results are amazingly enlivening. Aligning our spirits and consciously exchanging energy with our beloved seems to inflate our own energy. Actively creating an energetic bond between us establishes a powerful love exchange. Such heart connections help bring us back to the center of our selves, where the treasure chest of our Soul resides. From this center, the inherent, inherited, and earned gifts that we have accumulated over lifetimes are most easily accessed and made available to us and to those whom we love and serve.

A simple but effective love exchange is to lie or sit facing your partner. Hold hands or embrace and look into each other's eyes for a minute or so. Use your eyes to send love and appreciation. Just gazing at each other consciously can result in heart expansion. Next, begin to breathe synchronistically with each other and allow your breath to deepen naturally. A friend of mine has heard this called "conspiration: to breathe with." After a few moments of breathing deeply together, begin to establish a flow of energy between your heart centers. Gene and I use a rainbow of light, or simply a sense of energy moving through each of us to the other in a circle. It doesn't matter how you perceive the flow, your intention to establish one is what counts. You may see or sense light, movement, warmth . . . whatever.

After a flow has been established between your hearts for a while, change your breath so that one partner breathes in as the other breathes out. As you inhale, visualize drawing energy from your partner's heart into your own. As you breathe out, imagine sending energy to your partner's heart center and feel him or her receiving it. After you have done this for a minute or two, give each other and hug and take off, leavened and lightened, to do the "bready" things of life.

One of the beauties of this exercise is that it can be done without a partner present. When desiring to share energy with someone at a distance, allow yourself to know that, because energy is real and measurable, he or she will receive what is sent even if he or she doesn't realize it consciously. This is especially great to do if you're having difficulty with someone.

It can also be used to soften or love-infuse a situation, circumstance, or even our Mother Earth. Working with a like-minded person, establish a flow between *your* hearts. Together, place the situation, person, or being to be blessed between you. Allow the love flow between you to circle, or figure eight, through the object or person to be blessed and energized.

You can also use this technique to energize yourself. If you're feeling anxious, depressed, or otherwise drained, establish a flow between your heart and the heart of a loving spiritual Being with whom you resonate. I often use teachers such as Christ, Mary, or my guardian angels. Asking for a love infusion and then opening to receive it—either from a living person or a spiritual being—opens our hearts and helps us learn to receive.

Another very powerful energy exchange, often overlooked because of its simplicity, is to give each other our undivided attention. Attention is a profound way to share love energy. Listening from an open heart is an extremely empowering and energizing love exchange. Attention is an aphrodisiac.

SEXUAL ENERGY EXCHANGES

It's very important that we unite our spirit with that of our mate before we bring our bodies together. Uniting our spirits can happen in many different ways, and you and your beloved will know which ways make you feel spiritually connected. You can begin a lovemaking session with any nonsexual energy exchange in order to align your spirits. Or gently gazing into each other's eyes and talking love-talk will join your spirits, as will praying together.

Because sacred sex creates a powerfully healing current between lovers, it can be used for deep healing for ourselves as well as anyone or anything else. We may want to devote the energy we create together to a particular sub-personality within one of us who is needful, or to a part of our relationship that is strained.

Tibetans participate in a death ritual of dedicating their life's final pain for the good and enlightenment of all beings. We can do a similar ritual with our shakti love energy. A wonderful way to engage in a healing ritual is to align your spirits *and* extend healing outside the two of you by dedicating the energy generated in your lovemaking to a specific person or cause. For instance, Gene and I might ask for the love energy exchanged between us be dedicated to whatever needs our children have. Or we have asked that the current of healing, shakti energy be sent to a part of the ecological system that tugs at our hearts. There are endless needs that we can choose to bless by the overflow of love energy created between us.

Energy is real, vibrant, and full of impact. We can use the beautiful healing energy of both the masculine and feminine, united in love, to heal a bigger circle. Then, not only will our love energy reignite and empower us, it can also become a tiny particle of universal healing. We two, through our sacred union, reach out to embrace and uplift a greater whole.

I want to share with you two simple techniques, gleaned from the Tantra workshop, that can enhance sexual enjoyment and increase the energy of love immeasurably.

In keeping with the Tantra ideal of ever-increasing energy exchange during lovemaking, men are encouraged to stop several times before the moment of orgasm and breathe the accumulated energy up from the genitals throughout the entire body, especially into their heart centers. The woman can assist by stroking her hands up her lover's body from the groin to the heart. Both partners can visualize the build-up of shakti energy spreading up through both the man's and woman's bodies. Not only does this technique prolong the length and pleasure of intercourse for both lovers, but it also helps keep the man from feeling spent or drained afterward.

Another wonderful energy exchange technique is for both lovers to stop actively moving while linked together, and imagine that the man's penis is a wand of light emanating sacred energy and filling every inch of his beloved with empowerment, healing, or whatever she asks for in the moment. With the male radiating and the female receiving a concentrated emanation of life-force energy, a spiritual bond is formed between lovers, a bond that extends beyond the bedroom into the realms of Soul. Cherishing each other through aligning spirits and exchanging energy in these ways revitalizes both partners by beautifully feeding our hunger for union.

TEMPLE GIFTS

When both the God and Goddess are enthroned in our hearts and the precious balm of Sacred Feminine Energy is welcomed into our lovemaking, we will be gifted by deep healing and the heart-lifting joy of sacred union with our chosen beloved. From the divine depths of our hearts and guts we are called to ascend the temple steps together and embrace the power and majesty of shared energy and sacred sexuality.

Chapter Thirteen

SACRED CIRCLES

A sacred circle of love knows no bounds,
being infinite in its sphere of influence.

$\mathscr{C}$ircles are a sacred symbol, the form used for many religious rites and spiritual gatherings. Not only is the sanctity of the circle exemplified in spiritual life, but we also refer to the family circle when speaking of those we love, whether inherited, acquired, or chosen as kin. And, of course, Mother Earth, Father Sun, and Grandmother Moon are all circular.

I have a pet theory about why circles are such nurturing symbols. First, with no beginning or ending, a circle is definitely feminine in character. A circle is whole and holy. But other reasons why it seems so sacred to me is that there is no hierarchy. When facing into the center of a circle, everyone can see everyone else. Eye contact, as well as body contact, is possible. Everyone around the circle is equally important, equally present, equally accessible. Similar to the adage that a chain is only as strong as its weakest link, each member of a circle is equally important in keeping the circle viable and intact.

Sacred partnership creates circles that embrace a far wider spectrum than we can imagine. In times when we need to "circle the wagons," other people can watch out for our backs. If our circle faces outward, every direction is visible to at least one member of the group. Ideally, a circle of family, friends, community, and cosmos will support and protect us whether metaphorically facing in or out. Wrapped in the safety of both small and ever-enlarging circles, we are free to become the unique beings that our souls long to be. *And* as members of various valuable sacred circles, we have the opportunity to bring our unique sparks of divinity to the central fire that then warms us all.

Balanced circles are composed of complementary opposites represented by dark, receptive feminine yin and light, dynamic masculine yang energies. The sacred circle within ourselves recognizes that yin and yang are not divided along gender lines, and *both* are essential for keeping the circle intact, and the fire, at its center, lighted.

In gathering at the sacred circle of family, the queen, or Feminine/Yin Energy brings her gifts of vision, intuition, connectedness, wisdom, and the understanding of what is good, true, and beautiful within *all* members of the circle. Her consort, the Masculine/Yang Energy picks up the torch ignited within the sacred circle and takes the light out into the world, where he accomplishes what needs to be done. Family circles can't exist without valuing both energies.

For instance, when I'm writing a book, the feminine/yin Muse within me first envisions the concept, ritualizes the process, and organizes the scattered ideas into a semi-manageable glob, but it is the masculine/yang part of me that spends endless hours in front of the computer, looking for the most significant words and the best way to bring the book into form. During this process, I rely heavily on my circle of friends and family for their feminine/yin energy, which supports, nurtures, and helps me hold the vision when I'm discouraged, exhausted, or fresh out of insight.

The fires of support and protection burning brightly within the sanctuary of the family circle stand as a lighthouse to guide us safely through the storms of life. It is our calling to complete the sacred circle of support not only by accepting blessings, but also by *becoming* a blessing. Each of us must feed both ourselves and our beloveds the feminine fruits of kindness, consideration, and reverence.

When each person within our sacred circle is protected, nurtured, and has his or her emotional needs met, everyone's energy is freed up to care about others in a meaningful, unselfish way. Therefore, a circle of supportive, loving relationships is one of the best ways for gathering up the energy to move out into the world in order to right the wrongs and balance the imbalances. The energy from such sacred circles shines as a beacon of possibility for others, and spreads an aura of kindness and compassionate caring from which miracles can spawn.

A Sustaining Sense of Roots

Margaret Mead, famed anthropologist, believes the family is a cultural reality that will survive time and change. She states, "No matter how many communes anybody invents, the family always creeps back." Why? Because we yearn for—and *need*—sacred circles of connection. Like trees in a forest, we need roots, connecting at deep, unseen levels that will hold us solidly to the ground of our being. Though wind and rain—crisis and calamity—may strip us bare of leaves, our roots carry a storehouse of energy available for new growth.

Roots anchor us in the soil of our being. Without strong roots we are vulnerable to every little breeze that comes along. Whether we agree with them or rebel against them, our families contain the rare material from which our roots are made. Returning—at least in our mind's and heart's eyes—to our original roots and gleaning what is positive from them helps us in creating sacred partnership with our beloved and forming a sacred family circle for our children.

Reclaiming what had beauty, value, and goodness in our past shores up the roots that we are sending down in our present and ensures their strength in the future. No matter how hard a childhood we may have had, there is value to be gained from it. Although we can never rectify the bad things that happened to us, we can alchemize them into the gold of strength gained through experience. Acknowledging the goodness from our past helps us forgive the difficult parts, let them go, and move courageously into strengthening the roots growing now.

It's wonderful when our family of origin provides supportive roots, but if it doesn't, we have the right, responsibility, and ample opportunity to create sacred family circles of our own. I have a note from Gene that I've carried in my wallet for eighteen years. It was written after an argument and says, "You are the most loving person that I have ever known, and if I or any of the kids lose sight of your love, that is our loss and not your problem. Just keep being natural, for you are appreciated!"

Obviously that sentiment was and is extremely important to me, or I wouldn't still be carrying it. Now, when I feel disconnected from Gene, I get out his note, tap into the long-term history of our relationship, and hold the note as a sacred trust in the fundamental strength and rootedness of our love. We can do similar tiny rituals with any member of our circle, living or dead.

FAMILY MYTHS

One of the things that often stands in the way of our feeling deeply rooted in our own families is the myths they perpetuate. Myths such as "girls don't need an education" and "children are to be seen and not heard" are not ones that foster the idea of equal value for each member of the circle.

A client of mine—who has a Ph.D. in psychology—still labors under the feelings generated by a family myth. While she was growing up, her mother often said, "It's a good thing Lucy is pretty because she isn't very smart." Ouch. In reality, Lucy is *very* smart, but still struggles to really grasp that awareness within herself because she was so indoctrinated by the myth of her pretty dumbness. As in Lucy's case, we all have family myths that affect us.

Myths about marriage are also prevalent in our society. Easily and quickly, we can come up with several examples of less-than-magical myths about marriage. Remember the warning to engaged couples about being saddled with the old ball and chain? Or the infamous myth about the inevitable war between the sexes? Or the pervasive belief that men and women can't possibly understand each other? It's rumored that Sigmund Freud's dying comment was, "What *do* women want?" If true, that last question does more to endear him to me than most of his other work.

In order to make sacred, supportive family circles, we need to reform any myths that trigger inappropriate reactions and feeling. Very importantly, we need to be vigilant about the myths we create about ourselves, our beloved, our children, our friends, and the world at large. If we are going to create myths—and we will—they might as well be wise, wonderful, and loving stories. Any myth that limits our potential or smudges our divine spark is one to be replaced. Myths, to be valuable, need to encourage soul expression and soul growth.

NIX HAPPILY EVER AFTER

One of the most detrimental myths that some of us innocently believe in our deepest heart of hearts is, "And they got married and lived happily ever after." Intellectually, we know that isn't really possible, but emotionally we often feel that it *should* be true. A belief in *constant* compatibility is a fairy tale that stands in the way of our willingness and ability to process difficulty by experiencing our feelings and communicating our way to greater understanding, acceptance, and love.

It seems to me that the movie *Love Story*, with its infamous comment, "Love means never having to say you're sorry" was built around the myth of happily ever after. Never needing to say you're sorry?! In your dreams. . . . Or, maybe, in heaven. In real-life love, both we and our heart-connections to each other are strengthened and humanized when we have the courage to recognize behavior that warrants an apology, take responsibility for our action, be sorry, and say it!

I love Goethe's comment that, "Marriage is an intense learning in which I go back home to spirit." He seems to understand that saying "I do" means that we often have the opportunity to trip over hot coals and through searing pain to make our way back home to spirit. My fantasy is that Goethe's marriage and family circle were probably very interesting and exceedingly growth-producing. As are most of ours.

Living happily ever after does not ensure much soul growth. But if we changed the myth to read, "And they got married and their love evolved and grew forever after," we would open ourselves to limitless possibilities about how to love. Freed by the wide spectrum of choices available in such a belief, we could embrace the reality that relationships need to include the willingness and ability to process, process, process.

HAIKU FOR OUR FAMILY

Like our relationship with our mate, our family is an alchemical vessel, a crucible for personal and spiritual transformation. Our soul tasks are to grow, flower, and fruit in our own unique ways and create a sacred family circle where the fires of individual creativity burn brightly. Ideally, family circles are places where the embers are gently fanned, and we are each encouraged to catch fire in the best, most distinctive ways for us individually. Paradoxically, we seem to have the optimal freedom for flowering when we stay firmly connected to the roots supporting our family circle. That doesn't mean that we live in each other's hip pocket; it just means that trust, support, and connection are a reality we rely on.

Sometimes differences can divide us if we're not careful to honor the sanctity of our circle and the roots grown in it. I'm sure that trees in a forest don't say to each other, "No, I'm sorry, you're an oak and most of us are willows; therefore, your roots can't be a part of our support system," or "Nope, you're too scrawny and your roots too puny so we're just going to ignore them when we intertwine with each other's roots. . . ." Trees encourage the intertwining and bolstering of all different types of tree roots. Because of that inclusive attitude, they are incredibly resilient.

I was reminded of this nature-based lesson of deeply rooted inclusion one summer when I was taking a transpersonal psychology class in which we were required to write a haiku poem and *sing* it to the group. Writing for a group was hard enough, but *singing?!* Oh, my gosh! Everyone's haiku needed to be nature-based with five syllables in the first and third lines and seven in the middle line.

Complicating my reluctance to write and sing the darn thing was the fact that I was feeling especially vulnerable. Our family was in a phase where religion and politics had created some division. I always feel quaky when the family is emotionally fragmented, and struggle with myself about being a less-than-perfect parent. As the following haiku quickly came to me, my soul-self seemed to say, "Look deeper, Sue!"

> *Wolves together stand,*
> *Howling soft and loud at Light,*
> *Singing family songs.*

In a heart centered way, this little haiku poem spoke to my soul. Having written it—and, yes, *sung* it in class—I was able to honor and accept our differences even when they resulted in discomfort between us. As a result, peace softly oozed into my heart. Then—and now—some of us were gray wolves, some white, and some black, but we were, no matter what, family. And always will be.

Shining Light Beings

Children are such gifts to us! They have an innate and natural hunger for spiritual things. At some level, I believe they remember the home they have just come from and are still deeply connected to God. With their soul connection still intact, they are like little spiritual tuning forks, and can help us refresh our spirit memories. We just need to look, listen, and accept what they offer. They radiate the light from which they've come. Being aware of their "clouds of glory," we can bask in their energy and take advantage of the healing and inspiration it offers.

When I was a single parent, my little boys helped bolster my faith on many occasions. At night, while they were saying their prayers, I always asked for their guardian angels to protect them. One morning, on a whim, I asked them if they ever saw their guardian angels. Both of them looked at me as if that was the dumbest question they'd ever heard, and answered, "Yes. Don't *you*?" A profound question that made me ponder how far I'd strayed from my deep and natural childhood connection with God. Thankfully, I had these two light beings, masquerading as impish, ornery little boys, to help me reestablish my heart tie with God.

SONGS FOR OUR CHILDREN

An ancient proverb, "The greatest gift a parent can bestow upon a child is roots and wings" rings true for the whole of our family circle—mates, parents, siblings, friends. Encouraging others to strengthen their wings, enabling them to fly toward their soul-song is, indeed, a great gift. But the ability to bestow such gifts doesn't spring from thin air. It comes from our commitment to grow and evolve on all levels of ourselves, our marriage, and our souls. From the taproot of our commitment to our own soul-song can come the energy and wisdom for great parenting skills—or at least the ability to be a good human *being* with our children, able to instill in them the confidence and desire to sing their own song.

TO BE OR NOT TO BE PARENTS

"Making the decision to have a child—it's wondrous. It is to decide forever to have your heart go walking around outside your body."
                                                                            —Elizabeth Stone

Many of us may already have several "hearts" walking around outside our bodies, whether we consciously chose to be a parent or not. No matter. It's never too late to choose to be the best parent that we can be. Children are our greatest challenges and biggest responsibilities, requiring a lifetime commitment.

Being a parent is similar to having a tattoo. Once we have emotionally tattooed "my child" on someone—whether biological, adopted, acquired, or chosen—that mark is indelibly with us. No matter how old we and our children get or how far apart we are in miles, ideologies, or feelings, the bond persists.

It's a fact of life; once a parent, always a parent. Parenting is a terminal condition that I'm pretty sure death doesn't interfere with much.

If allowed to be, children can become our best teachers. Fresh from the Source and untainted by society, they open vistas to us that we may have long forgotten. Margery Williams, in her heart-warming story, *The Velveteen Rabbit,* succinctly states what children do for us when she has the wise nursery Skin-Horse tell the toy rabbit, "When a child loves you for a long, long time, not just to play with, but REALLY loves you, then you become Real." Loving and learning from our children helps us live from our heart-center, which plants our feet directly on the road to Real.

But if you're a control freak, think long and hard before you have children, unless control is an obsession you want to overcome. Children turn our well-oiled, calm lives into a kaleidoscope of color and chaos. It can be a wonderful turmoil as well as a heart-wrenching one. Therapist, author, and parenting expert Bobbie Sandoz, says, "Our children bring us our highest highs and our lowest lows." Control suggests detached objectivity, and it's darn near impossible to be detached or objective about our out-of-body hearts!

PARENTING PERFECTION AIN'T NECESSARY

Most, if not all, of us truly want to be good, kind, and loving parents. We try and we succeed. But we also fail because we are not, nor are we going to be this go-round, perfect. We can do our best to love our kids *consciously,* and that's as good as it gets. We can work on ourselves as human beings in order to clear our hearts and open them up to express more love to our children, but we won't always feel or be loving. Ain't possible. And the good news is, ain't necessary either.

I don't know about you, but I beat myself up over my real and imagined failures as a parent more than I do over anything else. Well, actually, at times I'm no slouch at beating myself about the head and shoulders for not being a wise, loving, and patient wife, friend, and teacher either. Although I'm infinitely better than I used to be, that insistent demon-voice inside still loves to snicker, "You are *bad*. You didn't say that lovingly. At best, you're not as good as you *should* be!" In other words, Not Perfect. Oh horrors!

I report this in a flippant way, but the corresponding feelings are anything but frivolous. I know I'm not alone in truly agonizing and suffering over whether the life I provided, or the way I was, was good for my kids. After all, we are a divorced step-family. There are wounds. There is pain. But there is also much love and a cherished extended family circle.

Given the fact that none of us received much parenting training, and some of us had even less natural inclination toward the maturity and unselfishness required, when our little ones appeared on the scene, most of us have done an adequate to marvelous job. I find Stephanie Coontz's book, *The Way We Never Were: American Families and the Nostalgia Trap,* very comforting in reviewing my parenting life. In it she discusses a study in which researchers looked at children from infancy to adolescence and were asked to predict which would have troubled adult lives. What they found was that the researchers consistently overestimated both the negative effects of early trauma and the positive effects of a "happy childhood," overlooking the possibilities for maturity and depth that can derive from early trauma, and the lack of motivation in many adults who had "trouble-free" childhoods.

These findings are not a license to decrease our desire to be wonderful parents or to give us permission to stop learning skills that help us with our kids. They are, instead, an encouragement to lighten up on ourselves and *enjoy* parenting these wonderful beings lent to us for a time. For comfort, read Ms. Coontz. For down-to-earth but from-the-heart how-to's I suggest *Parachutes for Parents: Learning to Parent from the Wisdom of Love,* by Bobbie Sandoz.

SECURITY AND SOUL GROWTH

Children need security. Security comes in many forms, such as respect for them as beings, setting and sticking with appropriate limits and boundaries, and consideration for feelings. But, to a child, the most important security is mom and dad, as *real* people, loving each other sometimes well and sometimes in faulty ever-so-human ways, but with a commitment to complementary partnership and the creation of a sacred family circle.

Like all of us, children feel most secure when the family is firmly committed to kindness and consideration for each other and is deeply rooted and stable. *One of the best ways to provide security for our kids is to truly love each other.*

I remember a particularly poignant example of that need for security based on love between the adults in the family. Gene and I were newly married and still very tentatively in the process of forging the step-family bonds. Gene became upset about something one of my boys said, and was in the process of bundling up his little girls to "take them somewhere where they were appreciated." It was a misunderstanding, and all of us, but especially Gene, were confused about what was happening. On her way out the door, seven-year-old Paige turned her big blue eyes to me and said, "Don't worry, Sue, he still loves you!"

Now this was a little girl who was not a great fan of mine at the time, but she was acutely sensitive to the need both of us had to feel secure in this family. She was not only reassuring me by assuring me of Gene's love, but herself as well.

We all benefit from a rock-solid foundation from which to fly and, for a child, the love and commitment between their parents or step-parents is the best and most secure base they can have. Not only are they reassured of that place when mom and dad pay attention to each other in loving ways, but seeing their parents' interaction is how they learn what love can be like between men and women. What we model, children take into their hearts and minds.

We also must do two other things. First, we need to do our own psychological work by healing old wounds and breaking the chains of self-, and other-, imposed limitations. Second, it's equally important that we do our *soul* work by living our conscious dreams—which *are* the songs of our souls—and uncover any yet-to-be-discovered subconscious ones, so that we might bring them to fruition. When we are emotionally healthy and live our dreams, we have more love and energy to give our kids, and we will not be constantly acting out of our own unfinished, unconscious business. Carl Jung said,

"Nothing has a stronger influence psychologically on their environment and especially on their children than the unlived life of the parent." In order to sing healthy and encouraging songs for our children, we must heal ourselves and learn to sing our own songs.

To create a climate of intimacy in which everyone in our sacred circle can march to the sound of their own drummer, we, the adults, need to set the tone not only by healing our wounds, but also by honoring our own excellence. One of the reasons parenting is both a blessing and a crucible is that children have the uncanny ability to mirror to us exactly what we need to work on or own up to. With flawless precision, they pirouette on our "buttons" at will. It can be crazy-making and we want to project blame onto them, but we need, instead, to look at ourselves. Carl Jung summed it up beautifully by writing, "If there is anything that we wish to change in the child, we should first examine it and see whether it is not something that could better be changed in ourselves."

Rebellion Without Cause

One of our culturally pervasive myths is that a child comes into life as an integral part of his family and must rebel in order to achieve autonomy. Although American and Western societies have fostered the notion that we need to separate from family in order to develop properly, that particular myth is now being called into question. Separating from family has never been a part of the more yin cultures of the East. In fact, Japanese myth believes that the infant is an alien at birth and needs to be slowly brought into and embraced by the family.

As we move toward a more connective feminine/yin model in our relationships, information is surfacing that shows children are actually more secure and well adjusted when they *don't* feel pressured to rebel and separate from their family circle, especially in their teens when they're trying to formulate who they really are as individuals.

Accepting rebellion and separation as natural seems to be a rather recent phenomenon. I didn't do it. Neither did Gene. When I questioned people of my generation whether they outwardly rebelled against their parents, the majority answered something like, "No way! They wouldn't have tolerated it." I rebelled a tiny amount, but never separated from my parents, not because they wouldn't allow it, but because I didn't *want* to. I relied on their presence, support, and love to sustain me through those tumultuous years. Even more than that, I liked them.

According to young people today, they're not that much different than I was. One recent survey conducted by The Zandi Group, a marketing consulting firm, says that 600 young people asked to name their role model "overwhelmingly named their parents." Another survey, conducted by the Roper polling organization, found that four generations of Americans, including the so-called Generation X, were remarkably similar in what they valued. Among the things valued most were prayer, job satisfaction, belief in God, and the importance of family. Where is the generation gap we've been led to believe is inevitable?

What we're learning is that children not only admire us, they absolutely need our support more than they need to rebel and separate. In an interview, Mary Pipher, author of the important book *Reviving Ophelia: Saving the Selves of Adolescent Girls*, states in answer to why so many girls seem to hate their parents and pull away from them in adolescence: "Just when girls most need the guidance of their parents, our culture sends them the message that they are to distance themselves from their families. Girls pull away from those people who love them most and who are fighting the hardest to save their true selves."

A boy's similar cultural predicament is illuminated in Olga Silverstein and Beth Rashbaum's book, *The Courage to Raise Good Men*, which discusses the issue of separation from the parents' point of view. "Believing we are not to 'smother' or 'thwart their growth' mothers, especially, withdraw from their sons."

Along that same line, Shere Hite's latest book, *The Hite Report on the Family: Growing up Under Patriarchy*, includes a very interesting "myth-buster" concerning how boys feel about being forced to separate from their mothers in order to be part of the gang. Ms. Hite discovered that the majority of the men (all under age 35) interviewed found the pressure to disassociate from their mothers around age ten to be extremely painful and difficult. Many men were still mourning the end of that first special, passionate relationship as adults. Another notable finding in *The Hite Report* was that 81 percent of men raised by single mothers found it easier to form good relationships with women later, as opposed to 40 percent of men from two-parent families. This leads me to believe that our cultural myth encourages women to back away from their sons when the father is present.

Emotionally, this can be just as hurtful for both child and parent as the outdated and silly notion, prevalent when I was a new mother, that we should "schedule" babies' feeding times in order not to spoil them. Unfortunately, many of us believed that unnatural rule as much as we believe the rebellion/separation myth. In reality, our children need us *both!* And they also need an extended circle of adults with whom they feel safe and comfortable, and from whom they can receive mentoring and supportive friendship.

Our sacred task as parents is to hold our children as our own but not claim ownership, to unstintingly give them our love as well as our genes, but not expect them to be replicas of ourselves. No matter what their age or gender, we are called to support, guide, and nurture our children, and be good models of love and responsibility for them. They are, after all, God's children, gifts coming *through* us in order to live the life they are called to live. When we can revel in who our children uniquely are, see the beauty of their souls and reflect it back to them so that they can feel loved, honored, and cherished for themselves, we will help equip them to move out into the world as courageous human beings, able to become the blessing they are meant to be.

From Mothering and Fathering to Mentoring

The cycles of our lives include many seasons. If we are fortunate enough, we will age beyond parenting into the cycle of mentoring and befriending our children and other young people as well.

We had a dog, Pua, who taught me a lot about the art of moving out of motherhood. When she was ready to wean her puppies, she just got up and moved when they tried to nurse. The tenacious little buggers held on for dear life as she sauntered away, but eventually they would lose their hold and drop off, complaining bitterly. But it didn't take long for these little pups to learn to eat different food and, eventually, move to different homes.

Pua had the wisdom to move to higher ground when it was time for her children to mature into a different cycle. What is higher ground for us as life moves forward? What might life-after-kids look like for us? A great way to find out is to explore our less active sub-personalities. Who has been waiting in the wings for her chance at center stage? What inner child has a long cherished dream yet to be fulfilled?

To use another animal analogy, a nest full of baby birds is noisy and demanding. As they fly—or are kicked—out of the nest, what new songs do Mom and Dad now have time to sing? Contrary to the popular myth about the trauma of the empty nest syndrome, most parents I know, no matter how devoted they are to their children, welcome reclaiming the nest as an adults-only habitat. Far from wringing their hands over the departure of the children, they clap them in willing celebration of the new freedoms and opportunities open to everyone involved.

One of the best ways to mentor anyone younger than we are is to age with enthusiasm and increasing wisdom, modeling the perks of aging for those who think they will never be old, demonstrating that the loss of one role invites others into our realm of experience.

DUET, QUARTET TO "INFITET"

In our highly mobile society, one of the good things that we've lost about "the good ol' days" is the security and solace of a large circle of extended family living close by. Often we don't have the built-in stability of the family root system that used to be the norm. Because of our transitory circumstances, we are now called to choose and create extended families. And we ought to, for humans are social animals and need each other to survive and thrive. Our days of rugged individualism have taken a toll on us, our kids, and families in general.

In order to regain a sense of community, it is extremely important that we develop circles of like-hearted people who can help us stay on our chosen path, personally, ethically, and spiritually. Being supported by a larger whole is infinitely precious—and necessary. Being a duet of sacred partnership is a deep and holy yearning, but we also need to expand that tight little circle to include not only our immediate families, but the whole as well. I like to think of it as moving from duet to "infitet." Embracing a larger circle does not diminish our most intimate ring of love. Instead, it can immeasurably enhance it.

WIDENING AND DEEPENING THE CIRCLE

A natural way to embrace a larger circle is to view everything with an awareness of soul-fullness, feeling the sacredness inherent in all beings, especially those closest to home, our partner, our family, and ourselves, but extending to the sacredness of all, inanimate and animate, the very ground we walk on and—hard as it may be—the flies that plague our picnics. When we can feel the interwovenness of the All, we move away from the disconnective notions of us/them and me/you to the alchemical honoring of what philosopher Martin Buber called I/Thou. Albert Schweitzer summed up this idea succinctly in the three-word credo by which he tried to live, "Reverence for Life."

From the reverence of I/Thou springs mutuality and respect, and from that, profound love and a sense of compassionate, caring connection. By embracing an I/Thou perspective within our own families, we will begin to create a sacred circle that will, hopefully, include others. Our primary relationships are a source of grounded, rooted spiritual connectedness. They bring heaven and earth together by marrying the energies of heart, soul, and body within the I/Thou of family life. From this reverent respect can flow much heart centered, healing love to our beleaguered planet and to all her children's kingdoms.

To help establish an I/Thou feeling between you and your beloved, or you and your children, first surround yourself with an egg of protective light, and then ask that anything sent toward you that is detrimental to your soul growth bounce back to the sender as a blessing. Sufficiently protected, open your heart and send loving energy to the hearts of your family members. Establish a sacred flow to the heart of your chosen Thou, and then create a circle—your love energy circling through their heart and then returning to your own. After the energy flow has been initiated and is well-established, imagine it resonating out into the world in ever enlarging circles of honor, respect, and awe-filled acceptance.

The beauty of sacred circles is that, once committed to, they immediately begin the alchemical process of altering the energy around them, widening and deepening in ever-increasing rings of light. The more we grow our *own* souls, the wider and clearer the path becomes for others to follow.

SHARING RITUAL AND CEREMONIES

An excellent way to grow our souls is to share rituals and ceremonies together, for they speak the language of the soul. During meaningful rituals, divine energy is absorbed not only by our brains but in our hearts and souls as well, much the same way that music speaks to our spirits in ways difficult to explain without sounding trite. Being involved in rituals and ceremonies, whether a tiny, solitary ritual or participation in a grand pageant, opens our hearts, connects us with our community and makes us more accessible to ourselves, others, and God.

Some ceremonial days are set aside on the calendar, sanctioned by our culture as special. They include religious holidays, such as Christmas and Chanukah, national celebrations such as Thanksgiving and the Fourth of July, and seasonal ones such as New Year's Eve. But we also have personal ceremonies important only to our sacred circles of family and friends. Weddings, births, birthdays, anniversaries, and deaths to name a few.

Our family-soul, as much as our personal soul, needs an infusion of sacred commemoration for personal milestones. We need to mark already accepted celebrations—and others such as individual initiations—with both revelry and solemnization. Empowerment, healing, and blessings flow from such ceremonies when they touch the hearts of those involved. Embraced with a sacred, joyful attitude, the planning, fun, frustration, and camaraderie of a ceremony can increase its value exponentially and influence us profoundly.

Scrooge, Eeyore, and the Grinch need to be banned from our celebrations. Let them stay home with their pessimistic bah humbugs and watch TV. Hand in hand, we can skip to the party with adventurous sub-personalities and our natural inner child who longs to be recognized by us and invited into our sacred circles. Only by coming to ceremonies with open-hearted wonder can we truly be touched by the mystical, meaningful, and magical elements inherent to even the simplest ritual.

Rituals are gatherings of the heart, whether we unite with just our own or congregate with many others. In the sacred circle of our ceremonies we bless, honor, and initiate our transitions and invite God's sacred fragrance to seep into all the nooks and crannies of our souls.

COMING FULL CIRCLE

Coming full circle means that we return to our original position. In life, our sacred task is to love well enough to come full circle to God, our source. Anything that opens our hearts to the mystery of the Divine and grows our souls in the direction of reunion with her adds to the union between our beloved, family, friends, and us. No matter what form it takes, touching our own divine, spiritual energy makes us a better lover. Love generates love. The more we feel and become love, the more we have to give. No matter how it is born within us, love will radiate outward to bless those whom we touch.

So, whether we experience an expansion of love energy from a ceremony or through an intimate connection with ourselves or a loved one, we become a more richly endowed vessel, and those around us can benefit from the overflow. As a sense of unconditional love and honor for all encircles our heart, that sacred circle will naturally become infinite in its sphere of influence.

Chapter Fourteen

EVOLUTION

OF THE

HEART

We are torchbearers for the light of God
and for the advent of heart centered living.

As with absolutely everything else, the evolution of our hearts from insecure self-centeredness to unconditional love and God-centeredness is a *process.* A process that begins with birth and ends—*if* it ends—we don't know where. The entire Mystery is not only unsolvable, but also largely unfathomable on this side of the veil. We are called to surrender to the gift of life trusting that God, as both our source and our destination, has our best interests at heart.

Individually, our main task is to open our hearts through the integration of our soul-self with our human-self, thereby inviting God to express herself through us. Our challenge in creating sacred partnership is similar in that we are not so much called to "do" our marriage as to "be" with our partner from our higher selves, to *become* an alchemical vessel of love, a sacred chalice from which healing and nurturing energy can pour.

GENTLY, GENTLY, GENTLY

Becoming a sacred chalice of love sounds pretty daunting, and it can be. Love is often hard to feel, be, and do. The key to opening our hearts and becoming love is to gently accept where and who we are at any given moment. The curious paradox is that when we accept ourselves just as we are, then we can change. One of the puzzles of soul growth is that we must love within us what appears to be soulless, or merely a shadow of the soul, before the luminosity of the Divine can shine through us.

We love ourselves to soul growth and heart opening much as we love a difficult child into happiness and appropriate behavior. In order to do our part in the renaissance of the soul and evolution of the heart, our main mission is to unconditionally love ourselves at all times and in all situations, to become a divine parent to ourselves so that we may, in turn, heal others through love.

If we open ourselves to the flow of unconditional love to and through us, we cannot be disappointed. Our human self only has glimpses and flashes of the radiant, flowing love of God, but our soul is effortlessly capable of such love. Each tiny glimmer, each momentary flash of divine love through us, inspires us to continue the process of opening our hearts and allowing the glimmers to become rays of positive, unconditional love.

As we struggle with and succeed in the evolution of our hearts, it helps to remember that growing our souls is similar to the maturation of a mighty oak tree. Like the acorn, we have a soul seed that has within it the majesty and magnificence of the oak and the essence of spiritual love. To grow, our soul needs gentle care, nurturance, and patience with the process just the same as the oak tree does.

We are learners and yearners in human form, and that makes us vulnerable and infinitely precious. In our evolution as heart centered spiritual beings, our job is to gently, gently, gently be the best *human* beings possible, and that includes a willingness to embrace our own failures and foibles and those of our beloved as well. In the center of our psyche is something eternally divine. We were divine before accepting this body and will be after we are released from it.

WE ARE TORCHBEARERS

Our deep and holy hunger for sacred partnership initiates an evolution of the heart within each of us. Conceived within our own self, our marriage, and our sacred family circle, this evolution eventually assumes an energetic consciousness of its own.

We, who yearn for and work toward sacred partnership, are the torchbearers. As philosopher Erasmus said, "Give light, and the darkness will disappear of itself." The light of our soul's growth and our commitment to ascending the temple steps to sacred partnership will illuminate crevasses of our world that we cannot even fathom.

We really have no way of knowing the extent of our effect on the whole. However, each of us, no matter who we are or what we do, makes a difference in the balance and harmony of our universe. To illustrate, I'd like to tell you two little stories.

MUSKRAT IN THE POND PHENOMENON

While reminiscing at a high school reunion, one of the returnees happened to mention a favorite Social Studies teacher. Most of the students remembered her well, and as they chatted about her, it became apparent that one exercise she'd had her classes do had made a huge impact on everyone. Knowing how hard teenagers can be on each other, the teacher had given each student a list of their classmates' names and asked them to write one nice thing by each name. She tabulated the comments and gave each student a copy of the nice things said about him or her. A surprisingly large number of the reunion participants still had their lists and knew exactly where they were! One man even carried his in his wallet to refer to when he felt downhearted. This thoughtful teacher's positive influence echoed down through the years, probably in a much more significant way than she had ever dreamed.

The other story is a personal one. Early one beautiful fall evening, I was leaning on the railing of a foot bridge watching the sun set over the Rocky Mountains. My attention was drawn to the pond in front of me. A black button muskrat nose had poked out of the water, its owner eyeing me curiously. The small movement was sending ever widening circles over the calm surface of the pond. One tiny little rodent nose was altering the entire reflection of the sunset.

Seeing this nature-painted picture, I was struck with a visceral awareness of something that I've known intellectually for many years: that, without a doubt, our actions and attitudes, no matter how insignificant they may seem at the time, modify the world around us just as this little animal, by a mere twitch of the nose, had changed how the mighty sun was reflected in his environment.

Realizing that we do make a big difference, and buoyed by sacred union with our soul-selves, our beloved, and the Beloved, we will be forever drinking from the well of renewal. Energized by the mystery of sacred partnership, we can more easily reap the rewards of love and expand our ability to share the harvest with others.

We are more powerful than we know. Our energy rings the globe in ways that we are only now becoming vaguely aware of. Are we radiating the gifts of love and sacred attitude? Are we transmitting joy and compassion? Are we a living blessing?

We have the power to choose to be a gift in and to our world.

SACRAMENT OF SERVICE

If we once catch a glimpse of the true, innate glory of ourselves as ordinary human beings, the magnificence of ordinary life, and the glory of the Creator who loved and laughed it all into existence, we will want to be in communion with the Whole through the unique sacrament of service. Fired from within, we will be inspired to hear our hearts' urgings and answer the calls of our souls. And it's a darn good thing because our Mother, brothers, and sisters need us badly. Transformation doesn't happen without our willing participation!

I've heard it said that gifts are given to be given away. As we come to know ourselves in an intimate and soul-full way, it will be easier for us to be attuned to what we care about *whole*heartedly, what we want to do for our world as a sacrament of love rather than an obligation or duty. When we discover, deep within us, our particular gifts of service, they will become an outward expression of our inner light. In Sufi poet Rumi's words we will, "Let the beauty of what you love be what you do."

According to psychology, spiritual mysticism, and myth, the process of our development from innocent child to wise elder, both as an individual and as a sacred partner, falls roughly into three phases:

1. *Separation*—In this phase, we become individuals, learn to live on our own two feet, so to speak. In this phase of *sacred* partnership, we work through our power struggles and find our own unique place in the sacred circle we are creating.

2. *Empowerment*—This is the time of our life when we own and activate our unique self and express our own excellence; we achieve. Sacred partnerships often raise families and carve out careers in this phase.

3. *Return to Serve*—Having accumulated wisdom through experience and soul growth, we give our energies to midwifing the evolution of spiritual unfolding for the larger whole. In this time for service, sacred partnerships continue to cherish the individuals while contributing their love energy to the good of greater causes.

One of the miraculous beauties of service is that it not only blesses the recipients but also circles back to bless the giver.

ALLIANCE FOR THE WHOLE

Like the muskrat, we are all intimately connected to the whole of our universe. And, who knows, maybe woven just as intricately into other universes yet to be discovered. The nature of the universe is connection and, yet, the patriarchal paradigm has for centuries fostered separation and domination. Author Al Bernstein said, "We treat this world of ours as if we had a spare in the trunk." We don't. Hopefully, the more heart centered we become and the farther we advance into sacred partnership, the more we will become partners with our world and treat her as the unique and *only* home that she is to us.

Only as we learn to come from our hearts in love—first for ourselves and our intimates—will the circles of love and responsible concern swell to become an alliance for the Whole. From the love and respect we learn to give ourselves will flow similar caring for Earth and all her children. As we learn more about the *in*ternal workings of our beings, we will naturally desire to change that which is destructive in the *ex*ternal. World peace may, indeed, be a matter of personal peace.

Each of us emanates from God, the ever-burning fire of Love. As sparks of the Divine, we separate from the flame and, held aloft by the heat of our souls, invent our own lives. But we are always God-sparks, an integral part of the larger whole, originally and inextricably related to all other divine sparks. Returning home to the awareness of our divine fire ignites our hearts with the flame of compassion and a passion to honor and protect all of our sisters and brothers—the two legged, four legged, winged, and finned—with whom we share the act of breathing, as well as our leafed, flowered, and inanimate kin.

As our deep and holy hunger for sacred partnership evolves into reality, flames of love will forge within our hearts the gentleness of compassion and the soft power of wisdom. Illuminated by the brilliance of intimacy, our souls will be unveiled and able to shine upon all who need their light. Healing and wholeness can only emerge from hearts centered in love and respect for the awesome Mystery of all life. And that is our sacred calling, to personify the grace of a heart centered life.

THE 12 GOLDEN GUIDELINES FOR HEART CENTERED MARRIAGE

1. *Live gently with yourself and others.*

2. *Remember that heart centered loving is an ongoing process graced by commitment, mutuality, and respect.*

3. *Look for the face of God in the faces you see—and don't forget the one in the mirror.*

4. *Honor, express, and heal your feelings.*

5. *Recognize that sexual love is a sacred exchange of healing and nurturing energy between you and your beloved.*

6. *Listen from your heart.*

7. *When speaking, it's always best to be heartful rather than hurtful.*

8. *Cultivate quiet and solitude.*

9. *Heal Mother Nature and allow her to heal you in return.*

10. *Be nice. Be kind. Be appreciative.*

11. *Look at life through the eyes of awe.*

12. *Laugh easily and laugh lots.*

SUGGESTED READINGS

A God Who Looks Like Me: Discovering a Woman-Affirming Spirituality, Patricia Lynn Reilly, Ballantine Books, 1995

A Marriage Made in Heaven or Too Tired for an Affair, Erma Bombeck, HarperCollins, 1993

Autumn of the Spring Chicken: Wit and Wisdom for Women in Midlife, Sue Patton Thoele, Conari Press, 1993

The Awakened Heart: Living Beyond Addiction, Gerald G. May, HarperSanFrancisco, 1993

Centering and the Art of Intimacy, Gay Hendricks and Kathlyn Hendricks, Simon & Schuster, 1985

The Chalice and the Blade: Our History, Our Future, Riane Eisler, Harper and Row, San Francisco, 1988

Conscious Loving: The Journey to Co-Commitment, Gay and Kathlyn Hendricks, Bantam Books, Inc., 1990

The Courage to Be Yourself: A Woman's Guide to Growing Beyond Emotional Dependence, Sue Patton Thoele, Conari Press, 1988

The Courage to Raise Good Men, Olga Silverstein and Beth Rashbaum, Penguin Group, 1994

The Four-Fold Way: Walking the Paths of the Warrior, Teacher, Healer, and Visionary, Angeles Arrien, HarperSanFrancisco, 1993

The Fragile Bond: In Search of an Equal, Intimate, and Enduring Marriage, Augustus Y. Napier, HarperCollins, 1990

Getting the Love You Want: A Guide for Couples, Harville Hendrix, HarperPerennial, 1990

Gifts From the Sea: An Answer to the Conflicts in Our Lives, Anne Morrow Lindbergh, Pantheon, 1955

Goddesses in Everywoman: A New Psychology of Women, Jean Shinoda Bolen, HarperCollins, 1985

Husbands and Wives: The Guide for Men and Women Who Want to Stay Married, Melvyn Kinder and Connell Cowan, Signet, 1990

In a Different Voice: Psychological Theory and Women's Development, Carol Gilligan, Harvard University Press, 1982

Intimate Partners: Patterns in Love and Marriage, Maggie Scarf, Ballantine Books, 1987

Intimate Strangers: Men and Women Together, Lillian B. Rubin, HarperCollins, 1984

Journey of the Heart: Intimate Relationship & the Path of Love, John Welwood, HarperCollins, 1991

The Liberated Man, Warren Farrell, Berkeley Publishing Group, 1993

The Magic of Conflict, Thomas Crum, Touchstone Books, 1988

Making It Through the Night: How Couples Can Survive a Crisis Together, Pat Quigley with Marilyn Shroyer, Conari Press, 1992

Making Peace in Your Stepfamily, Harold H. Bloomfield and Robert B. Korg, Hyperion, 1993

Men Are from Mars, Women Are from Venus, John Gray, HarperCollins, 1993

Now that I'm Married, Why Isn't Everything Perfect? Susan Page, Little Brown, 1994

Parachutes for Parents: Raising Children for a Better World, Bobbie Sandoz, Family Works Publications, 1995

The Partnership Way: New Tools for Living and Learning, Healing Our Families, Our Communities and Our World, Riane Eisler and David Loye, Harper and Row, San Francisco, 1990

Passive Men, Wild Women, Pierre Mornell, Ballantine Books, 1971

Please Understand Me: Character and Temperament Types, David Keirsey and Marilyn Bates, Gnosology Books Ltd., 1984

Reviving Ophelia: Saving the Selves of Adolescent Girls, Mary Bray Pipher, Putnam Publishing Group, 1994

Sacred Eyes, L. Robert Keck, Knowledge Systems, Inc., 1992

Sexual Secrets: The Alchemy of Ecstasy, Nik Douglas and Penny Slinger, Destiny Books, 1979

SoulMates: Honoring the Mysteries of Love and Relationship, Thomas Moore, HarperCollins, 1994

Tantra: The Art of Conscious Loving, Charles and Caroline Muir, Mercury House, Inc., 1989

Two Part Invention, Madeleine L'Engle, Crosswicks, Ltd., 1988

Unconditional Love and Forgiveness, Edith R. Stauffer, Triangle Publishers, 1987

The Way We Never Were: American Families and the Nostalgia Trap, Stephanie Coontz, Basic Books, 1992

We Can Work It Out: Making Sense of Marital Conflict, Clifford Notarius and Howard Markman, Putnam, 1993

The Woman's Book of Confidence: Meditations for Trusting and Accepting Ourselves, Sue Patton Thoele, Conari Press, 1992

The Woman's Book of Courage: Meditations for Empowerment and Peace of Mind, Sue Patton Thoele, Conari Press, 1991

You Just Don't Understand: Women and Men in Conversation, Deborah Tannen, Ballantine Books, 1990